Naming, Nece

Naming, Necessity, and More

Explorations in the Philosophical Work of Saul Kripke

Edited by

Jonathan Berg

palgrave
macmillan

First published 2014 by
PALGRAVE MACMILLAN

Palgrave Macmillan in the UK is an imprint of Macmillan Publishers Limited, registered in England, company number 785998, of Houndmills, Basingstoke, Hampshire RG21 6XS.

Palgrave Macmillan in the US is a division of St Martin's Press LLC, 175 Fifth Avenue, New York, NY 10010.

Palgrave Macmillan is the global academic imprint of the above companies and has companies and representatives throughout the world.

Palgrave® and Macmillan® are registered trademarks in the United States, the United Kingdom, Europe and other countries.

ISBN 978-1-349-48624-3 ISBN 978-1-137-40093-2 (eBook)
DOI 10.1057/9781137400932

A catalogue record for this book is available from the British Library.

Library of Congress Cataloging-in-Publication Data
Naming, necessity, and more / [edited by] Jonathan Berg University of Haifa, Israel.
pages cm
Includes bibliographical references and index.
ISBN 978-1-349-48624-3
1. Kripke, Saul A., 1940—Congresses. 2. Philosophy—Congresses. 3. Necessity (Philosophy)—Congresses. 4. Reference (Philosophy)—Congresses. 5. Meaning (Philosophy)—Congresses. 6. Wittgenstein, Ludwig, 1889–1951—Congresses. I. Berg, Jonathan, 1954– editor.
B945.K794N36 2014
191—dc23 2014024475

Typeset by MPS Limited, Chennai, India.

Transferred to Digital Printing in 2014

Contents

Acknowledgments

The editor and publishers are grateful to the publishers who have granted permission for the following papers or portions or versions thereof to be reprinted here: Chapter 2: Buzaglo, Meir 'Masoret velashon' ['Tradition and Language'], in his *Safa lane-emanim* [*A Language for the Faithful*], Jerusalem: Keter Books and Mandel Foundation, 2008. Chapter 3: Dresner, Eli 'Over-Assignment of Structure', *Journal of Philosophical Logic*, 33 (2004), 467–80, publisher: Springer. Chapter 5: Salmon, Nathan 'Personal Identity: What's the Problem?', in his *Metaphysics, Mathematics, and Meaning: Philosophical Papers*, vol. I, Oxford/New York: Oxford University Press, 2005, pp. 192–225. Salmon, Nathan 'Trans-World Identification and Stipulation', *Philosophical Studies*, 84 (1996), 203–23, publisher: Springer. Chapter 8: Shagrir, Oron 'Kripke's Infinity Argument', *Iyyun: The Jerusalem Philosophical Quarterly*, 57 (2008), 3–24. Chapter 9: Horwich, Paul 'Kripke's Paradox of Meaning', *Polish Journal of Philosophy*, 3 (2009), 23–32, reprinted in his *Truth–Meaning–Reality*, Oxford/New York: Oxford University Press, 2010, pp. 99–112.

Preface

The chapters in this volume derive from the conference 'Naming, Necessity, and More', held at the University of Haifa in 1999, in honor of Saul Kripke on the occasion of his being awarded the degree of Doctor of Philosophy *honoris causa*. Arranged under the topics of naming, necessity, meaning, skepticism, and logic, the papers (apart from his own) relate to Kripke's writings to varying degrees, sometimes very closely, and sometimes taking his work merely as a point of departure. Either way, they bring new insight to Kripke's work, attesting to its great depth, extraordinary richness, and lasting significance.

The first part of the collection concerns names and rigid designation. Kripke famously argues 'intuitively' (*Naming and Necessity* (*NN*), 49) that proper names are rigid designators. Hanoch Ben-Yami asks whether Kripke's rigidity claim might instead be derived from more basic facts about our use of proper names. He argues that it can on the basis of the principle of the independence of reference, which says that the reference of a name is independent of what is said in the rest of the sentence in which it occurs. He argues that this principle also provides explanations of other aspects of our use of referring expressions, such as the *strong* rigidity of proper names, the use of names of fictional characters, the use of definite descriptions in modal contexts, and the use of natural kind terms. He goes on to consider how Kripke's conception of rigid designation might be threatened by the existence of names shared by more than one individual. After considering and rejecting a number of possible solutions, including one suggested by Kripke himself, Ben-Yami proposes a way of restricting the notion of rigidity to what he calls 'token rigidity' and thereby avoiding the problem posed by shared names.

Kripke's picture of how our use of names is grounded in chains of communication prompts Meir Buzaglo to develop a dialogue between Kripke and the medieval Spanish Jewish philosopher and poet Rabbi Yehuda Halevi on how names are handed down from one speaker to another. The starting point is the classical distinction, most commonly associated with Pascal, between 'the God of Abraham, Isaac, and Jacob' and 'the God of the philosophers'. Halevi construes the Tetragrammaton – composed of the four Hebrew letters *Yod, Hey, Vav, Hey* – as a name of the former, and other names as names of the latter; and he insists that 'the

Tetragrammaton is a name exclusively employable by us, as no other people knows its true meaning'. This leads Buzaglo to wonder how the chains of communication by which names are passed on could possibly be confined in principle to just one group of speakers. What is there to prevent a 'philosopher' from acquiring the name for the God of the patriarchs? Buzaglo proposes a solution based on the role of a community's traditions, or forms of life, in determining reference. In particular, the acquisition of a name may be restricted to individuals who follow the community's traditions with regard to who is to be recognized as a semantic authority.

The second part of the book deals with necessity. Eli Dresner aims to show how certain kinds of talk of possible worlds are just instances of a general fallacy he calls 'the measurement-theoretic fallacy of "over-assignment of structure": the unwarranted assumption that every numeric relation holding among two (or more) numbers represents some empirical, physical relation among the objects to which these numbers are assigned as measures'. An example of this fallacy would be to think that if one body has a temperature of 20 °C and another has a temperature of 10 °C, then the first is twice as hot as the second. After showing how this fallacy arises in philosophical discussion of the reducibility of arithmetic to set theory and in the ascription of full-blown intentional states to pre- or nonverbal creatures or machines, Dresner turns to possible worlds semantics. Useful as it is in talking about necessity and other modal notions, possible worlds talk may lead to questions such as how many possible worlds there are, and whether there can be numerically distinct possible worlds that are identical – as well as questions about possible worlds as real objects. Dresner argues that such illegitimate questions arise from fallaciously transferring the superfluous structure in systems of possible worlds back to the philosophical discussion of the modal notions that the possible worlds talk was brought in to explain.

In one of the most widely discussed footnotes in 20th-century philosophy Kripke suggests how one might prove a version of the principle that 'if a material object has its origin from a certain hunk of matter, it could not have had its origin in any other matter' (*NN*, 114, n. 56). This is the starting point for Teresa Robertson's discussion of what is sometimes called 'Chisholm's paradox': how can the claim that a given artifact could not have been originally made from wholly different matter be retained together with the view that a slight variation in its material origin is *possible*? Robertson examines solutions proposed by Graeme Forbes, Nathan Salmon, and David Lewis, rejecting the first in favor of what she calls the 'Salmon–Lewis solution', which she argues is better implemented by Salmon than by Lewis.

Moving now from origin essentialism to individual essentialism, we have Nathan Salmon's discussion of the problem of personal identity, which he argues splits into two. What he calls the 'essentialist' problem seeks a criterion of personal identity involving metaphysical necessity, while the 'reductionist' problem seeks a criterion involving logical necessity. Discussing three variations of brain transplant cases, Salmon proposes a criterion based on the continuation of the same brain functioning as a solution to the essentialist problem. On the other hand, he claims to solve the reductionist problem by rejecting it on the basis of considerations of impossible worlds and a proof of the determinacy of identity.

The third part of the volume contains two chapters on meaning. Gilead Bar-Elli suggests taking the target of *Naming and Necessity* as not merely the description theory of names, but – more significantly – as any cognitivist conception of meaning and reference-determination. Behind the main arguments of *Naming and Necessity* Bar-Elli sees what he calls a 'modal conception of meaning', whereby meaning is '*intrinsically modal*, in that the mastery and understanding of simple sentences involve understanding their truth conditions in counterfactual situations'. He argues that, properly understood, Frege's cognitivist conception of meaning is not ruled out by Kripke's modal conception.

In my own contribution to the volume I explore what David Kaplan has dubbed the 'Twilight Zone' – the area Kripke warns of at the end of his discussion of Pierre, 'where our normal apparatus for the ascription of belief is placed under the greatest strain and may even break down'. I try to clarify what the Twilight Zone is, how we get into it, and what we should do about it.

Part IV of the book deals with Kripke's discussion of Wittgenstein's skepticism about rule-following. Oron Shagrir discusses Kripke's infinity argument, claiming that it does not rule out a dispositional account of meaning, neither for perceptual terms, such as 'horse', nor for mathematical terms, such as '+'. Nevertheless, he suggests that Kripke's argument does show that it is wrong to think of symbol machines as being disposed to computing infinite functions, such as addition. The moral he draws from the argument is that 'the dispositionalist cannot fully rely on symbol machines to account for the meaning of arithmetical terms'.

Paul Horwich proposes a deflationary reply to Kripke's skeptic. Instead of looking for a *direct* explanation of how a word's having some underlying non-semantic property makes it true of exactly the things in its extension, Horwich shows how we can get an *indirect* explanation by making use of the deflationary schema which implicitly defines 'true of' – for example 'w means DOG $\rightarrow$ (x)(W is true of x $\leftrightarrow$ x is a dog)'. Using the deflationary schema in this way would seem to obviate the arguably impossible task of harboring infinitely many intentions about how to use a word.

Mark Steiner takes up Kripke's comparison of Wittgenstein's skepticism with that of Hume's. Steiner finds much in common between the two: both reject philosophical explanation and theories; both favor the views of the common man over those of the professional philosopher; both view philosophy as a struggle against superstition; and both use skeptical arguments, not to establish the position of the skeptic, but to attack academic philosophy and its explanatory pretensions. From this perspective Steiner analyzes Hume's arguments against 'necessary connections' and the causal theory of perception, and Wittgenstein's rule-following paradox, his argument against private language, and some of his arguments against mathematical Platonism.

In Part V Kripke's chapter crosses the frontiers between logic, history of logic, and philosophy of logic. He shows how Godel's incompleteness theorem '*could* have, and perhaps *should* have' been the inevitable result of a certain historic line of thought. After a brief review of Godel's own proof, highlighting the 'almost magical way' it yields the crucial undecidable formula that in effect says of itself that it is unprovable, Kripke takes us down a road, beginning with the paradoxes of set theory, that shows that the unrestricted comprehension schema leads to a contradiction. The road continues to Grelling's paradox – seen as a version of Russell's paradox, satisfaction replacing membership – which, in turn, after we replace satisfaction by provability, leads to a straightforward construction of what in effect is Godel's statement G – which Kripke concludes could actually be called Godel's form of the heterological paradox. Anyone who remembers going through Godel's proof for the first time cannot help but appreciate the elegance and simplicity of the route Kripke shows us.

Notes on the Contributors

Gilead Bar-Elli is Professor Emeritus of Philosophy at the Hebrew University of Jerusalem. His main fields of research are philosophy of logic, philosophy of language, classical analytic philosophy, philosophy of music, and Jewish philosophy. His books include *The Sense of Reference: Intentionality in Frege* (1996), *Fathers of Analytic Philosophy: Frege, Russell, Wittgenstein*, vols I, III (2009, in Hebrew), and *Truth, Belief, Secularity and Idolatry* (2010, in Hebrew).

Hanoch Ben-Yami is a professor in the Department of Philosophy of the Central European University in Budapest. His philosophical publications include papers on logic, language, mind, time and causality in special relativity, medical ethics, Wittgenstein, and also a satirical play on experimental philosophy. Ben-Yami's current research is mainly in two areas. He has been developing a new logic, closer than the predicate calculus to natural language, with a formal system and with applications to plural logic, modality, and more. He is also working on a book on Descartes, in which he shows that some of Descartes' most important philosophical innovations are the product of a variety of influences, coming from the technological, scientific, mathematical and other disciplines of the time, and which were not developed by the method Descartes declared he was following in the *Meditations*.

Jonathan Berg teaches in the Department of Philosophy at the University of Haifa and has held visiting appointments at UCLA, the University of Pittsburgh, Simon Fraser University, the University of Bristol, the University of London, Georgetown University, and the Graduate Center at CUNY. His publications include *Direct Belief: An Essay on the Semantics, Pragmatics, and Metaphysics of Belief* (2012), and *Applied Logic: A Guide to the Principles of Argument* (1998, in Hebrew).

Meir Buzaglo is a lecturer in the Department of Philosophy at the Hebrew University of Jerusalem. After finishing his graduate studies in mathematics he wrote a dissertation on Solomon Maimon's philosophy, later published as *Solomon Maimon: Monism, Skepticism and Mathematics* (2002). While visiting Hilary Putnam at Harvard University in 1992 he began work on *The Logic of Concept Expansion* (2002). Since 2002 he has turned his attention to the link between the foundations of physics and metaphysics. Buzaglo has also worked on issues of Jewish identity, which brought him to a project on faithfulness as a key to the variety of contemporary Jewish identities, presented in *A Language for the Faithful* (2008, in Hebrew). Buzaglo is now combining his interest in Jewish identity with pure metaphysics in his research on Maimonides, where he is trying to develop a Neo-Maimonidean world view.

Eli Dresner is an associate professor in the Philosophy and Communication Departments at Tel Aviv University. His areas of interest are the philosophy of language, philosophy of logic and computing, and the philosophy of communication. Among the journals in which his papers have been published are *Synthese, Linguistics and Philosophy, Mind and Language, The Journal of Philosophical Logic,* and *The Journal of Philosophy.*

Paul Horwich is a professor of philosophy at New York University. He has published the following books: *Probability and Evidence* (1980), *Asymmetries in Time* (1987), *Truth* (1990; 2nd edn 1998), *Meaning* (1998), *From a Deflationary Point of View* (2004), *Reflections on Meaning* (2005), *Truth–Meaning–Reality* (2010), and *Wittgenstein's Metaphilosophy* (2012).

Saul A. Kripke was the author of pioneering results in modal logic while still in high school. He continued to develop and extend these insights in subsequent technical work. With 'Identity and Necessity' and *Naming and Necessity* – two published lectures given in the early 1970s that became classics almost upon publication – his work turned towards the philosophical implications of his formal investigations. Then and now, his work is marked by formal rigor coupled with an engaging and accessible prose style.

Teresa Robertson is Associate Professor of Philosophy at the University of California, Santa Barbara. Her primary interests are in topics that fall into the areas of metaphysics and philosophy of language. She has published articles on origin essentialism, the sorites paradox, and reference to kinds. She owes a great debt to Saul Kripke for the philosophical education she received from him while she was a graduate student at Princeton.

Nathan Salmon is Distinguished Professor of Philosophy at the University of California, Santa Barbara, where he has taught for 30 years. As both an undergraduate and a graduate student at UCLA he took several courses and seminars with Kripke. He later became Kripke's colleague, both at Princeton University and later still at the Graduate Center of CUNY, where he taught as a regular visiting distinguished professor from 2009 to 2012 and where he has served on the advisory board of the Saul Kripke Center.

Oron Shagrir is Vice Rector and Professor of Philosophy and Cognitive Science at the Hebrew University of Jerusalem. His current research aims at understanding the claim that the brain computes. He is the editor, with Jack Copeland and Carl Posy, of *Computability: Gödel, Church, Turing, and Beyond* (2013), and is the author of many articles and book chapters on computation and supervenience. Journals in which he has published articles include *Mind, Philosophy and Phenomenological Research, Philosophical Studies, Philosophy of Science,* and *the British Journal for the Philosophy of Science.*

Mark Steiner taught at Columbia University from 1970 to 1977, and then until his retirement at the Hebrew University of Jerusalem, where he was Chair of the Philosophy Department for a good part of the 1990s. His books include *Mathematical Knowledge* (1974), *The Applicability of Mathematics as a Philosophical Problem* (1998), and an edited Hebrew translation of Hume's *Treatise* (2013). He has written a number of articles and lectured widely on Wittgenstein. Lately he has been working in Guangzhou, China.

Part I
Naming

1
Why Rigidity?

Hanoch Ben-Yami

Introduction

According to Kripke, proper names in natural language are rigid designators. That is, a proper name that designates some object in our world, designates the same object in every possible world in which that object exists (*Naming and Necessity* (*NN*), pp. 48–9) and does not designate any different object in any other possible world (more on this last clause below). For example, the proper name 'Plato' is a rigid designator, since in a sentence describing a counterfactual situation, for instance,

> Plato would not have been a philosopher had he died as a child.

it designates the same individual that it designates in sentences about the actual world, namely Plato.

The rigidity of proper names might seem to be a *contingent* fact about natural language: it might seem that a language in which names are *not* rigid designators should be possible. Indeed, the literature usually presents the claim that proper names are rigid as empirical, derived not from theory but from observation. Stanley, for instance, explicitly writes that the thesis that names are rigid is 'an empirical claim about natural language' (1997, p. 566). The question then arises: why are the proper names of *our* natural languages rigid? This question, which is never raised by Kripke, deserves some attention.

By contrast to Kripke, I will attempt in this chapter to derive rigidity, or something close to it, from more basic facts about our use of names. It will turn out that rigidity is a necessary property of names.

Attempts to derive rigidity from some more basic facts about language exist in the literature. Kaplan, for instance, has asked:

> How could rigid designation not be based on some deeper semantic property like direct reference? It couldn't be an accident that names were rigid and descriptions were not. (1989, p. 571)

As this paragraph indicates, Kaplan tried to derive rigidity from his idea of direct reference. I tend to think, however, that his concept of direct reference is insufficiently clear. Yet examining it critically is a topic for a different work, so I shall not discuss here his attempted derivation.[1] I shall take a different route in this chapter.

The principle of the independence of reference

How do we use proper names in modal sentences? In ordinary language, names are used to describe possible situations mainly in sentences beginning or structured like, for instance, the following incomplete ones:

> Socrates could have ...
> Plato might have been ...
> Aristotle could not have been ...
> If Socrates had been ..., then Plato couldn't have ...
> It could have been the case that Socrates, but not Plato ...

And so on.[2] That is, we refer to people and 'modally' predicate of them various things, namely, we express this ascription not by the copulas 'is', 'was', 'will be', etc., but by modal ones like 'might', 'could' and so on. Or we may modally deny them some properties; or again, we may modally ascribe these properties only conditionally; etc. And the reference of names used in the description of the possible situation is independent of what is said in the rest of the sentence containing them.

This idea, that the reference of a name is independent of what is said in the rest of the sentence in which it occurs (the principle of the

---

[1] For a concise presentation of Kaplan's derivation and a survey of the literature on the relation between rigidity and direct reference, see section 2.1 of LaPorte (2006).

[2] For brevity's sake, I restrict my examples to names of people, and ignore names of animals, places, etc.; I do not think there is any significant modal distinction between all these uses.

independence of reference, or PIR), can be clarified and demonstrated as follows. Suppose someone intends to say that Aristotle might have been a physician instead of a philosopher. She starts saying that, but is interrupted after having said only 'Aristotle might have been'. Although failing to say anything about Aristotle, she did refer to him. The reference of 'Aristotle' is determined independently of what she intended to say about him. Similarly, if we did not hear clearly what a speaker has said, yet did hear him say 'Aristotle', we may know to whom he referred: the referent is determined independently of those parts we failed to hear. Reference is even independent of the fact that we talk about what is merely possible and not actual, or vice versa: if one was interrupted after having said only 'Aristotle ...', or 'Aristotle, as you all know ...', then one has referred to Aristotle, while what one said does not determine whether the situation one intended to describe was actual or merely possible.

That is why I gave above *incomplete* sentences as examples: the reader knew who is mentioned in those partial sentences, although they specified no situation – actual, possible or impossible. This shows that the reference of a name occurring in any of those sentences is independent of the way the sentence containing it might be completed.

Here is a chess picture of the logic of discourse. We first take some chess pieces: this is reference by means of proper names, and in this way the identity of the particulars we talk about is determined. We then arrange these pieces on the board: this is the description of a situation, either actual or merely possible, which is specified by the rest of the sentence. The identity of the chess pieces we pick is independent of the way we later arrange them.

Why is the reference of names independent of what is said in the rest of the sentence containing them? The reason is that, first, unlike definite descriptions and demonstrative phrases, names have no descriptive content, which could relate them to other things mentioned in the sentence. Second, unlike pronouns and definite descriptions, names are not used as anaphors and therefore they cannot have their reference depend on the reference of other phrases in the sentence in the way the reference of anaphors does. And I don't see any other way – with one possible exception soon to be discussed – in which the reference of a phrase might be dependent on other words or phrases in the same sentence. Of course, it cannot be ruled out that I have failed to notice some special construction which does generate such dependence. Yet this would not *refute* the principle but only show that it does not apply to all possible uses of names; and it is also likely that in such constructions names indeed would *not* be rigid.

The fact that names are different in these aspects from definite descriptions, demonstrative phrases, and pronouns is of course not contingent: we *consider* as names those singular terms that are not pronouns nor have their reference determined by the meaning of words that compose them in the way that the reference of definite descriptions and demonstrative phrases is. Consequently, the PIR is not a contingent fact about names.[3]

Phrases that share some features both with names and with definite descriptions do exist, in the form of definite descriptions that have grown capital letters: 'The United Nations', 'Central European University', and so on. Apart from some special cases, the description here has to apply to the thing named, although it does not participate in determining the reference of the phrase. It seems that this standardized use of the capitalized description also prevents it from relating to other parts of the sentence in a way that might influence its reference. So it seems the PIR does hold even for this limiting case of names.

Notice that I have not claimed that the PIR applies *only* to names: other terms and phrases *may* have their reference depend on other words and phrases in the sentence, but it *need not* be so. This is indeed the case with many uses of pronouns, definite descriptions and demonstrative phrases. I shall return to this below.

Before proceeding with additional points, let us consider two objections that might be raised to the PIR. First, as I have maintained that the reference of a name is independent of what is said in the rest of the sentence containing it, its reference should be determinable independently of what is said by the rest of that sentence. But suppose someone says, 'Zeno invented the Arrow Paradox': the audience might know that he is talking about Zeno of Elea and not Zeno the Stoic precisely by relying on other parts of the utterance; in this case, by relying on the fact that the Arrow was mentioned, a paradox invented by Zeno of Elea. Accordingly, contrary to what the PIR claims, a name's reference might be determined by what is said in the rest of the sentence containing it.

---

[3] I was once given the following example as an alleged case in which a name is used as an anaphor: 'Josephine would marry only a man called "Ernest" who is tall and handsome. Ernest is a lucky man!' I am not sure whether this sentence is acceptable, but even if it is, it shows that there is some special and probably exceptional use of names in which reference *is* dependent on what it said earlier in the discourse (as is the second occurrence of 'Ernest' in this example). Notice also that the reference of that anaphoric name would change across possible situations and that it will not be rigid, a fact that supports the derivation below of rigidity from the independence of reference.

This objection, however, confuses a semantic point with an epistemic one; and although it correctly describes the epistemic point, it does not apply to the semantic one, in which we are interested here. The audience indeed may come to *know* to whom a speaker referred with a name or expression by reliance on the meaning of other parts of the sentence uttered; this is the epistemic point. However, *it should be possible* to determine the reference of the name independently of this procedure; this is the semantic aspect of the independence of reference. After all, it is possible that the speaker made a mistake and ascribed the invention of the paradox to Zeno the Stoic. To ascertain whether he is right (Elea) or mistaken (the Stoic), it should be possible to determine to which Zeno he referred without reliance on what he said of him. And this is the idea expressed by the semantic principle of the independence of reference.

The second objection to the principle runs as follows. Suppose I *introduce* a name for a person, saying, for instance, 'Let this baby be *John Smith*'. The reference of 'John Smith' *is* determined, in this case, by what is said in the part of the sentence preceding it, in apparent disagreement with the PIR. However, when such a sentence is used in a naming event, the name is only *mentioned* in the utterance; the naming speech act, if successful, makes a *future use* of the name possible. The form of the sentence should not mislead us into thinking that the name is used to refer in the specific utterance concerned: the sentence could be substituted in that context by 'I name this baby "John Smith"', where the mentioning is explicit. Yet even if one does not accept this response to the apparent counterexample, then we have here an exception to the PIR only in the special case in which a name is introduced into language with a specific reference.

Turning back to rigidity, if the PIR is accepted, then names can be shown to be rigid in the following sense. According to the principle, the reference of a name is determined independently of what is said in the rest of the sentence containing it. Consequently, if what is said by the rest of the sentence makes it necessary to consider a variety of possibilities in order to determine its truth-value, the reference of the name that the sentence contains is determined independently of these possibilities and is therefore the same for all. The name is therefore rigid.

In one place in NN, while critically discussing the alleged problem of transworld identity, Kripke comes close to explaining rigidity in a way similar to the way developed here. He writes:

> We do not begin with worlds ... and then ask about criteria of transworld identification; on the contrary, we begin with the objects,

which we *have*, and can identify, in the actual world. We can then ask whether certain things might have been true of the objects. (*NN*, 53)

I believe this passage expresses the same aspect of modal discourse Kripke characterized earlier in his book (*NN*, 44) by claiming that possible worlds are stipulated. Now 'beginning with the objects' may be read as expressing figuratively the idea of the independence of the reference of names of what is said in the rest of the sentence. In this respect my derivation of rigidity may develop a line of thought found in *NN*.

Yet we should also note some differences. I have attempted to derive rigidity from a more general principle of the reference of names. Nothing of this sort is found in Kripke's work, which argues 'intuitively' for the rigidity of proper names (*NN*, 49) by means of examples alone.

Another difference between what Kripke says in the quoted passage and the approach developed here is that only according to the former do 'we begin with the objects, which we *have*, and can identify, in the actual world'. On the view developed here we may 'begin' with objects that do not really exist, objects which we do not have in the actual world. We shall see some examples of this below, where I shall also note some further related differences.

Lastly, in the quoted passage Kripke is trying to explain rigidity, but I shall eventually suggest the PIR as an *improvement* on the rigidity claim. So far, the PIR has been used to support and derive the rigidity of proper names. However, I shall now turn to difficulties in the accepted conception of rigidity. These difficulties might lead us to consider the PIR as expressing more accurately than the concept of rigidity the facts about names that the latter was meant to capture.

Rigidity vis-à-vis independence of reference applied to other aspects of name use

In this section I will show that describing by means of the concept of rigidity the principles governing the reference of names and other referring expressions involves several layers of contingency, which is unexplained by theory – contingency which disappears once we adopt the PIR.

Let us consider the following sentence:

(1) If Abraham hadn't met Sarah, Isaac wouldn't have been born.

Here we describe a possible situation in which Isaac would not have existed. All the same, the name 'Isaac' in (1) clearly designates Isaac. This reference is straightforward according to the PIR: the designation of 'Isaac' is independent of what is said in the rest of the sentence; in particular, it is independent of whether its designatum would have existed in the situation specified by the rest of the sentence. 'Isaac' may therefore designate, when used in (1), the same person whom it often designates when used to talk about the actual world, namely the second patriarch.

On the other hand, according to the rigidity claim, the question of the designation of 'Isaac' in (1) is still unsettled. The question is the following. When we use a name to talk about a possible situation in which the person that the name designates when used to talk about the actual world does not exist, whom does the name designate, if it still designates at all? Kripke's definition of rigidity in *NN* leaves this question unanswered:

> A designator rigidly designates a certain object if it designates that object wherever the object exists. (48–9)

Nothing is said on what, if anything, is designated when talking about possible situations in which the object does not exist. At that stage of his thought Kripke was at least occasionally inclined to define rigidity so that in worlds where the object does not exist the name does not designate anything:

> When I use the notion of rigid designator ... all I mean is that in any possible world where the object in question *does* exist ... we use the designator in question to designate that object. In a situation where the object does not exist, then we should say that the designator has no referent. (1971, p. 173)

However, as is made clear by what he writes in *NN*, he was also occasionally inclined to think that even in such situations the name might designate the same object. On page 78 Kripke gives the following example: 'If you say "suppose Hitler had never been born" then "Hitler" refers here, still rigidly, to something that would not exist in the counterfactual situation described.' This example of course necessitated changing in *NN* the explanation of rigidity I just quoted from the 1971 paper.

This example and the change of definition demonstrate that the idea of rigidity of names does not naturally dictate how they should function when talking about possible situations in which what they otherwise name does not exist. And from the *NN* example we see that Kripke came to think that proper names are not only rigid, but form a sub-class of rigid designators. Indeed, in a seminar delivered much later at the Hebrew University in Jerusalem (in April 2000), he elaborated the concept of rigidity as follows. A designator, he defined, 'is *strictly* rigid if and only if there is an *a* such that it designates *a* in *all* possible worlds' – including, as he explicitly said there, worlds in which *a* does not exist. And names in natural language, he maintained, are *strictly* rigid.[4]

We see that in order to capture the semantics of proper names in natural language, we need to distinguish several kinds of rigidity. Moreover, Kripke does not explain *why* proper names should be *strictly* rigid and not form a different sub-class of rigid designators. He presents their being strictly rigid as an unexplained empirical fact about natural language, a fact which is not necessitated by their rigidity, let alone by their being names. The theory of the rigidity of proper names contains several unexplained layers of contingency.

By contrast, as we saw above, this 'strict rigidity' of proper names is derived a priori from the PIR. So we have here a reason for preferring the characterization of the behavior of names by means of the idea of the independence of reference over its characterization by means of the concept of rigidity.

Let us also examine proper names of a different kind: names of fictional characters. They not only turn out to be 'rigid', but they also show, *pace* Kripke, that we do not have to 'begin with the objects, which we *have*, and can identify, in the actual world'. We may say, for instance:

(2) If Sherlock Holmes had existed, some unsolved crime mysteries in Victorian Britain would have been solved.

Here we 'begin' with a merely possible entity, taken from the world of Conan Doyle's novels, a character that does not exist and whom we cannot consequently identify in the actual world, and then say something about what could have happened.[5] In the contemplated counterfactual situation,

---

[4] Strictly rigid designators were earlier called *obstinately rigid designators* by Salmon (1981, p. 34).

[5] Kripke argued that, 'granted that there is no Sherlock Holmes, one cannot say of any possible person that he *would have been* Sherlock Holmes, had he existed' (*NN*, p. 158; 2011, p. 59; 1973, Lecture 2). I find his argument there invalid (Ben-Yami, 2010), but justifying my position would constitute too large a digression given the aims of this chapter. Since Kripke's position on fictional characters is far from being generally accepted, I believe it is worth considering here the consequences of a plausible alternative position for the rigidity claim. Similarly, Kripke argued that fictional characters *do* exist in our world, but as some kind of abstract objects (2011, pp. 62ff.; 1973). Again, the fact that this view is far from being generally accepted and that it would take too much space to discuss it here allows me, I believe, to examine the consequences for the rigidity claim of a more plausible position that I adopt without argument, namely that Sherlock Holmes simply *never* existed. But of course, if some do accept Kripke's views of fictional characters, this should make them reject my last example.

the name designates the same detective it designates when talking of the world of Doyle's novels, so it presumably exhibits some kind of rigidity. That it behaves in this way is again on the rigidity approach a contingent fact empirically observed, while it is derivable from the PIR.

I shall now examine the use of definite descriptions in modal contexts. Unlike names, definite descriptions, in virtue of their descriptive content, may allude to what is said in other parts of the sentence, in which case their reference may be partly determined by what is said there. Consider, for instance, the sentence

(3) If elections had been postponed, the person who would then have been prime minister would have faced an impossible situation.

The definite description 'the person who would then have been prime minister' in the consequent refers to a person who would have been prime minister in the situation specified in the antecedent, so its reference is partly determined by what is said there.

However, as noted above, the definite description *need not* contain material that mentions what is said in the rest of the sentence, in which case its reference would be independent of that, and it would exhibit the same rigid behavior as names do. This can be seen in the following example:

(4) The prime minister wouldn't have been elected had his opponent been a better rhetorician.

The phrase 'the prime minister' refers to someone who in the situation described would not have been the prime minister, namely the actual prime minister. Its reference in the merely possible situation is identical to its reference in the actual world, and it should therefore be classified as rigid. (The same applies to demonstrative phrases.)

Kripke himself was 'tentatively inclined' to reject the view that definite descriptions are sometimes rigid (1971, p. 176, n. 11). He thought that any such alleged rigid use could be handled 'by Russell's notion of scope' (*NN*, pp. 59–60, n. 22), presumably by analyzing definite descriptions as quantified constructions. But if, unlike Russell and together with Frege and Strawson, we do consider such descriptions to be singular terms occurring in the logical argument position, then the notion of scope cannot be applied to them. On this view of definite descriptions, the former example *is* a case of what Kripke should regard as their rigid use.

Why is the definite description in sentence (4) used rigidly? From the fact that proper names are rigid it does not follow that any definite description should be. We again have on Kripke's approach an unexplained empirically observed fact about natural language; yet another layer of contingency. By contrast, this fact can again be derived from the PIR: in the case when the reference of a definite description does not depend on what is said in the rest of the sentence, the description will exhibit the same rigid behavior as names do, namely, its reference will be constant across different circumstances of evaluation.

I will conclude this section by examining the application of the PIR to terms of a different kind, which Kripke also claimed are rigid: terms of natural kinds and phenomena. Kripke's examples were 'gold', 'heat', 'light', 'molecular motion', 'pain', 'my being in such and such a brain state', and 'yellowness' (*NN*, pp. 128, 136, 139, 148; 1971, p. 189). Presumably he would agree that names of biological types are also rigid, since in his discussion of their meaning he does not distinguish these from the former cases. We can therefore assume, with the literature, that 'tiger', 'feline', etc. are supposed to be rigid as well.

What this rigidity could amount to has puzzled the literature. Since the tigers and the pieces of gold that exist in our world need not have existed in all possible situations, and since there might have existed some tigers and pieces of gold that do not actually exist, the reference of 'tigers' and 'gold' is not the same across possibilities. In face of this problem, Donnellan (1983) suggested that a rigid general term designates a kind, and that this stays the same across possibilities. Yet Donnellan's suggestion empties the notion of the rigidity of general terms of any content, for if we adopt it *all* general terms will turn out to be rigid.[6] Devitt and Sterelny (1999, pp. 85–6, 312) have suggested that natural kind terms have what they called rigid *application*, namely, if such a term applies to an object in the actual world then it applies to that object in every possible world in which it exists. But this is unacceptable. A queen bee is presumably a natural kind, but whether a bee develops into a queen depends on what it is fed; thus, a queen bee need not have been a queen bee, and the term 'queen bee' does not apply to it across possibilities. Similarly, due to radioactive decay, a piece of matter can change from being predominantly one kind of stuff to being predominantly a different kind of stuff, in which case a natural kind term does not apply to it any longer. Consequently,

---

[6] See LaPorte (2000) for an attempt to overcome this problem, and Schwartz (2002) for criticism.

natural kind terms need not have rigid application. Kripke's claim that some general terms are rigid thus seems either empty of content or wrong.

The discussion above may shed light on the confusions involved. I have derived the rigidity claim for proper names from the PIR, and also showed that this principle can explain more aspects of the behavior of proper names as well as of definite description than can the rigidity claim. Turning to general terms, all words and phrases considered by Kripke do not have a descriptive content that may allude to other parts of the sentence containing them. Their meaning, like that of names and unlike that of definite descriptions, should therefore be independent of what is said in the rest of the sentence containing them. Since they are general terms, however, this should apply to their *meaning* and not to their reference or extension: their extension may vary between possible situations, but not their meaning. Moreover, the principle applies not only to natural kind terms but to other general terms as well. Accordingly, if we see the rigidity claim as an unclear expression of the PIR, then applying this principle, with appropriate changes, to general terms shows in what sense their behavior is similar to that of proper names and why they seemed rigid to Kripke.

To review the discussion so far, we have seen that the claim that names are rigid is derivable from the principle that the reference of names is independent of what is said in the rest of the sentence containing them. We also saw that one can derive from this principle additional facts about the use of names, definite descriptions, and general terms, which are unexplained by the rigidity claim. The PIR is thus more general than the rigidity claim. In the next section I shall show that the rigidity claim, as formalized by Kripke, involves a difficulty that should make us modify it and consider it as more limited in scope than often thought, while this difficulty does not face the PIR.

A problem with rigidity

Names obviously do not always have the same reference: 'Zeno', for instance, is used to name both Zeno the Stoic and Zeno of Elea. And the name 'Zeno' used in a modal sentence to name Zeno the Stoic ('Zeno would have remained a merchant had he not visited Athens') has a different reference from the same name used to name Zeno of Elea in a non-modal sentence ('Zeno invented the Arrow Paradox'). So if we apply the accepted definition of rigidity literally – a term is a rigid designator if in every possible world, the actual one included, it designates the same object (*NN*, p. 48) – it follows that proper names are not rigid: the proper name 'Zeno' may designate different people when used to talk about the actual world and a merely possible situation, as the example demonstrates.

Yet one is bound to feel that this apparent refutation of the rigidity of proper names obviously gets something wrong, although it does seem effective against the application of the concept of rigidity as literally formulated by Kripke and the subsequent literature. Accordingly, we must conclude that the standard, Kripkean definition of rigidity is insufficiently clear; we need to patch it up somehow in order to express correctly what was originally meant by the idea and avoid this apparent difficulty. So what does it mean, that names are rigid?

Kripke was aware of this difficulty when he wrote the Preface to *NN*. He first suggested:

> For language as we have it, we could speak of names as having a unique referent if we adopted a terminology ... according to which uses of phonetically the same sounds to name distinct objects count as distinct names.[7] (*NN*, pp. 7–8)

This 'homonyms' response is indeed the first one I have usually encountered when raising the above-mentioned difficulty.

However, this move trivializes the claim of rigidity: according to it names would be rigid *no matter how they are used*. To see this, consider a language in which the reference of a name in any specific utterance is arbitrarily determined, independently of any other use of the same name in any other utterance. If, following Kripke's suggestion, we considered two phonetically or orthographically identical words as being the same name only if they had the same reference, then in this language Kripkean names would still be rigid. So Kripke's suggested terminology seems to empty the claim that names are rigid of any content. If we wish that claim to say something significant about names, it seems the concept of rigidity should be saved in some other way.

Kripke of course did not think that a mere change of terminology would overcome the difficulty. He goes on to claim that, however we treat such 'homonymous' names when we talk about the truth conditions of a sentence, it must first be fixed who the names it contains name (*NN*, pp. 8–9). But at least prima facie, this does not answer our difficulty: the reference of 'Zeno' in a modal sentence can be fixed in several different ways, and in each case it differs from the reference of the name in some non-modal sentences; so the definition of rigidity

---

[7] See Kaplan (1977, p. 562) for a similar suggestion.

still does not apply. Nor does Kripke show how his claim solves our difficulty: he immediately proceeds to assert that once it is fixed which proposition a sentence expresses, it would, on Russell's account of names, fail to conform to the rule of rigidity – as if the issue of what rigidity means has already been settled. So it might seem we cannot find in Kripke's response an answer to our difficulty. We shall reconsider these passages of the Preface later, but first let us discuss some other attempts to resolve the difficulty.

One certainly can overcome the problem – in theory rather than practice – by, say, adding indices to names, distinguishing '$Zeno_1$' from '$Zeno_2$', and stipulating that the former will be used to refer in all contexts only to Zeno the Stoic, the latter only to Zeno of Elea. In this way the modified proper names will be rigid according to Kripke's definition. But the rigidity of the *modified* proper names does not explain in what sense *ordinary* proper names are rigid, while Kripke's claim was about the latter. And the stipulation would make the modified names rigid, no matter how ordinary names are used. Moreover, stipulations can be introduced in a variety of ways: we could also stipulate that '$Zeno_1$' names only Zeno of Elea in non-modal contexts and only Zeno the Stoic in modal ones, and in this way render our modified names *non*-rigid. So the theoretical availability of stipulations is neither here nor there when we consider the rigidity of names in natural language.

Should we say that if the name 'Zeno' is used in a modal sentence with the same *meaning* it has in a non-modal one, it then has the same reference, and that *that* is what is meant by rigidity? This is the way Fitch – the only author apart from Kripke of whom I am aware who discusses this difficulty – tries to overcome the problem (2004, pp. 43–6). Our examples of different uses of the name 'Zeno' above, which apparently demonstrated that the name is not rigid, would not be, according to Fitch, uses of the name with the same meaning, and therefore they are merely apparent counterexamples. Yet the talk of the meaning of proper names cannot help us here, as will become evident once we consider what this meaning could be.

First, if we identify the meaning of a proper name with its referent, we will again be arguing in a circle: names are rigid, i.e. the same name refers to the same individual in modal and non-modal sentences, because we count names as the same only if they refer to the same individual in modal and non-modal contexts. As we saw above, this definition empties the rigidity claim of any content.

On the other hand, if what one had in mind in talking about the meaning of a proper name were some kind of description, or perhaps a vaguely bound cluster of differently weighted descriptions, then this would commit one to a version of the description theory of names. This option is of course unavailable to Kripke, who is not only the most renowned critic of the description theory, but in fact uses the very idea of rigidity to argue against that theory (*NN*, Preface and Lecture I). Moreover, the description theory of names is indeed highly problematic: those of us who find Kripke and Donnellan's arguments from ignorance and error[8] sound (*NN*, pp. 80–7; Donnellan 1972) should of course reject it.[9] Finally, I am not acquainted with any other conception of the meaning of a proper name that could help Kripke answer this difficulty. Accordingly, appealing to the meaning of a proper name does not look like a promising way of saving the original idea of rigidity.[10]

Would it help if we substituted for the meaning of a proper name Kripke's idea that a name's reference is determined by a communication chain beginning with the introduction of the name in a naming event (*NN*, Lecture II)?[11] A name's being rigid would then mean that it refers, in modal and non-modal contexts alike, to the referent to whom the chain to which it is appropriately related leads. This attempt would be in agreement with a footnote Kripke added to his suggestion to individuate names according to their reference: 'two totally distinct "historical chains"', he writes, 'that by sheer accident assign phonetically the same name to the same man should probably count as creating distinct names despite the identity of referents' (*NN*, p. 8). But this attempt, I think, would run into similar difficulties. The name 'Zeno' belongs to several communication chains: one leading to Zeno the Stoic, another to Zeno of Elea, and many additional ones leading to other people

[8] I use Devitt and Sterelny's term (1999) for the argument; Salmon (1981) calls it the *semantic* argument.

[9] I think there are also other important considerations against the description theory, which I intend to develop in a separate work.

[10] Yet it is worth noting that if one does adhere to a description theory of names, then one can coherently reformulate the idea of rigidity by relying on the meaning of the name as expressed by the description associated with it – an approach unavailable to those who reject the theory. Whether that could save the claim that names are rigid will then depend on the soundness of Kripke's modal argument against description theories of proper names.

[11] Almog (1984) has powerfully argued that the communication chain cannot be taken as belonging to semantics, but that its role is pre-semantic. If that is so then the communication chain obviously cannot be substituted for the *meaning* of a name, as suggested in the text. For the sake of argument I ignore this difficulty in this chapter.

named 'Zeno'. Moreover, a person using 'Zeno' in a specific utterance to refer to the Stoic philosopher might do that in a context in which some other Zeno has also been discussed, and perhaps he was reminded of Zeno the Stoic precisely because of that other Zeno, so his current use of the name is also related to the chain that leads to the other Zeno. The question consequently arises, when such a person says, 'Zeno would have remained a merchant had he not visited Athens', as to what determines to which of these chains this token of 'Zeno' is related? If the chain is determined by identity of reference, then this again would make names rigid no matter how they are used, so this cannot be what the rigidity claim amounts to. Neither can Kripke determine the chain by the description one would give of the named person, because that would endow names with descriptive meaning, an option he rejects. And I am unaware of any other option of determining a communication chain that could save the rigidity claim. So I do not think reliance on communication chains can help Kripke here.

In view of the difficulty of identifying the *meaning* of a name with an appropriate description, should we perhaps allot the description only the more modest role of *fixing the reference* of the name, and classify two tokens of phonetically or orthographically the same expression as being of the same name just in case their reference is fixed in the same way? This would not do either, for the following reasons.

We cannot demand, for this classification of names, identity of the descriptions that speakers supply or would supply for fixing the reference, for even the same speaker might supply different descriptions on different occasions: 'The inventor of the Arrow Paradox', 'The inventor of the Achilles Paradox', 'Parmenides's most famous follower' and other descriptions may be equally forthcoming, and on this approach would bring about an undesirable multiplicity of names. Neither can we classify names by the cluster of the descriptions available to the speaker, for this would result in different people using different names, even when all use 'Zeno' to refer to Zeno of Elea. And if we counted two ways of fixing the reference as the same just in case they yielded the same referent, then again we are classifying names according to identity of reference, and names would turn out rigid no matter how they are used. So neither can the way reference is fixed help us here.

All the responses discussed above to our difficulty, which were shown to be unsatisfactory, are either found in the literature or were given to me by professional philosophers. They therefore show, I believe, that even if this difficulty can be satisfactorily settled, the concept of rigidity as currently used is in need of clarification.

Let us try a different approach to the problem. The problem arose when we compared the uses of the same name across different sentences and tried to see in what sense the name is then rigid. We can call this type of rigidity *inter-sentential rigidity*. We failed to find an acceptable sense of 'same name' in which names are inter-sententially rigid. However, we may try instead to introduce a notion of a name *token* being rigid, *token rigidity*.

The attempt to ascribe rigidity to name tokens would go as follows. When determining the truth-value of a modal utterance containing a name, the truth-value of the utterance should be evaluated in every (relevant) possibility, and in each such evaluation the name designates the same object, which is also the object it designates in the actual world. This is a non-trivial property of the modal discourse, which is independent of the use across utterances of name tokens, and therefore does not involve any problematic need to classify token names into name types.

Although this is an important observation on modal discourse, it is problematic as an interpretation of *all that was meant* by rigidity. First, several passages of *NN* strongly support the claim that Kripke thought rigidity is inter-sentential and characterizes not only name tokens. Consider, for instance, the following:

> When I hear the name 'Hitler', I do get an illusory 'gut feeling' that it's sort of analytic that that man was evil. But really, probably not. Hitler might have spent all his days in quiet in Linz. In that case we would not say that then this man would not have been Hitler, for we use the name 'Hitler' just as the name of that man, even in describing other possible worlds. (This is the notion which I called a rigid designator in the previous talk.) (*NN*, p. 75)

The talk of use here suggests recurrent use, and not only the occurrence of one token in one sentence; and it is hard to see how to make sense of this passage when only one token is being considered. Accordingly, Kripke was probably thinking of rigidity not only as token rigidity. Moreover, Kripke maintained that the idea of rigidity makes sense also when applied to sentences containing *no* modal or other operator, such as 'Aristotle was fond of dogs' (*NN*, pp. 6–12). The attempt to clarify rigidity by applying it to name tokens in modal contexts alone would thus make it more limited in meaning than was intended by Kripke.

Let us reconsider Kripke's remarks on rigidity in the Preface to *NN* to see whether he succeeded in conferring on rigidity any additional meaning. On pages 6–12 of the Preface Kripke contrasts, in order to clarify the idea of rigidity, the following two sentences:

(5) Aristotle was fond of dogs.
(6) The last great philosopher of antiquity was fond of dogs.[12]

A proper understanding of (5) and (6), he writes, involves an understanding both of the conditions under which they are in fact true, and of the conditions under which a counterfactual course of history would be correctly described by them. The rigidity thesis, he continues, is simply that (5) correctly describes a counterfactual situation just in case *the same man* who should be fond of dogs in order for (5) to be *in fact* true, namely Aristotle, would have been fond of dogs in that counterfactual situation. By contrast, for a counterfactual course of history to make (6) true, *a different man* than the one who should be fond of dogs to make (6) in fact true might have had to be fond of dogs.

The way the designation of the proper name in (5) is determined is indeed different from the way the designation of the definite description in (6) is – this is Kripke's claim that names are not implicit definite descriptions, which I am not contesting. The question is: in what sense might the reference of the subject term of (6) change while that of (5) remains constant as regards counterfactual situations? Once the reading of both sentences is determined, as Kripke assumes on pages 8–10, both make a claim about the actual world and both are about Aristotle. To change the referent of the definite description of (6), we need to change the context in which that referent is determined. Namely, to use Kaplan's terms, we need to consider not only different circumstances of evaluation but *different contexts of utterance*. Only in such different contexts might 'the last great philosopher of antiquity' stand for a person different from Aristotle.

However, once we change the context of utterance, the referent of 'Aristotle' might also change; and this is so on any theory of how the reference of names is determined, Kripke's own communication-chain picture included. To convince ourselves of that, consider how we would set about verifying (5) in that case. Someone asserts in our presence, 'Aristotle was fond of dogs'. We first have to find out which Aristotle he is talking about: we have to fix the intended reading of (5); this is granted by Kripke (*NN*, p. 9). We therefore find out to which communication chain the speaker is related; for instance, he met the name

[12] For the sake of argument I pretend that Aristotle was the last great philosopher of antiquity.

'Aristotle' in a specific introductory book entitled *Aristotle*, and he now uses the name intending to refer to the same person to whom the author of that book referred. In the actual world, this communication chain leads back to Aristotle; but in a different context of utterance it might lead to a different person, and then the referent of 'Aristotle' in (5) would be different from its actual referent.

Notice that I am *not* confusing here (i) a *modal* assertion made in the actual world about a possible situation and (ii) an assertion that might have been made in that possible situation about that situation (this is a confusion Kripke rightly warned against (*NN*, p. 77)). Rather, we are considering what the name in the non-modal sentence (5) would have designated had its context of utterance been different, as it *has to be* in order for the reference of *the definite description* of (6) to change the way Kripke wishes it to change. And the name might then have also designated a different person.

It is easy to see that we shall have similar variability of reference with context of utterance for any available account of the reference of names. Accordingly, no acceptable sense of rigidity can be extracted from considering these examples.

I therefore suspect that the only sense of the rigidity claim that can be maintained is the token-rigidity in modal sentences we considered above, which I claimed is a particular case of the PIR. We could not save any additional sense of that claim, although it seems Kripke did mean it as implying more than just token rigidity.

To conclude, the PIR is more general in scope than Kripke's rigidity claim and can explain more linguistic phenomena than can the latter. It is also justified by considerations on the nature of names. Moreover, the rigidity claim, as understood by the literature, is unclear between inter-sentential and token rigidity, of which only the latter can be maintained; and Kripke's claim to demonstrate the phenomenon of rigidity in non-modal assertions cannot be maintained. The work that the concept of rigidity was meant to do is done better by the idea that the reference of names is independent of what is said in the rest of the sentence containing them.[13]

---

[13] This chapter has profited from comments made by Kripke on a talk delivered at a conference held in Haifa in 1999, and from attending Kripke's seminar given at the Hebrew University during the second semester of the academic year 1999–2000. I am also indebted to Michael Devitt, Peter Hacker, John Hyman, Ran Lanzet, Josep Macià, Genoveva Marti, François Recanati, Zoltan Szabo, and Zsófia Zvolenszky for comments on earlier drafts; to discussions in several forums in which I presented material leading to this chapter; and to my students in seminars I gave at the Central European University in Budapest.

The research leading to these results has received funding from the European Commission's Seventh Framework Programme FP7/2007-2013 under grant agreement no. FP7-238128.

References

Almog, Joseph (1984) Semantical Anthropology. *Midwest Studies in Philosophy* IX: 479–89.

Ben-Yami, Hanoch (2010) Could Sherlock Holmes Have Existed? *Croatian Journal of Philosophy* 10: 175–81.

Devitt, Michael and Kim Sterelny (1999) *Language and Reality: An Introduction to the Philosophy of Language*, 2nd edn. Cambridge, MA: MIT Press.

Donnellan, Keith (1972) Proper Names and Identifying Descriptions. In D. Davidson and G. Harman (eds) *The Semantics of Natural Language*. Dordrecht: Reidel.

Donnellan, K. (1983) Kripke and Putnam on Natural Kind Terms. In C. Ginet (ed.) *Knowledge and Mind: Philosophical Essays*. Oxford: Oxford University Press, 88–104.

Fitch, G.W. (2004) *Saul Kripke*. Chesham: Acumen.

Kaplan, David (1977) Demonstratives. In Joseph Almog, John Perry and Howard Wettstein (eds) (1989) *Themes from Kaplan*. Oxford: Oxford University Press, 481–563.

Kaplan, David (1989) Afterthoughts. In Joseph Almog, John Perry and Howard Wettstein (eds) *Themes from Kaplan*. Oxford: Oxford University Press, 565–614.

Kripke, S. (1971) Identity and Necessity. Reprinted in A.W. Moore (ed.) (1993) *Meaning and Reference*. Oxford: Oxford University Press, 162–91.

Kripke, S. (1973) Reference and Existence, unpublished typescript, The John Locke Lectures, Oxford .

Kripke, S. (1980) *Naming and Necessity*. Oxford: Blackwell.

Kripke, S. (2011) Vacuous Names and Fictional Entities. In his *Philosophical Troubles: Collected Papers, vol. I*. Oxford: Oxford University Press.

LaPorte, J. (2000) Rigidity and Kind. *Philosophical Studies* 97: 293–316.

LaPorte, J. (2006) Rigid Designators. In Edward N. Zalta (ed.), *The Stanford Encyclopaedia of Philosophy*. http://plato.stanford.edu/entries/rigid-designators/.

Salmon, N. (1981) *Reference and Essence*. Princeton, NJ: Princeton University Press.

Schwartz, S. (2002) Kinds, General Terms, and Rigidity: A Reply to LaPorte. *Philosophical Studies* 109: 265–77.

Stanley, J. (1997) Names and Rigid Designation. In B. Hale and C. Wright (eds) *A Companion to the Philosophy of Language*. Oxford: Blackwell, 555–85.

2
Tradition and Language

Meir Buzaglo

Introduction

This chapter attempts to present a dialogue between Saul Kripke and the medieval Jewish philosopher and poet, Rabbi Judah Halevi, on the naming of God. By 'dialogue' I do not mean the application of Kripke's concepts to Halevi's notions. My intent is to engage them in a dialogue that requires the modification of Kripke's theory of a chain of communication through an examination of Halevi's differentiation between the names of God. This involves the classical distinction between 'the God of Abraham, Isaac, and Jacob' and 'the philosophers' God'.

In the first, interpretive, section, I will introduce Halevi's position and his claim that there is a name of God that is inaccessible to philosophers. It turns out we can shed light on his position *not* in terms of Frege's distinction between sense and reference, but rather by focusing on the way names are handed down from one speaker to another. In the second section I will place this view within a general picture on names. The impossibility of transferring a name to philosophers is not a singular phenomenon which is true only for a name of God, but a general phenomenon more likely to arise when we take into consideration the role played by tradition in the creation of language.

Part I: the question

Halevi's point

In the fourth part of his book, *Kuzari*, Halevi distinguishes between the different names of God. The major distinction is between 'Elohim' (אלוהים, i.e. God, but in a noun form usually reserved for plurals in Hebrew) and 'Jehovah' (the Tetragrammaton יהוה, or YHWH). The designation 'Elohim' is also used to denote judge or ruler. Halevi explains that the name 'Elohim' can appear with the definite article and therefore indicates a quality. In contrast to this, the second name for God, or rather a family of names, of which the most outstanding is YHWH, is not considered as denoting a quality:

> And there is no name more precise or important than the one indicated by the letters YHWH. It is a proper name with which one refers to God not by indicating His role or His qualities, but by using a name special to Him. It is as though someone would ask who is this Elohim that is to be worshipped – the sun, the moon or the heavens ...? And the answer is: YHWH. It is as though you point at a certain person and call him by a proper name, e.g. Reuben, or Simon. (*Kuzari*, IV, &1)

In addition (*Kuzari*, IV, &3), Halevi says several other things concerning the difference between the divine names:

a. That which is expressed by 'Elohim' can be known through ratiocination.
b. That which is expressed by 'YHWH' is envisioned internally and directly by the prophets.
c. The name 'YHWH' is associated with salvation, while the name 'Elohim' functions at the level of theoretical knowledge about the world and, as such, it is not connected to human need.

This is how Halevi introduces the classical distinction between the God of the believer and the philosophers' God, which, in several respects, seems to anticipate Pascal's distinction between the philosophers' God and the God of Abraham, Isaac, and Jacob. Indeed, some of the characteristics he injects into this distinction support this reading. However, Halevi also adds something that Pascal does not mention, and which is what interests me in this chapter. Halevi claims that the philosophers are not qualified to speak of God by mentioning the Tetragrammaton (YHWH). Consider the following:

> Thus He singled us out by the words: 'So the Lord alone did lead him, and there was no strange god with him' (Deut. 32:12). The Tetragrammaton is a name exclusively employable by us, as no other people knows its true meaning. (Ibid.)

I shall call this 'Halevi's point'.

The problem of intelligibility

The distinction between the two names, 'Elohim' and 'YHWH', surprisingly reminds us of Russell's distinction between knowledge by description and knowledge by acquaintance.[1] However, the attribute mentioned at the end of the excerpt raises a difficult question. How is it possible that a certain name could be restricted to a particular community of speakers, i.e. the prophets *and* their followers? What prevents a name acquired by some individual to pass on to any other human being? What is it that provides a certain group with access to some name and enables it to use this name in reference to God, while denying other groups the same possibility? Alternatively, in a more positive vein: Which philosophical theory might render Halevi's point intelligible?

First attempt: calling and referring

One way to understand Halevi's point is to consider the role of names in calling forth someone, rather than in formulating propositions about the bearer of the name.[2] Thus, when the prophet invokes God by articulating the name YHWH, he attests to the special relationship that exists between him and God. This notion is supported by Halevi when he says that the name YHWH denotes a special relationship between the people of Israel and their God (ibid.). Just as not everyone is entitled to call some person 'sweetie' or 'daddy', so not everyone may call God by the name YHWH. This name is only available to His servants.

However, this is not a satisfactory answer. First, Halevi seems to hold that even propositions such as 'I am YHWH who brought you out of Egypt' are inaccessible to philosophers. Second, even if we assume that YHWH signals a relationship, this does not necessarily make it an exclusive term. For example, when speaking to a child, one can ask: 'Is daddy at home?' In this case, the word 'daddy' does not denote the kinship between the speaker and his or her own father.[3]

---

1 Russell, as a faithful atheist, would not think of subjecting his theory to such use.

2 There is, of course, a Kabbalistic discourse on the Name into which I will not go here, one reason being, among others, that it is not at all clear that the expression 'Name' is indeed used in the sense of a name. Indeed, in that discussion a prominent place is accorded to the letters of which the name is composed and to their forms, while the role of a name in designating an object is taken to be less essential.

3 Certainly, we could argue that when speaking of the name of God we are prone to face anomalies. While I am sympathetic to this claim, I am well aware that by not placing the anomaly within the context of a wider picture, it may put an end to any philosophical discussion on the names of God.

A Fregean way out

Another natural way to understand Halevi's restriction is to consider it in terms of the Fregean sense vs. reference. According to this suggestion the designation 'YHWH' conveys a different sense than does the counterpart name 'Elohim', and while the former is restricted to believers the latter is accessible to philosophers. To analyze this possibility let us first read Halevi's parable of the lights:

> The sun is only a single body, whilst those receiving their light from it differ in the way they absorb its light. The most fitted to annex its luster are the ruby and the crystal, as well as pure air and water, whose light is called penetrating. Glittering stones with polished surfaces have a reflected light. As for all other things, the light they receive has no special name. Now, the name 'Elohim' corresponds to this general light, as I have explained earlier, while the name YHWH corresponds to penetrating light. (*Kuzari*, IV, &14)

To follow the suggestion offered here we will have to read each light as a way God is given to us, i.e. as a Fregean sense. But there is one important difference: Halevi speaks of different types of light, with some of them superior to others. In this hierarchy, a particular light may penetrate the entire personality of the recipient, while some other light may remain completely outside it. Such a difference is not found, or at least was not developed for Frege's notion of sense.

But this is not a crucial difference. Frege, at least according to one interpretation, claims that not all senses are accessible to all people. I am not accessible to others in the same way that I am accessible to myself when I refer to myself with the word 'I'. And, even more clearly, the way a congenitally blind person grasps the sense of 'light' is different from the way it is grasped by someone who can see. This holds true even though for both of them 'light' has the same reference. Indeed, the difference between 'light' for a blind man and 'light' for someone who can see is analogous to the difference between 'the morning star' and 'the evening star'.

If we read Halevi with Fregean eyes, we can make considerable progress. As far as the name of God is concerned, one sense of God is accessible to the people of Israel and another is open to philosophers. This suggests that, at a later point in time, it would be possible to remove any essential difference between the Israelites and other people, and assert that the different names of God correspond to different senses. That is to say, all religious traditions worship the same God, but they grasp different senses of Him: The light Jews receive from the name YHWH is different from the light received by the Moslems from the name 'Allah'. This is, in fact, a widespread view.

Still, the attempt to interpret Halevi according to Frege involves several problems. These problems do not stem from the fact that much of the mystical in Halevi is not grasped by Fregean thought; that does not seem to me so problematic.[4] One problem is that there is no parallel between the blind man and the philosopher. In the case of the blind man, we have a ready explanation why he cannot grasp some meaning. If, for example, we assume that seeing a red light is the way to grasp the reference of 'red', we understand that being blind is a handicap that affects the grasping of this sense. Yet, what is it about Jews that makes them different? We can stipulate that Jews have a different biology; however, this would be an ad hoc addition, one that Halevi might have accepted, but which does not appeal to me.[5]

The selectivity of transmission

The second problem is even more difficult. It concerns Halevi's thesis that the Jewish tradition of the Sinai Revelation is reliable and the best proof for the validity of the Jewish faith. For if the Revelation were sound evidence, it should be possible for every rational human being, philosophers included, to be convinced by this proof. Halevi, however, claims that the fact that the Revelation is an empirical proof of the Jewish faith makes the latter valid only for the Jews.

---

[4] As in many cases, the dialogue with 'odd' positions can be productive. We may suggest to Frege a ranking of different senses of the same object. Though both the blind person and the person with complete vision perceive the sense of color expressions, one may hold the position that the sense perceived by the latter is better than that perceived by the former, who actually depends on the latter. One way to define this dependence is by resorting to the way we verify sentences which use these senses. We can also extend this idea to the distinction between the sense I attach to my own name and the sense that somebody else has of my name. But it is not easy to apply it to the difference between the sense of '$7 = 6 + 1$' prior to the reduction of arithmetic to logic and after Frege's analysis of this sentence. This matter, however, goes beyond the concern of this chapter.

[5] Indeed, it is difficult to see what that physical difference might be. Could this be a matter of a special sensory perception? Not likely, since it is said 'no man shall see me and live'. Moreover, this sensory augmentation might lead to the materialization of God.

What makes the situation even more complex is the identification Halevi draws between subscribing to a tradition and possessing empirical evidence for the existence of God:

> In the same way God commenced His speech to the assembled people of Israel by saying: 'I am the Lord your God who led you out of the land of Egypt.' Note that He did not say: 'I am the Creator of the world and your Creator.' Now in the same style I spoke to thee, Prince of the Khazars, when thou did ask me about my creed. I answered by letting thee know what is that thing that binds me and binds all the people of Israel, the very thing that became clear to the Israelites first from the sight of eyes [ראות עיניים], and afterwards through uninterrupted oral tradition, which is equal to the former. (*Kuzari*, I, &25)

'Sight' here is a misleading metaphor, for only our ancestors saw with their own eyes whatever they saw, though they can communicate to us, who have never witnessed the Sinai Revelation, the name YHWH.[6] However, if they can communicate this name to us, what can stop them from communicating it to a philosopher?!

At this point, we come close to the notion of the chain of transmission from an unexpected direction. Halevi knows that he has to link his point on the inaccessibility of YHWH to the chain of transmission. Otherwise, only the original prophets would have access to the name YHWH. He tries to do so within the framework of his own epistemology, by identifying the transmission of the name with the actual witnessing of this experience. Reading Halevi's point in terms of Frege's distinction between sense and reference does not help us understand why the name YHWH cannot transcend the limits of the Jewish community. The limitation on intersubjectivity that Halevi imposes on the name 'YHWH' stems from the impossibility of communicating the name, rather than from

---

[6] At any rate that is what emerges at first glance. However, it may well be that I am missing here some crucial point. Maimonides ,too, in speaking of Moses' prophecy and its advantage, adds that we have witnessed with our eyes. Perhaps the difference between eye witnessing and tradition, which was already defined by R. Sa'adiah Gaon, was not acceptable to Maimonides and Halevi; thus they espoused a different epistemology, in which tradition is a natural continuation of the actual experience of seeing. One can also connect this with ideas about memory and personal identity: just as memory is a natural continuation of sensory evidence, so my own memories blend with those of my community and together we form a commonly shared repository of memories.

some special perceptual or even conceptual machinery that is supposedly found among the Jews.[7]

Ought implies accessible

Upon rereading Halevi, one may find a direction to follow that does not assume the above epistemology. Halevi explains that only those who are commanded by the Lord may use the name YHWH. Anyone who is not obliged to serve God in this way can use it. In Halevi's words:

> Therefore, philosophers have no proper name for God, a name by which they refer to Him alone. Only the man who has hearkened to the word of God, and His edict, and His warning, and His declaration that He shall benefit his servants and punish the rebellious, can call Him by a proper name. (*Kuzari*, IV, &3)

There is something in the chain of transmission that limits the name of God to one single community. Thus, if we want to understand Halevi, we must add a constraint on the chain of transmission that hands down the name. This constraint is the exclusive nature of the transmission. Not every person can serve as a link in the chain that transmits the name of YHWH. It is not enough that the recipient of the name is willing to refer to God by articulating this name (YHWH); he or she also has to view the commandments as pertaining to him or her personally.

---

[7] What is certain is that one should not rely on the beliefs of the philosophers and of the observant Jews in order to exclude some people from gaining accessibility to the name, while making it accessible to others. Recently, Barelli (1999) argued that whoever denies the existence of God and reads the Bible must face a problem for he or she cannot understand any discussion about God. Barelli substantiated his claim by resorting to Fregean and Wittgensteinian constraints on the use of words. As far as Frege is concerned, the given constraints cannot be of any assistance to Halevi's argument. A phrase may or may not have a sense and a reference. If it has a reference, then both the atheist (who in this case replaces the philosopher) and the believer can refer to the name, and perhaps they can understand it too. Conversely, if the phrase has no reference, then neither the religionist nor the atheist can refer to it. In the same vein, if a philosopher does not believe in the existence of divine Revelation, this is not supposed to prevent him from grasping the sense of phrases that include the name of God, if indeed the Revelation took place. The philosopher, let's say that he is Fregean, would say that there is no thought here, though he would then be subject to an opposite error: he would think that there was no Fregean thought while at the same time he would apprehend such thought. Indeed, when a mathematician thinks that the names of numbers do not stand for objects, while in fact they do, he still grasps the numbers or the meaning of claims about them, against his judgment.

Between transmitting and sharing

Here is one attempt to draw a picture that is implicit in Halevi, and which may be used to account for it. I propose to distinguish between two ways to pass on a word from one link of a chain to another: transmitting and sharing. The second way is selective while the first is not. Names that are accessible to all humans are transmitted. Such a name is, for instance, 'Gödel'. Other names are not accessible to all humans. They are passed on only to the members of a given community. These individuals, through their education within the community, share its values and collective identity and are therefore entitled to receive the name. Verses such as 'YHWH delivered the people of Israel from Egypt and gave them the commandments' and 'YHWH was revealed to his people in Mount Sinai' are intended for internal use in the community.

The Holon–Bat-Yam question

There are two objections to be made here. The idea of a name shared only by a specific group of speakers brings to mind the idea of a name used by only one person and thus brings us closer to the idea of a private language. Now, it has been argued that a language that *in principle* is open to only one person is problematic. If so, what about a language used exclusively by two persons? Is that, too, problematic in terms of the argument against a private language? Similarly, what is wrong with saying that only the Israelites, or the Sufis, for that matter, understand each other?

To answer this question we must check whether the assumptions that are employed by the private language argument suffice to prove the stronger version: that a language that in principle is open to two persons is impossible. However, I cannot deal with this problem just yet.

And there is another problem. How can we categorize the thesis that only the one who has been commanded, or has certain inclinations of his or her own, can use some particular name of God. The question here is not factual. The thesis that only someone who is specifically inclined has access to the name YHWH, and the difference between transmitting and sharing, seem intuitive to me. The problem is that I see no way of placing this statement in a more general context, unconnected with the use of the name YHWH. Is there, then, something distinctive about this particular name? Must we accept the distinction between sharing and transmitting as one of the anomalies of the discourse about God?

The second objection can be made explicit by considering what I have dubbed the 'Holon–Bat-Yam question'. Suppose that one fine day a booming voice of some hidden power is heard on the beach of Bat-Yam and this voice commands all the inhabitants of Bat-Yam, specifically, to stop eating hot dogs with mustard. Now, let us suppose, furthermore, that some of the inhabitants do indeed follow this commandment, and that some of the arguments of Pascal's wager apply here. In other words, these residents could argue that abiding by this edict is more profitable to them than other possibilities, especially if the power had threatened dire retribution against transgressors. This is what Revelation may look like to a philosopher. As to the recipients of the Revelation, the question that arises is as follows. What would hinder the residents of Bat-Yam from passing on the name of this power to their acquaintances in the neighboring town of Holon, who were not personally commanded by this power, and are not inclined to follow this edict? Moreover, if the residents of Bat-Yam can name this power, why cannot the residents of Holon follow suit? What is the difference between this and the case where a new sea creature is discovered and named by the residents of Bat-Yam? Couldn't the residents of Holon use this name? Even if this creature has actually spoken to the residents of Bat-Yam, there seems to be no hindrance to passing the name of this creature on to the residents of Holon. And if the residents of Bat-Yam can communicate the name of this creature to the residents of Holon, what bars the people of Israel from communicating their name for God to the philosopher?

Selectivity and form of life

It would be natural to make a leap here to Wittgensteinian ideas about the deep relations between the meaning of words and the form of life in which they are embedded. Prima facie, such a view might serve as the background to the distinction between sharing and transmitting: if one does not belong to a community and participate in its form of life one cannot use the word with the meaning attached to it by the members of the community. Yet, though I *accept* this line of thought, this account does not suffice to give a complete reply to the Holon–Bat-Yam question. After all, we do translate words from one language to another. On the other hand, we are engaged in a language game in which we translate words from one form of life to another. If 'milk' and 'cow' are translatable from one language to another, why not transfer the name of God from one community to another?

Part II: the creativity of transmission

Natural kinds

To solve this problem, we must leave the name of God for a moment and focus on chains of reference in general, but this time keeping an eye on the possible intervention of tradition. Instead of a chain that starts with one person we will imagine two representatives of different traditions. A Jew and a Gentile are standing next to a bottle of liquid. One calls it '*halav*' and the other calls it 'milk'. After this baptism, they both return to their respective communities and carry on with their lives. We may also assume that, from then on, they trade in milk and discuss it from time to time. They can also translate this word 'milk' as '*halav*'. The next generation inherits the term and handles the substance. Now, it should be noted that with words such as 'milk', if some material is identical to milk, then it is milk. *Both* the Jew and the Gentile acknowledge this truth and therefore they consider 'milk' and '*halav*' as interchangeable. Yet, 2,000 years later, an interesting thing happens: a Jew and a Gentile are standing beside a new bottle of liquid. The Gentile says that it is milk, but the Jew denies this. The Gentile claims that this liquid is chemically identical to the substance labeled as 'milk' by his forefathers; therefore, it must be the same thing. But the present-day Jew says that the mere fact that the two products have the same chemical composition does *not* establish their identity. A product with exactly the same chemical composition as milk could still be considered '*parve*' – neither dairy nor meat – and as such it would not be milk.

What has happened here is this. One person (the Jew) perceives milk as necessarily being a material that came from a cow or another animal; the other does not do so. Accordingly, the former does not perceive the non-dairy liquid as milk, while for the latter the opposite holds true.

Division of labour and selectivity

This difference may be understood in terms of Putnam's *division of labor.*[8] Putnam believes that one should consult an expert to determine whether, for instance, some material is made of gold. Yet, in our case, in one community the expert is the rabbi, while in the other it is the scientist. In one tradition, it is generally true that if the laws of nature cannot differentiate between A and B then A is the same matter as B,

[8] The claim that the division of labor is an important component of the description of the manner in which the reference of words that designate natural kinds is established was contested by Kripke, who attributed no significance to experts (Kripke 1986). My use here of the notion of experts is useful for didactic purposes: one can see that it is the decision made by the entire community that stands behind the expert's authority. Nevertheless, as can be understood from my discussion in this chapter, I do not consider, in contrast to Kripke, that the expression 'a is the same as b' is established in the baptism ceremony.

while the other tradition replaces this principle by substituting the laws of God for the laws of nature.

One way to describe what is going on here is to view the current difference between the Jew and the Gentile as mirroring the original state of affairs dating back 2,000 years. This means that back then, in the primal stage, the difference already existed, regardless of the fact that when the Jew and the Gentile were on the mountain, there was no clear indication of a semantic discrepancy, nor did their behavior in their respective communities give any hint of such difference. It is only from the perspective of later generations that we can notice any difference.

There is a second way to understand the role of tradition in shaping language. The chain of reference is not a neutral vehicle for the transmission of a well-determined meaning but, rather, tradition develops and shapes the meanings of the words that are handed down from one generation to another.

The openness of reference

The second possibility is far more appealing to me. A community can give rise to several traditions, and if each one is a transparent vehicle for transmitting meaning we would end up by claiming that at the time of the baptism ceremony, and in fact at every point of time, we have only ambiguous terms. This entails that no one has ever meant something definite, which seems to me a *reductio ad absurdum* of the first view.[9]

When speaking of meanings, tradition is active and is not merely uncovering a fixed meaning. Of course, practically speaking, there is

---

[9] If we accept the first view we may end up claiming that there is nothing at all to suggest that, at the moment of baptism, the original speakers were actually referring to milk. Neither the composition of the given liquid, nor the condition of the *community* at that time, can serve as an indication of such meaning. For it can be safely assumed that, at the time of the baptism, the speakers had no knowledge of chemistry, nor were they aware of the religious injunction concerning the Jewish dietary laws. Thus, it wasn't at all apparent to these speakers that the same substance was to be interpreted, in generations to come, in terms of its chemical composition or origin. To establish what someone means at any given time, we do not look into his or her mental situation or explore the dispositions of the community to which he or she belongs. Instead, we have to examine the way the community has evolved. Thus, if one community uses something, and another community, not unlike the first one in any definable sense, uses the same thing, and both communities name the thing in question, then even if, at the given time, they share the same dispositions with regard to that particular object, they may still mean two different things by the respective names given to it.

no problem in finding an equivalent term for 'milk'. I can say that, for a Jew, milk is 'what can be milked from a cow, and not what is chemically identical to such a product'. At any given time, I can make such an approximation, but no approximation can ever apply at all times. I am not saying that the language of a given community is incommensurable with the language of another community; all I am saying is that an enduring translation is impossible. The living power of tradition prevents this.

We can make this account more poignant. There is a trivial sense in which every translation is good only for its time. Since the different expressions in any human language continually undergo a change in meaning and are subject to other transitions, there is no reason to assume that, once a translation is established, it would keep abreast of these ongoing transformations. Yet, there is a further difference. When we speak of Jewish tradition, we should bear in mind that the rabbi who rules that something is not milk, does not thereby change the language, nor does he see himself as inventing a new expression or usage. In pronouncing his ruling, he is striving to figure out what his forefathers meant by the term 'milk'. According to the second approach, that which stresses the role of tradition in *developing* meaning, the rabbi redefines '*halav*' in a way that emphasizes its relation to a cow – just as the theory of general relativity redefines 'straight line' with 'a geodesic trajectory'.

A generalization

What is said here about 'milk' applies as well to 'oil', 'wool', 'linen', and 'meat'. Moreover, there is no reason why this cannot be extended to 'pork'. The scientist may claim that a creature with the same DNA pattern as a pig is a pig, while the religious Jew may say that a pig, in the full sense of the word, must be an issue of a sow. The same applies to ducks, and any other animal. It should be noted that the rabbi's decision is not made independently of scientific facts. He may well consult the scientist, but there is nothing in the scientific information he receives which could deterministically specify what the rabbi's decision would be.

He thus may state that although a liquid may look and taste like milk, and may even have the same chemical composition as milk, this does not necessarily mean that it is indeed milk. In fact, the rabbi is extending what Kripke has said about gold. Just as there is gold and there is fool's gold, so there is real milk, which originates from a living cow, and there is 'scientists' milk', which is actually *parve*.

Chains of reference are active

There is some openness in Kripke's conception which allows for this idea. Undoubtedly, if not for Kripke, we could not even begin to deal with such an idea. For if we were captivated by Russell's or even Frege's theory, we would have to speak of changes in meaning as a natural outcome of every development in tradition. In this way, we would blur the distinction between replacing the meaning of a term and shaping its meaning by tradition.

However, we must add one improvement: Kripke saw science as a magnifying lens of fixed meanings. This is incorrect in two respects. First, it works only within traditions that give an important role to science; second, neglecting the first qualification, one may think that chains of reference are passive vehicles for transmitting meanings. In many issues, science gives the final verdict. But even where this applies, we shouldn't forget a prior, subtle decision on the part of the community to allow science to decide on such matters. We identify a gem with its chemical structure, and this has had a tremendous impact on the trade in gems, for it is now possible to produce them in the lab. On the other hand, nothing and no one in the whole world can determine a priori that we will treat synthetic gems as favorably as we treat natural ones.

Here is an example that is easy to cope with. For the racist, at least one who pretends that his or her racism is based on scientific standards, a clone of an Aryan is always an Aryan. For the Jewish rabbi, on the other hand, an Aryan clone can be Jewish and, conversely, a clone of a Jew is not necessarily Jewish. This does not impose any limitations on science. It simply shows that the community dictates whether or not science should determine meaning. Such determination of a second order has not been recognized by Kripke.[10]

Back to the Holon–Bat-Yam question

I hope the reader can see how this consequence may help us answer the problem left open at the end of the previous section. The impossibility

---

[10] This shows up in Kripke's critique of the particular place of the community of experts in fixing the reference. Kripke claims that while experts do not establish the extension of the term 'gold' they are likely to be of great assistance in establishing whether a certain material is made of gold. When I define gold as 'that material which is like this object' and point to gold, and when a researcher defines it in the same manner, the exact same extension of the word 'gold' is, in any case, established. But here Kripke ignores the openness in the meaning of 'X is made of the same material as Y'.

of transferring a word from one community to another is not a peculiar phenomenon. The residents of Bat-Yam and those of Holon belong to the same semantic community. Should a monster suddenly appear on the seashore of Bat-Yam, the residents of other Mediterranean towns, including those who believe in the existence of extraterrestrial creatures, will regard it in more or less the same way. However, in the hypothetical case of milk, or as far as the name of God is concerned, the different semantic communities determine reference in compliance with different authorities. In Halevi's terminology, the philosopher submits to rational deduction, while the religious person submits to shared prophetic Revelation.

Philosophy in a sovereign community

Now, at last, we can understand what Halevi is doing. He confronts the philosopher and tells him that divinity matters are not subject to scientific investigation. By taking this approach he also indicates what the Jews have actually been doing, at least up to his time. In addition, he tries to convince them to keep doing the same thing, and he does so by raising arguments at different levels. At this point, he mobilizes the well-known fundamentals: strong religious feelings, comments on the restricted power of reason, which is always prone to doubts, and the information accessible to him about the Revelation. The philosophical state of mind, along with its inherent skepticism, cannot lead to redemption, which is what religious practice is all about.

Halevi's argumentation did not resolve the issue conclusively. For Spinoza, who succeeded Halevi by several centuries, the stories of the Revelation do not involve any certainty and, furthermore, after Descartes we have come to believe that seeing is not a supreme judge, and it is actually reason which does not err. The Jewish community had historically opted for Halevi's interpretation, and not only rejected Spinoza's views, but also excommunicated him. By making this decision, tradition had its say. It proclaimed: I prefer Halevi's direction to that of Spinoza. This is where the sanctified set of values, the loyalties, and the historical-political situation of the community enters the scene and determines the formation of the conventions on how to interpret God. However, things could have happened differently. Spinoza could have given rise to a tradition that goes hand in hand with the scientific spirit and purifies God from 'irrelevant remnants', the product of the exegetic tradition. Halevi could not have known that the Jews, whether the secular or even the religious ones, would not always subscribe to a non-scientific orientation. Indeed, the rabbi and a number of philosophers can give us good answers on many important matters; but neither the rabbi nor the philosopher can decide for us whom we should consult.

References

Barelli, G. (1999) Secularizing the Talmud (A'l Talmud Tora She-hulan). *Alpaim* 17, 9–23.

Halevi, J. (1969) *Book of Kuzari*, trans. Hartwig Hirschfeld. Brooklyn: P. Shalom.

Frege, G. (1960 [1892]) On Sense and Reference. In Peter Geach and Max Black (eds) *Translations from the Philosophical Writings of Gottlob Frege*. Oxford: Basil Blackwell, 56–79.

Kripke, S. (1972) *Naming and Necessity*. Oxford: Basil Blackwell.

Kripke, S. (1986) A Problem in the Theory of Reference: The Linguistic Division of Labor and the Social Character of Naming. In *Philosophy and Culture (Proceedings of the XVIIth World Congress of Philosophy)*. Montreal: Editions du Beffroi, 241–7.

Putnam, H. (1979) The Meaning of 'Meaning'. In his *Mind, Language, and Reality: Philosophical Papers, Vol. 2*. Cambridge: Cambridge University Press, 215–71.

Part II
Necessity

3
Over-Assignment of Structure

Eli Dresner

Over-assignment of structure

Twenty is two times ten. The length of a body of 20 centimeters is twice the length of a 10 centimeter body. But is the temperature of a body at 20 degrees centigrade two times the temperature of a body at 10 degrees centigrade? No, it is not. This is easy to see by converting the temperatures into Fahrenheit: 20 degrees centigrade is 68 degrees Fahrenheit; 10 degrees centigrade is 50 degrees Fahrenheit; and thus the first temperature is no longer two times the other. As these are the same two temperatures that are being measured, each time in a different scale, we conclude that there is just no fact of the matter in the temperature reality of one body's temperature being x times the temperature of the other.[1]

We see there is a difference between the way numbers are used to measure length and the way they are used to measure temperature. In the measurement of length the numeric 'fact' that 20 is 2 times 10 represents a physical relation between any two bodies to which these numbers are assigned (as lengths), while in the case of temperature measurement the same numeric fact does not represent a similar physical relation defined in terms of temperature. But how can we tell which numeric properties are relevant to temperature measurement, and which properties are not? And why are we using a system of measurement that could easily mislead us into making false claims, such as that a 20 degree centigrade day is twice as hot as one that is 10 degrees centigrade?

The answer to the first question is implicit in the scale change from centigrade to Fahrenheit. This scale change involves a switch in the

[1] The existence of absolute zero will be ignored in this discussion; let us suppose we live before its discovery.

temperature that is assigned zero, and a change in the temperature interval that is the unit of measurement, i.e. one degree. What is left invariant under this change are only *interval relations* among temperatures. (For example, the interval between 30 and 10 degrees centigrade is two times the interval between 20 and 10 degrees centigrade, and this relation between the two intervals will be the same after the change to Fahrenheit.[2]) And indeed, in temperature measurement all that needs to be represented are interval relations – this is all there is 'out there' in temperature reality. Therefore the only 'numeric facts' that are of relevance to temperature representation are those concerning interval relations among numbers; other facts are superfluous.

In fact, these observations entail that the right algebraic structure for measuring temperature is not the numbers, but rather what is called a (single dimension) *affine space* – an abstract mathematical entity whose elements have no numeric size at all, but rather only have numeric interval relations among each other.

The second question raised above was why it is that we use a system of measurement that represents temperature reality fallaciously, in the sense of imputing to this reality aspects that it does not have. The answer to this question follows from the above: (i) in order to represent temperature we need a mathematical entity among whose elements there are interval relations; (ii) the numbers consist of such an entity; and therefore (iii) we use the numbers for the purpose of temperature measurement, even though they have more structure than what we actually need. Admittedly, the affine spaces would have been more suitable for the purpose at hand, having no structure beyond what is needed, but these spaces are obscure mathematical entities, and are far from being intuitive. The numbers, on the other hand, are familiar and well known to us from their many other uses, such as the measurement of length.

In order to describe this situation in a more precise and general fashion, let me appeal to the theory of measurement.[3] Measurement starts with a set of physical objects and some empirically defined relation on them (for example, we can empirically verify which of a given pair of

---

[2] Similarly, the interval between 20 and 0 is two times the interval between 10 and 0, a relation that will be preserved by the change to the Fahrenheit scale. What was noted above is that the relation between 20 and 10 (a relation between temperatures, not temperature intervals) is not preserved by the scale change.

[3] I shall be relying here on Krantz et al. (1971–89).

objects is longer by putting them next to each other).[4] The set of objects in question together with this basic relation comprise an *empirical relational structure*, which may satisfy various axioms; for example, the relation 'longer than' (on a given class of objects) turns out to be transitive and asymmetric. And now (only now) come the numbers: due to the properties of the empirical relational structure there is a homomorphism – a structure preserving mapping – from this structure into the numbers. That is, there is a function assigning numbers to objects such that the empirical relations among any pair (or sequence) of objects is mirrored by numerical relations among the numbers assigned to these objects. The measurement of some property of the constituents of a given domain consists in finding such a homomorphism.

The predicament discerned above in temperature measurement can be stated now more accurately. What is required for measurement is only a *homomorphism* from the empirical structure to the mathematical one (i.e. the numbers), not an *isomorphism* between the two structures. That is, the empirical structure must be mapped onto the mathematical one *but not necessarily the other way around*: there could be extra structure in the abstract mathematical entity that does not reflect anything in the empirical structure being measured. Thus the mathematical entity used in measurement need not be tailor-made to the phenomena it is supposed to represent (as affine spaces are tailor-made for temperature measurement), but rather could be richer in structure. This possibility allows for generality and uniformity, in that it enables us to represent a variety of non-isomorphic phenomena (i.e. empirical structures) by a single, rich, and well-understood mathematical entity – such as the real numbers. The drawback is that this freedom opens the door to imputing to the real-world phenomena a structure that is not in them.

We are now in a position to define the fallacy of *over-assignment of structure*. Let E be an empirical structure, A an abstract structure, and F a homomorphism embedding E into A. Furthermore, let $e_1, \ldots, e_n$ be elements of E, and $a_1, \ldots, a_n$ the A-elements assigned to $e_1, \ldots, e_n$ (respectively) by F. (That is, $a_1 = F(e_1), \ldots, a_n = F(e_n)$.) Finally, let $\varphi(a_1, \ldots, a_n)$ be a relation on A that is *not* defined in terms of a structure that is preserved by F. An *over-assignment of structure from A to E through F* is an inference

[4] It is usually required that the set of objects in question be closed under some operations; for example, in length measurement we want closure under concatenation.

from $\varphi(a_1, \ldots, a_n)$ to the conclusion that an analogue relation $\varphi^*(e_1, \ldots, e_n)$ obtains in *E*.[5]

In the temperature example, *E* is the relational structure of physical objects with temperature relations among them, *A* is the real numbers, and '$\varphi(10,20)$' is the (correct) claim that 20 is two times 10. The fallacious inference from this claim is that an object at 20 degrees centigrade is two times as hot as one that is 10 degrees centigrade. As another example let *E* be some empirical linear ordering, *A* the natural numbers, and φ a quantitative relation on the numbers; thus 4 is two times 2, but from this fact we cannot infer any quantitative relation between the second and fourth place in a given linear ordering.

Over-ascription of structure, as defined above, can be described either as (meaningful and) false, or as meaningless. In what follows the latter option is chosen: statements like 'this object is twice as hot as that one' seem to be better characterized as senseless than as false, just as, for example, the statement 'this number is sweeter than that one'; however, nothing substantial depends on this classification. Note, though, that even if claims involving over-assignment are viewed as meaningless, so-called second-order assertions (or beliefs) to the effect that such claims *are* meaningful (and true) may still be described as false, or mistaken.

The over-assignment of structure in philosophical arguments

I have presented over-assignment in the relatively narrow context of measurement, but I claim that this phenomenon is of a wider scope: it occurs in both formal and non-formal settings in various philosophical discussions. Let me first characterize this phenomenon more generally, and then give three examples.

It is quite often attempted in philosophical discussions to reduce a given set of concepts *E* to another set *A*, or to analyze one such set *E* through the use of another, *A*, or, which is more modest, to apply a conceptual framework *A* to a domain of discussion *E*. I believe it is clear that all such moves consist, albeit implicitly and non-formally, in establishing the existence of a homomorphism from *E* to *A*. That this

[5] An indication (or criterion) that $\varphi^*(e_1, \ldots, e_n)$ does indeed involve over-assignment is that there exists another homomorphism from *E* to *A*, say *G*, such that according to *G* we would be prompted to conclude $\sim\varphi^*(e_1, \ldots, e_n)$. (That is, $b_1 = G(e_1), \ldots, b_n = G(e_n)$ and $\sim\varphi(b_1, \ldots, b_n)$.) I am indebted here to the referee of the *Journal of Philosophical Logic*.

is indeed so is clearest in the case of outright reduction: if we replace each concept from *E* with a logical combination of concepts from *A*, then the replacement function is obviously a homomorphism, because, by the definition of reduction, it allows for the representation of the conceptual relations in *E* within *A*. Now in the analysis of *E* in terms of *A* (whichever way, exactly, 'analysis' is understood) and in the application of *A* to *E* we have a similar situation. That is, although we might not want to swap the concepts of *E* with those of *A*, we are also clearly committed in these cases to some kind of structural representation relation leading from *E* to *A*, a relation that makes *A* applicable to *E* (or *E* analyzable in terms of *A*). This relation is a homomorphic mapping. Therefore in all these methodological set-ups (reduction, analysis, and application) there arises the possibility of over-assigning structure: the (possibly implicit) homomorphism from *E* to *A* requires the reflection of *E*'s structure in *A*, but it does not assure us that all of *A*'s structure is applicable to *E*.[6]

It could be asked why we put ourselves in danger of committing this fallacy; i.e. why not try to establish only *isomorphisms* among conceptual domains, and avoid the tricky homomorphisms altogether. The answers to this question have already been given. First, the richer conceptual domain *A* might be more familiar to us than one that is designed to represent the phenomenon *E*. Second (and relatedly), the rich structure of *A* could be adequate for representing a variety of non-isomorphic *E*s, thus allowing for generalization and uniformity.

We see there is a trade-off here between generalization and accuracy. The application of rich conceptual tools to some given domain allows for generalization (i.e. for connections between this domain and others), but it opens the door to over-assignment. On the other hand, a representation of one domain with an isomorphic one is harder to find,

---

[6] It could be objected that in the case of outright *reduction* (as opposed to analysis and application) over-assignment is impossible, because in reduction one domain is claimed to be *identical* with (a part of) another, and therefore trivially isomorphic to it. This objection should be conceded in the case of, for example, scientific reductive claims (such as the one from gas theory to statistical mechanics); however, in other domains of inquiry, such as philosophy and mathematics, the force of reductive and identity claims is much less explicit and clear. (See examples 1 and 3 below.) Hence legitimate reduction *could* involve over-assignment, or, alternatively, one could insist that over-assignment and reduction are incompatible, and take any manifestation of over-assignment as an indication that would-be reductions are in fact fallacious. (This line is taken in some of the examples below.) In any case, the concept proves to be a useful tool.

and might be of lesser value, or of no value at all (because it does not permit generalization). Let me now present three examples, in ascending order of complexity.

Example 1

There are several reductions of arithmetic to set theory; one of the best known is von Neumann's (1967 [1923]), in which 0 is equated with $\varnothing$ (the empty set) and $n+1$ is defined inductively as $n \cup \{n\}$, but there are others. Obviously a reduction of arithmetic to set theory consists in a homomorphic embedding of the natural numbers into the richer domain of sets, and therefore it opens the door to the assignment of superfluous structure: the sets representing the numbers may have inclusion and membership relations among them that do not mirror any properties of the natural numbers represented. (In von Neumann's reduction, for example, for all n we have both $n+1 \supset n$ and $n+1 \ni n$.) Inferring that the natural numbers bear similar inclusion and membership relations among them would obviously be a case of over-assignment; however, nobody is really tempted to make this fallacious move (Benacerraf 1983).

Example 2

In everyday talk we often ascribe full-blown human intentional states to very young infants, to animals, and sometimes even to machines. Such ascriptions appear also in philosophical discussions. I will now argue that this is another example of over-assignment of structure.

First, note that any such intentional ascription involves a homomorphic embedding of a certain domain – the 'mental economy' of some animal – into the framework of intention, i.e. the web of human desire and belief.[7] When we ascribe intentional states to, for example, an animal, we apply to its mental states the conceptual framework usually used to describe what people think and want, and such an application amounts (albeit implicitly) to the claim that there is a homomorphism from the mental system of that animal to our own. For example, 'The cat wants to play with the red ball' enables us to use the standard intentional web within which the desire ascribed to the cat is embedded in order to make inferences concerning that cat's behavior and mental

[7] See e.g. Dennett (1987) and Davidson (1984). (Davidson (pp. 224–5) explicitly compares radical interpretation to measurement.) Of course, there are those who would claim that there is more to intentional ascription than such a homomorphism (and would eschew talk of 'mental economy' altogether), but nobody should deny its existence.

states, such as 'If I give the ball to the cat it will play with it', or 'If I give the ball to the cat it will be happy'. These inferences rely on the assumption that there is some homomorphism between the cat's system of belief, desire, and action and ours.

This homomorphism raises the possibility of over-assigning structure by imposing too much of the human intentional structure onto the animal, i.e. making inferences concerning the animal's states of mind and the connections among them that are allowed by our intentional idioms, but that go beyond the actual, real structure of the animal's 'mental economy'. (The (epistemic) question of how we can know when structure is over-assigned is difficult, of course, and will not be addressed here; the point being made here is logical.) Thus it was acknowledged above that ascribing to the cat a desire to play with the red ball is useful, in that it supports *some* legitimate inferences regarding the cat's future behavior and other states of mind; there are other inferences, however, that are allowed when the *X* who wants to play with the red ball is a (sufficiently developed) human, but that are unwarranted in the case of the cat. For example, when *X* is a human we can infer from the above ascription that he wants to *play* with the ball, as opposed to having some 'serious business' with it (e.g. wanting to fix it); in the case of the cat, on the other hand, the opposition between play and serious business would seem to be meaningless, and therefore any inference involving it unwarranted.

The above claims, concerning unwarranted ascriptions of (full blown) intentional states, also apply, *mutatis mutandis*, to some ascriptions of content to *utterances*. As an example from contemporary philosophy, consider J. Perry's interpretation of Wittgenstein's builders' parable (Perry 1994).[8] Perry's objective in this paper is to disprove the view (held by Davidson and others) that the meaning of subsentential expressions is derived from the role they play in complete sentences. (Let us label this view 'sentence priority'.) In particular, Perry wants to show that even if we accept the claim that linguistic expressions acquire meaning through their use in interpersonal communication, sentence priority still does not follow. For this purpose he appeals to Wittgenstein's famous builders' scenario, which is often understood as showing how meaning can be derived from use. His argument is the following (ibid., p. 28). (1) The builders' utterances ('slab', 'block', etc.) are utterances of *nouns* – this is their meaning for the builder and his assistant. (2) These

[8] The following remarks rely on a more detailed discussion of Perry's paper presented in (Dresner 2002a).

expressions' 'nounhood' is not derived from their role in complete sentences. (3) Therefore sentence priority fails.

Premise (2) in Perry's argument is justifiable only if we assume (as Wittgenstein stipulates) that the four construction expressions are all that the two builders ever say to each other and to others – otherwise the 'nounhood' of the four expressions could be derived from their role in complete sentences, uttered in other circumstances. However, if we make this assumption then all we know about the builders is that one reacts differentially to the other's verbal behavior, as many animals (and some machines) do. To claim in this case that the expressions are used by the builder as *nouns*, i.e. as designating (kinds of) *objects*, is therefore a case of over-assigning structure: we do not know enough about the minds of these (outwardly human) creatures to justify the assumption that their mental life is rich enough to substantiate such a claim.[9] Thus premise (1) is unjustified.

Perry supports his first premise as follows. The builders' utterances convey complete propositional contents, he says, but almost all of this content is implicit in the circumstances of the interaction and thus is not part of the meaning of the expressions uttered themselves. In particular, the fact that the builder orders his assistant to bring him a stone of some kind is clear before anything is said, and therefore the function of the expressions uttered is only to designate the kinds of stones that should be brought, i.e. they are nouns. However, this is yet again over-assignment. If all we know about the builders is that they engage in the interaction described, then we cannot be sure that *for them* there is propositional content of any kind implicit in the circumstances (as there may be for us). Certainly we do not make a similar claim concerning the fax machines of Note 9 and their circumstances. Thus the builders' systems of states of minds concerning the situation could, most probably, be embedded within our intentional system, but they need not be as rich.[10]

---

[9] In order to see this, note that when two fax machines exchange synchronization messages and settle on an agreed transfer speed we certainly do not hold that the messages really designated the right speed *for the machines themselves*; if indeed we say so it is an (innocent, in this case) anthropomorphization – an over-assignment of structure.

[10] Note that according to the above considerations it would be an over-assignment to think of the builder's expressions also as complete sentences, expressing full-fledged propositions (if, as we assume here, the four expressions are all that the builder ever utters). Thus, for example, Quine's famous hypothetical field-linguist would seem to be at fault if he translates an utterance of 'Gavagai' by an unknown (albeit a human-looking) creature into a sentence ('Lo, a rabbit'): at least on first encounter, until further linguistic interaction is observed, such a translation is unjustified (Quine 1960, pp. 26–30). Quine, however, does not seem to acknowledge this point.

Note that it is not claimed here that the mere ascription of the above-considered intentional states to the builders (or to the cat) is wrong (or meaningless), as it was not claimed above that saying of an object that it is 20 degrees centigrade is wrong. Rather, the claim concerning the assignment of the number 20 to an object as its temperature was that such an assignment is too rich and thus could lead to a mistaken assertion of senseless claims (if used uncritically); similarly, the claim made here is that the assignment of full-blown intentional states to the cat or to the builders is in fact too rich, and that it does lead to mistakes.

Also, note how the trade-off mentioned earlier is illustrated in this example. On the one hand, the application of the rich human intentional system to a wide variety of sub-human domains is highly useful: such an application allows for overarching generalization, and it is carried out utilizing a structure that is well known and familiar to us. (The alternative would be to create a tailor-made system of descriptions of mental states for each kind of sub-human creature; obviously we do not have a clue how to achieve this feat, and even if we did the result would lack generality.) On the other hand, the free ascription of full-blown intentional states makes over-assignment possible.

Example 3

The third example is that of possible-worlds semantics. There is no doubt that possible-worlds talk is useful in capturing our intuitions concerning such modal notions as necessity and possibility (as there is no doubt that the real numbers are useful in measuring temperature). However, just as the use of numbers in temperature measurement gives rise to nonsensical questions, so does possible-worlds talk give rise to questions that seem to go beyond our modal intuitions. Here are some examples:

(1) How many (metaphysically, logically) possible worlds are there?
(2) For two propositions p and q, are there more possible worlds in which p is true than worlds in which q is true?
(3) Are there two (or more) possible worlds that are identical but numerically distinct?

All these questions are expressible in the framework of possible-worlds semantics, but they should be avoided in philosophical discussions of modality because our intuitions tell us that they are inapplicable to our modal notions – there is no fact of the matter about any of them, as there is no basis on which to decide whether 20 degrees centigrade is or is not two times as hot as 10 degrees centigrade. Thus at least some questions about the cardinality of classes of possible worlds cannot be made intuitive sense of, yet talk of any kind of objects of modality (such as possible worlds) imputes content to all such questions – once you have objects, you can certainly count them.[11] Therefore objectification goes beyond the logical structure of (at least some of) our modal locutions.

This conclusion can be supported in the same way its temperature-theoretic counterpart was. Comparisons of size among temperatures are not preserved under permissible scale transformation (e.g. from centigrade to Fahrenheit); this fact is an indication that size relations among numeric temperatures do not represent any feature of temperature reality itself. Similarly, it is easy to see that there are transformations within the possible-worlds framework that alter cardinalities, but that are nevertheless permissible – i.e. make no difference to our intuitions vis-à-vis some of the modal notions. Consider S5, for example, and let *G* be the transformation that duplicates every possible world, i.e. creates (or assumes there exists) for every such world another that is identical to it but numerically distinct. If *S* is a concrete model of S5 then *G*(*S*) will be another such model, induced by *G* in a natural fashion.[12] Clearly *S* captures our intuitions correctly (concerning a certain modal notion) if and only if *G*(*S*) does; yet, if *S* is *finite*, then *S* and *G*(*S*) assign, to every consistent sentence, sets of worlds of different cardinality.[13] As before, this is an indication that cardinality considerations (and hence full-fledged objectification) go beyond the structure of 'modal reality' itself (according to our intuition).[14]

---

[11] Admittedly, there are cardinality questions vis-à-vis modality that we do make intuitive sense of, e.g. when saying 'you have two possible options here'. However, such locutions do not involve direct talk of possible worlds and they can be paraphrased without appeal to an objectual analysis of modality.

[12] Each additional world will join the equivalence class of the accessibility relation to which its 'parent' belongs.

[13] Similar arguments apply to models of any cardinality; for example, for *S* of cardinality κ, repeat the argument with a *G* that duplicates each possible world 2^κ times.

[14] Recall that after the full structure of the real numbers was shown to be 'too rich' for temperature reality it was noted that structures of a different kind – i.e. affine spaces – are 'just right' for temperature; that is, affine spaces have no structure that goes beyond what is required for representing temperature-induced relations among objects. It could be asked now whether similar such structures exist in the modal case. The answer to this question is positive: in many cases *algebraic formal semantic systems* consist in an alternative to possible-worlds frames that does not involve objects of modality of any kind. (In a system of the algebraic mold each sentence is assigned an element of a given algebraic structure – typically an expansion of a Boolean algebra – instead of a set of possible worlds; the semantic properties of sentences are captured in this framework by the properties of the algebra elements assigned to them.) The formal interplay between world frames and algebraic structures is well known, but its philosophical significance is often overlooked; it is discussed in more detail in Dresner (2002b).

Possible-worlds systems are richer in structure than (at least some of) the modal empirical structures they represent. (A concrete example is metaphysical necessity.) Therefore the use of such systems opens the door for the transfer of superfluous structure from these systems back onto the philosophical discussion of modality. Now the fact that questions about the cardinality of possible-worlds sets are indeed avoided in philosophical discussion would seem to suggest that structure is not actually over-assigned.[15] However, many of those who finesse the above meaningless questions concerning metaphysical modality (and possibly other modal notions) nevertheless hold that modal notions should be analyzed as involving implicit quantification – over possible worlds, or other entities. This position takes various forms, from D. Lewis's full-fledged realism about possible worlds, to all kinds of ersatzism (according to which worlds are merely linguistic or conceptual constructions). What is common to all these variants is that they give conceptual priority to talk about objects of modality over the primitive modal notions; that is, according to these accounts some kind of quantification underlies our intuitions of what is or is not necessary. This outlook already imputes to the modal subject matter more structure than there is in it.

Note that the thrust of the claim is not metaphysical – it is not against the postulation of any kind of objects, be they real or abstract – but rather logical, or methodological: the fact that the logic of some (or possibly all) of our modal notions can be homomorphically embedded within a domain of (modal) objects does not imply that these notions should be subject to reifying explication or analysis.

It should be acknowledged that there are, of course, modal notions that do involve implicit or explicit quantification. Modality of place ('somewhere', 'everywhere'), for example, clearly appeals to quantification over spatial positions, and some (of which I am not one) might also claim that physical necessity and probability are modalities that should be understood as implicitly quantifying over some kind of entities. However, these observations are consistent with the foregoing discussion: the fact that for some modal notions a reifying analysis does not consist in over-assignment does not imply that this is the case for other modal notions.

We are thus led to notice again the trade-off between generality and accuracy. On the one hand, the framework of possible worlds is rich

[15] Thus the notion of *filtering* is introduced in order to avoid questions about identical but numerically distinct worlds; this is an example of an effort explicitly made to avoid questions of the kind alluded to above.

enough to absorb a wide variety of modal notions: we can use this framework to capture our intuitions concerning different modalities and make insightful and important generalizations. Moreover, this rich and general framework is well known and familiar, so it is beneficial to discover that it is applicable to the obscure domain of modality. For all these reasons Kripke's possible-worlds semantics is the great achievement that it is. However, the down side is the loss of a clear view of how much logical structure there actually is in each specific modality.

It is not denied, then, that talk of, for example, metaphysically possible worlds is useful and illuminating, and should not be given up. However, it has been shown how such an admission is consistent with an anti-reifying view of some of the modalities for which possible-worlds talk is useful. Thus we have a new theoretical grounding for a so-called deflationist position vis-à-vis possible worlds: a basis for using possible worlds as a conceptual tool without commitment to their existence as entities that underlie modality. (The suggested view is *not* eliminativist or reductionist concerning the modal aspects of the world; it just rejects the claim that these aspects must be analyzed objectually.)[16]

This account opposes fictionalist theories of possible worlds, which have been the subject of heated debate in recent years. We do not view ourselves as engaged in fiction when we use real numbers to measure temperature, and similarly there is no fiction involved when we talk of possible worlds; in both cases we employ a structure that goes beyond what we are really committed to, but it would be misguided to label the extra structure as fictive. There is no implicitly shared (yet disbelieved) *story* according to which 20 degree centigrade days are twice as hot as 10 degree centigrade days – once the danger of over-assigning structure is pointed out to us we just dismiss this statement. Similarly, there is no fiction behind our possible-worlds talk – once it is acknowledged that the application of reifying idioms to (some) modal locutions over-assigns structure we steer clear of its unwarranted implications, e.g. statements to the effect that possible worlds exist.

Bearing this in mind, however, it should be acknowledged that there is some affinity between the view presented here and what is sometimes called *timid fictionalism* (Rosen 1990), i.e. the position that claims involving (fictive) possible worlds rely on (and are just used to capture) more basic facts of modality. (This is opposed to so-called *strong fictionalism* (Nolan 1997), according to which things are the other way around,

---

[16] See also Dresner (2002b).

i.e. modal facts are reduced to facts about possible worlds.[17]) Both the measurement theoretic account presented here and timid fictionalism give priority to our 'raw' modal judgments over possible-worlds talk, and then try to explain our ability to use the latter kind of talk without being committed to the existence of possible worlds. The explanation provided in this chapter has been shown to be general and natural, I believe, relating possible-worlds talk to other cases of over-assignment of structure; it should therefore be preferred over its artificial, seemingly ad hoc, fictionalist alternative.

The foregoing considerations are in accord with most of Kripke's own remarks concerning the metaphysical and logical status of possible worlds, as presented, for example, in the Preface to the second edition of *Naming and Necessity* (Kripke 1980). Consider what Kripke says about the reduction of the modal notions to quantification over possible worlds (p. 19, footnote):

> I do not think of 'possible worlds' as providing a *reductive* analysis in any philosophically significant sense, that is as uncovering the ultimate nature, from either an epistemological or a metaphysical point of view, of modal operators, propositions, etc., or as 'explicating' them. In the actual development of our thought, judgments involving directly expressed modal locutions ('it might have been the case that') certainly come earlier. The notion of a 'possible world', though it has its roots in various ordinary ideas of ways the world might have been, comes at a much greater, and subsequent, level of abstraction. In practice, no one who cannot understand the idea of possibility is likely to understand that of a 'possible worlds' either. Philosophically, we by no means need assume that one type of discourse is 'prior to' the other, independently of the purpose at hand. The main and original motivation for the 'possible worlds analysis' – and the way it clarified modal logic – was that it enabled modal logic to be treated by the same set theoretic techniques of model theory

[17] Patently all arguments raised against fictionalist theories of modality are directed only against strong fictionalism; thus these arguments do not apply to the account presented here. For example, it is argued that the fictionalist provides us with no reasons to pick one possible-worlds fiction over another as the basis of our modal judgments (Baldwin 1998, 72–5), and that the seemingly linguistic nature of the fiction involved (whatever it is) leads the theory into the same troubles as those faced by linguistic ersatz theories (Nolan 1997); clearly these objections cannot be leveled against a position in which modal statements are irreducible.

that proved so successful when applied to extensional logic. It is also useful in making certain concepts clear.

Kripke rejects a reduction (or analysis) of necessity and possibility to quantification over possible worlds, as I have here. Although he says 'directly expressed modal locutions' and possible-worlds talk should not be given philosophical priority one over the other, still he admits that in several respects the former are, in fact, prior to the latter: the direct modal locutions 'come earlier' in the development of our thought, and understanding them is a prerequisite to having any idea as to what possible worlds are. Again, this accords with the foregoing discussion. Also, note that in the last few lines of the paragraph quoted above Kripke describes the motivation behind the introduction of possible-worlds semantics in almost exactly the same terms as those used here, i.e. as an application of the rich framework of set theory to modality. In this chapter this application has been placed in a much wider context and thus, hopefully, characterized and understood better.

Finally, consider another remark of Kripke's (ibid., p. 18): 'Certainly the philosopher of "possible worlds" must take care that his technical apparatus not push him to ask questions whose meaningfulness is not supported by our original intuitions of possibility that gave the apparatus its point.' As it appears in the text this remark calls for elucidation: what questions are those whose meaningfulness is questionable, and why is it that an apparatus that is (justifiably) claimed to be useful gives rise to such meaningless questions? The foregoing discussion provides complete answers to these questions. Our philosophical intuitions concerning the modal locutions, as captured by a series of deductive systems, were homomorphically embedded by Kripke into a formal system that is too rich in structure. Applying the full structure of the system to the philosophical subject matter yields senseless questions, but using the system critically is very fruitful and helpful, since it involves a conceptual framework of which we have a very good grasp (i.e. object talk). These two are compatible, as they are in temperature measurement.[18]

[18] I would like to thank Donald Davidson, Saul Kripke, Thomas Nagel, Stephen Neale, Carl Posy, Nathan Salmon, and Bruce Vermazen for their comments, and the referee of the *Journal of Philosophical Logic* for his many insightful remarks and suggestions.

References

Benacerraf, P. (1983) What Numbers Could Not Be. In P. Benacerraf and H. Putnam (eds) *The Philosophy of Mathematics*. Cambridge: Cambridge University Press, 272–94.

Baldwin, T. (1998) Modal Fictionalism and the Imagination. *Analysis* 58, 72–5.

Davidson, D. (1984) Reality without Reference. In D. Davidson, *Inquiries into Truth and Interpretation*. Oxford: Clarendon, 215–55.

Dennett, D. (1987) *The Intentional Stance*. Cambridge, MA: MIT Press.

Dresner, E. (2002a) Wittgenstein's Builders and Perry's Objection to Sentence Priority. *Dialectica* 56, 49–64.

Dresner, E. (2002b) Measurement Theoretic Semantics and the Semantics for Necessity. *Synthese* 130, 413–40.

Krantz, D., D. Luce, P. Suppes, and A. Tversky (1971–89) *Foundations of Measurement*, vols 1–3. New York: Academic Press.

Kripke, S. (1980) *Naming and Necessity*. Cambridge, MA: Harvard University Press.

von Neumann, J. (1967 [1923]) Zur Einfuhrung der transfiniten Zahlen. *Acta litterarum ac Scientiarum Regiae Universitatis Hungaricae Francisco-Josephinae (Szeged), Sectio Scientiarum mathematicarum* 1, 199–208; reprinted in van Heijenoort, J., *From Frege to Godel*, Cambridge, MA: Harvard University Press, 346–54.

Nolan, D. (1997) Three Problems for 'Strong' Modal Fictionalism. *Philosophical Studies* 87, 259–75.

Perry, J. (1994) Davidson's Sentences and Wittgenstein's Builders. *Proceedings and Addresses of The American Philosophical Association* 67, 23–37.

Quine, W.V. (1960) *Word and Object*. Cambridge, MA: MIT Press, 26–30.

Rosen, G. (1990) Modal Fictionalism. *Mind* 99, 327–54.

4
Modal Paradox

Teresa Robertson

1 Introduction

Albert, the table at which I work, was originally made from some particular wood, nails, and glue. It could have been originally made from slightly different matter: if the carpenter who originally made Albert had picked up and used a few nails that were different from the ones she actually picked up and used in the construction of Albert, the resulting table might still have been Albert. But origin essentialism claims that although the difference in original material constitution that I just described *is* a possibility for Albert, *not all* differences in original material constitution are: if the carpenter received a shipment of entirely different pieces of wood, boxes of nails, and bottles of glue on the day of Albert's manufacture and went on to construct with these items a table just like Albert in shape and size and so on, the resulting table would not have been Albert.

We have here a pair of intuitions:

[P] Slight variation in the original constitution of a material object is possible.

[E] Total variation in the original constitution of a material object is not possible.

Origin essentialism, the claim that an object's (material) origin is essential to it, has in recent years enjoyed a fairly widespread acceptance (due in part of course to Kripke's having a very strong intuition in favor of it). When I first heard the claim that origin was essential, I took it to mean that a table, for example, couldn't have had any different material origin, no matter how slight the difference. But, it turns out that most advocates of origin essentialism have been careful to formulate their claims in such a way that [P] is not obviously violated. In *Naming and Necessity*, Kripke suggests only that the table in the lecture hall could not have been made from a '*completely* different block of wood' and that Queen Elizabeth could not have originated from a '*totally* different sperm and egg' (Kripke 1972/1980, p. 113, my change of emphasis). These claims, which are in keeping with [E], do not obviously conflict with [P].

But, do [P] and [E] nonetheless conflict in some less than obvious way? Although I (1998) have argued that the *arguments* that have been used to support (claims like) [E] sit ill with (claims like) [P], I have not said that (claims like) [P] and (claims like) [E] themselves conflict. However, one can construct a paradox that suggests that the intuitions do, after all, conflict with one another. The paradox arises because [P] – and [E] for that matter – if true, does not *just happen* to be true as a matter of contingent fact; rather it *has* to be true. [P], if it holds at all, holds not only for material objects that actually have been or will be made, but for any material object that could be made. [P] is necessary. Actually something more – perhaps stronger, depending on your views – should be said about [P]: it is not only necessary, but it is necessarily necessary and necessarily necessarily necessary, and so on.[1]

Let's call the hunk of matter from which Albert was originally made '*h*'. Let *n* be the number of molecules in *h*. Let $h, h_1, h_2, \ldots, h_n$ be a sequence of different hunks of matter, each hunk differing from its immediate predecessor only in the replacement of one molecule by a distinct molecule of the same kind, so that that h_1 'overlaps' *h* by all but one molecule, h_2 'overlaps' *h* by all but two molecules, and so on through h_n which does not 'overlap' *h* at all.

[1] That whatever is necessary is necessarily necessary (or what amounts to the same thing, on the assumption that every proposition has a denial opposite to it in truth value, that whatever is possibly possible is possible) is the cornerstone of S4 modal logic, whose characteristic axiom schema is $\ulcorner\Box\phi \rightarrow \Box\Box\phi\urcorner$ (or, in an alternate axiomatization, $\ulcorner\Diamond\Diamond\phi \rightarrow \Diamond\phi\urcorner$). The theorems of S4 are a subset of the theorems of S5, which is the standardly accepted system of logic for metaphysical modality. Hence, *according to S5* (and S4), if [P] is necessary, it is necessarily necessary and necessarily necessarily necessary, and so on. But what if one does not accept S5 (or S4)? One might still think that *[P] and [E]*, if true, are necessary, necessarily necessary, and so on without thinking that this is (logically) the way it is for *all* necessary truths. Suffice it to say that everyone whose views I will be discussing here does in fact think that [P] and [E], if true, are necessary, necessarily necessary, and so on.

Here then is the paradox, which for ease of exposition, I present in the familiar language of possible worlds.[2] Since Albert was originally made from h, we can infer via [P] that Albert could have been manufactured from h_1. In other words, there is a possible world in which Albert was originally made from h_1. Eliminating the abbreviation, there is a world, which is *possible relative to* (or, in alternative terminology, *accessible from*) the actual world in which Albert was originally made from h_1. Call this possible world 'w_1'. Now consider [P] again. It doesn't *just happen* to be true. Not only does it hold in the actual world, it holds in w_1 as well: if Albert had been originally made from h_1 – as in fact it could have been – then Albert could have been originally made from h_2. In other words, there is a world, possible relative to w_1, in which Albert was originally made from h_2. In still other words, there is a world, which is possible relative to a world that is itself possible relative to the actual world, in which Albert was originally made from h_2. For short, there is a *possibly possible* world, w_2, in which Albert was originally made from h_2. Now consider [P] again. Not only does it hold in the actual world and in w_1, it holds in w_2 as well: if Albert *had been* originally made from h_2 – as it *possibly could* have been – then Albert could have been originally made from h_3. In other words, there is a world, possible relative to w_2, in which Albert was originally made from h_3. In still other words ... We can continue on in this way until we reach a world, w_n, which is possible relative to w_{n-1}, in which Albert was originally made from h_n. If the relation of being possible relative to is transitive, that is, if whatever is possibly possible is also possible, then w_n is possible relative to the actual world, which is just to say that Albert could have been originally made from h_n. But h_n has no matter at all in common with the hunk of matter from which Albert actually was originally made. Thus [E] has been violated.[3] Obviously this presents a puzzle for anyone who holds

---

[2] I do this at the risk of presenting the paradox in a way that would be objectionable to David Lewis. If we simply stipulate that 'possible world' is synonymous with 'maximal ways things could have been', then Lewis should not object to this way of setting out the paradox. (For more on this issue, see Section 5.) Consider it so stipulated.

[3] This paradox is sometimes called 'Chisholm's Paradox'. I am not sure whether the name is appropriate. The paradox with which I am concerned may loosely be described (borrowing words from David Lewis) as one in which a chain of little differences in the original constitution of a given artifact add up to a big difference in the original constitution of the artifact. Chisholm (1967) presents a puzzle in which, by gradual changes over a number of possible worlds, two individuals in the actual world, Adam and Noah, are supposed to swap all their

that whatever is possibly possible is possible and that both [P] and [E] are conceptual truths that are not only true but necessarily true (and necessarily necessarily true and so on).

It will be useful to write this paradox in the language of quantified modal logic.[4]

[MP] (a modal paradox)

(The superscripted numerals indicate the number of times a given operator is repeated. 'Mah_1' is read 'Albert is originally made from h_1' or 'h_1 originally materially constitutes Albert'.)

(1) $\Diamond Mah_1$

(2) $\Box(Mah_1 \rightarrow \Diamond Mah_2)$

(3) $\Box\Box(Mah_2 \rightarrow \Diamond Mah_3)$[5]

.

.

.

(n) $\Box^{n-1}(Mah_{n-1} \rightarrow \Diamond Mah_n)$

(C1) $\Diamond^n Mah_n$

(C2) $\Diamond Mah_n$

(n+1) $\sim\Diamond Mah_n$

Obviously, one can solve this paradox by rejecting [P] (and so rejecting (1) through (n)). And equally obviously one can solve this paradox by rejecting [E] (and so rejecting (n+1)). My concern here though is to examine some (purported) solutions to the paradox that (at least appear

---

properties (well, as many as they can), so that the end result is a world that is indistinguishable from the actual world, 'except for the fact that the Adam of [the last world] may be traced back to the Noah of [the actual world]' and vice versa. In later work, Chisholm (1976) offers a problem more like the paradox presented here. Lewis says that he does not 'distinguish [the] paradox about origins from Chisholm's original paradox' (Lewis 1986, p. 244). Salmon (1986, note 1) though expresses some reservation about calling the paradox about origins 'Chisholm's Paradox'. It seems to me safest simply to drop the name and note (as I am here doing) that the paradox I discuss is akin to the one(s) given by Chisholm.

[4] There is at least one difference between the paradox I gave in 'the language of possible worlds' and [MP]. The original presentation had as a premise that whatever is possibly possible is possible. [MP] in effect deems that premise a *logical truth* that is reflected in the *inference* from (C1) to (C2).

[5] '$\Box\Box(Mah_2 \rightarrow \Diamond Mah_3)$' states of the proposition expressed by '$(Mah_2 \rightarrow \Diamond Mah_3)$' that it is necessarily necessary, that is, that it holds on all worlds possible relative to worlds that are themselves possible relative to the actual world. And similarly for other 'stacked box' statements.

to) honor [P] and [E] – solutions that don't blame the paradox simply on a conflict between [P] and [E]. (When I speak of rejecting/honoring these principles, I mean rejecting/honoring them as conceptual truths that are true, necessarily true, necessarily necessarily true, and so on.) Broadly speaking there are in the literature two general approaches meeting this constraint. One approach simply denies that (it is a logical truth that) whatever is possibly possible is possible and hence rejects the inference from (C1) to (C2). According to the other approach, it is a logical truth that whatever is possibly possible is indeed possible, and this (alleged) fact allows [MP] to be recast as an argument that is formally similar to (standard formalizations of) classical sorites paradoxes; the thought then is that the modal paradox would be amenable to one's favored solution to sorites paradoxes in general. In Section 2 I present the solution offered by Graeme Forbes (notably 1983, 1984, 1985, and 1992), who takes the second approach. In Sections 3 and 4, I present the solutions offered by Nathan Salmon (notably 1981, 1986, and 1989) and by David Lewis (1986), who both take the first approach. In Section 5, I address some mistaken criticisms that Salmon and Lewis have made of each other's solutions. In Section 6, I offer criticisms of Ferbes's solution. Section 7 contains my concluding remarks.[6]

2 Presentation of Forbes's solution

[MP] has the feel of a sorites paradox. Forbes's (1983, 1984, 1985, 1992) solution takes this quite seriously: what I call 'step 1' assimilates formally our modal paradox to standard sorites paradoxes; what I call 'step 2' offers a solution to the latter; and what I call 'step 3' thereby offers a solution to the former as well. I will explain each step of Forbes's solution in turn.

Step 1: the assimilation

In spite of the undeniable fact that our modal paradox feels something like a sorites paradox, in fact [MP] bears very little formal resemblance to (standard formalizations of) sorites paradoxes, one of which is exhibited below.

[SP] (a sorites paradox)
('g_1' through 'g_n' are names for the individuals in a succession of shorter and shorter people. 'Tg_1' says that g_1 is tall.)

[6] The postscript to this chapter was written 13 years after my original talk at the June 1999 conference in Haifa. I have made some changes to the paper as originally given, but I have tried not to change its general thrust, even though I would now approach the material somewhat differently.

(1) Tg_1
(2) $Tg_1 \rightarrow Tg_2$
(3) $Tg_2 \rightarrow Tg_3$
.
.
.
(n) $Tg_{n-1} \rightarrow Tg_n$
(C) Tg_n
(n+1) $\sim Tg_n$

Clearly there is nothing in [SP] that corresponds to the stacking of necessity operators in [MP]; thus the two are formally quite different. Forbes points out though that in the standardly accepted system of logic for metaphysical modality, S5, [MP] can be recast as [MSP] below.

[MSP] (a modal sorties paradox)
(1) $\Diamond Mah_1$
(2) $\Diamond Mah_1 \rightarrow \Diamond Mah_2$
(3) $\Diamond Mah_2 \rightarrow \Diamond Mah_3$
.
.
.
(n) $\Diamond Mah_{n-1} \rightarrow \Diamond Mah_n$
(C) $\Diamond Mah_n$
(n+1) $\sim\Diamond Mah_n$

When I say that [MP] can be recast in S5 as [MSP] I mean that the like-numbered premises of each argument are S5-equivalent to one another. [MSP] has only one conclusion, (C), whereas [MP] has two, (C1) and (C2), because (C1) and (C2) are S5-equivalent.[7]

[7] There are four systems of (propositional) modal logic that are relevant to the current discussion: T, B, S4, and S5. (Propositional modal logic is adequate for our current purposes. The 'conversion' of [MP] to [MSP] does not turn on quantification or the subject-predicate structure of the relevant sentences.) All may be given axiomatically as systems whose inference rules include modus ponens and necessitation and whose axioms include every instance of the K(ripke) axiom schema $\ulcorner\Box(\phi \rightarrow \psi) \rightarrow (\Box\phi \rightarrow \Box\psi)\urcorner$. An axiomatization of the system T results from adding to this that every instance of the axiom schema $\ulcorner\Box\phi \rightarrow \phi\urcorner$ is an axiom. This characteristic axiom schema for T corresponds to models in which the accessibility relation between worlds is reflexive. An axiomatization of the system B results from adding to the axiomatization of T that every instance of the axiom schema $\ulcorner\phi \rightarrow \Diamond\Diamond\phi\urcorner$ is an axiom. This characteristic axiom schema for

[MSP] does have the same form as [SP]: where [MSP] has the 'predicate' '◊*Ma*' (or 'possibly originally constitutes Albert'), [SP] has the predicate 'T' (or 'is tall'); and where [MSP] has the names of individual hunks of matter (h_1 through h_n), [SP] has names of the individuals (g_1 through g_n).

Step 2: the solution to standard sorites paradoxes

Sorites paradoxes are often called paradoxes of vagueness, since they are thought to arise from the sort of vagueness that gives rise to the prospect of borderline cases. In the case of [SP], the vague predicate is 'is tall'.[8] Vague predicates may usefully be contrasted with a predicate like 'is even' as predicated of an integer. Satisfying this predicate is plausibly seen as an all or nothing affair: any integer either satisfies it (completely) or does not satisfy it (at all), that is, any integer is either even or not. There is no prospect of an integer's being a borderline case for evenness. No integer is 'sort of' (or indeterminately) even.

Forbes thinks that vague predicates can be satisfied to a full range of degrees. For our purposes, we can think of these degrees as real numbers between and including 0 and 1. Forbes thinks that since Kareem Abdul Jabbar is taller than Michael Jordan, Jabbar satisfies 'is tall' to a higher degree than does Jordan.[9] Nonetheless both satisfy 'is tall' to a fairly high degree, and to a higher degree than does Bill Clinton, for example.

B corresponds to models in which the accessibility relation between worlds is symmetric. (So in any B-model, the accessibility relation is both reflexive and symmetric.) An axiomatization of the system S4 results from adding to the axiomatization of T that every instance of the axiom schema ⌜$\Box\phi \rightarrow \Box\Box\phi$⌝ is an axiom (or equivalently by adding to the axiomatization of T that every instance of the axiom schema ⌜$\Diamond\Diamond\phi \rightarrow \Diamond\phi$⌝ is an axiom.) This characteristic axiom schema for S4 corresponds to models in which the accessibility relation between worlds is transitive. (So in any S4-model, the accessibility relation is both reflexive and transitive.) Finally, an axiomatization of the system S5 results from adding to the axiomatization of T that every instance of the characteristic B axiom schema is an axiom and that every instance of the characteristic S4 axiom schema is an axiom. (So in any S5-model, the accessibility relation is an equivalence relation. Typically, a defender of S5 has in mind that every world is accessible to every world. A formula is true in all S5-models of this restricted type if and only if it is true in all S5-models.) Equivalently, one can add to the axiomatization of T that every instance of the characteristic axiom schema for S5, ⌜$\Diamond\phi \rightarrow \Box\Diamond\phi$⌝, is an axiom.

[8] I do not intend to suggest by the words 'vague predicate' that I think that vagueness resides in language rather than in the world. A predicate may be 'vague' because the property or concept associated with it is vague.

[9] To give a more specific reference than just the four works cited at the beginning of this section, I refer the reader to Forbes (1985, p. 170). It may be worth noting that apparently none but perhaps the tallest person (or people) is tall to degree 1.0.

Now, if the idea of degrees of predicate satisfaction makes sense, then so should a corresponding idea of degrees of truth, according to which the sentence 'Kareem Abdul Jabbar is tall' is true to a higher degree than the sentence 'Michael Jordan is tall'. Sentences involving vague predicates can be wholly true or wholly false or somewhere in between, just as individuals can satisfy vague predicates completely or not at all or to some degree in between.

Traditionally we work with a two-valued logic, in which sentences are either wholly true or wholly false. Forbes thinks that this is appropriate whenever our predicates are sharply defined, as they are in mathematics. But, he thinks, if we keep to tradition when the sentences with which we are concerned admit of many values besides absolute truth and absolute falsity (because the predicates involved admit of various degrees of satisfaction), we are bound to get into trouble. And that trouble comes, for example, in the form of sorites paradoxes. The paradox arises because we treat sentences with 'in between' truth values as if they were sentences with values 0 and 1 only. So, Forbes turns to a logic that he thinks is appropriate for sentences whose truth values are between 0 and 1. The 'truth tables' Forbes (1985, pp. 170–1) adopts are given below.

$$
\begin{aligned}
\text{val}[{\sim}p] &= 1 - \text{val}[p] \\
\text{val}\ [p\ \&\ q] &= \min\ \{\text{val}[p], \text{val}[q]\} \\
\text{val}\ [p \vee q] &= \max\ \{\text{val}[p], \text{val}[q]\} \\
\text{val}\ [p \rightarrow q] &= 1 - (\text{val}[p] - \text{val}[q]), \text{ if val}[p] > \text{val}\ [q] \\
&\ 1 \text{ otherwise}
\end{aligned}
$$

It is easy for the reader to verify that these 'truth tables' yield the familiar results in cases where the sentences involved have values 0 and 1. The crucial clause, for present purposes, is the one for the material conditional. To get a feel for the idea behind it, consider two conditionals in which the antecedent is 'more true' than the consequent: (i) if Kareem Abdul Jabbar is tall, then so is Michael Jordan; and (ii) if Kareem Abdul Jabbar is tall, then so is Bill Clinton. It makes some intuitive sense to say that the first conditional is more true than the second, which to some degree explains why the clause for the arrow is written as it is.

According to Forbes, validity in this many-valued logic is not a matter of preservation of absolute truth, as it is in two-valued logic; rather it is a matter of preservation of degree of truth. An argument is valid just in case 'there is no assignment of degrees of truth to its sentence letters such that the value of the conclusion falls below that of the lowest-valued premises' (ibid., p. 171). Again, it is easy for the reader to verify that this yields the usual results in cases where the sentences of the argument all have values of either 0 or 1.

Forbes thinks that once we make the move to a many-valued logic, we will see that sorites arguments are in fact *invalid*.[10] This claim seems implausible at first, since the only inference pattern that sorites arguments ultimately involve is modus ponens, which surely is a paradigm of a valid inference pattern. But, Forbes points out, modus ponens is *not*, according to his definition of validity, a valid inference pattern, since it does not preserve degree of truth. To see this, consider a case where the antecedent of the conditional premise has value 0.6 and the consequent has value 0.4. In this case the premises of a modus ponens argument will have values 0.6 (for the premise which consists of the antecedent of the conditional alone) and 0.8 (for the conditional premise, since 1 minus the difference between the antecedent and the consequent is 0.8), while the conclusion will have value 0.4 (which is the value of the consequent of the conditional alone), which is lower than the value of the lowest valued premise. Here the premises are 'mostly' true and the conclusion 'mostly' false.

Our initial intuitions about any sorites paradox are that the reasoning involved is legitimate, since modus ponens is above reproach; that all of the premises are true; but that the conclusion is false. In a way, Forbes's solution respects these intuitions: modus ponens *is* above reproach in cases in which the sentences involved are wholly true or wholly false; all of the premises in a sorites argument are (at least) very nearly true; and the conclusion of a sorites argument is very false (perhaps even wholly false). Because modus ponens is, in the cases we are most familiar with, a valid inference pattern, we are lulled into thinking, wrongly, that it is always valid. In this way, Forbes proposes to explain the seductiveness of sorites paradoxes while yet depriving them of their power.

Step 3: the extension of this solution to [MSP]

To my mind, the extension of the solution is quite straightforward, and here is what I take it to be. [MSP] and [SP] both have the same general form, which is displayed below.

(1) $\varphi\gamma_1$
(2) $\varphi\gamma_1 \rightarrow \varphi\gamma_2$
(3) $\varphi\gamma_2 \rightarrow \varphi\gamma_3$

---

[10] For a criticism of Forbes's characterization of validity and of his characterization of his own solution, see Salmon (1986, pp. 105–6).

.
.
.

(n) $\varphi\gamma_{n-1} \rightarrow \varphi\gamma_n$
(C) $\varphi\gamma_n$
(n+1) $\sim \varphi\gamma_n$

It is clear then that the 'predicate' '◊*Ma*' (or 'possibly originally constitutes Albert') should play the same role in the modal paradox as the predicate 'T' (or 'is tall') plays in the sorites paradox, since each is the appropriate substituend for φ. Just as different people satisfy 'is tall' to varying degrees, so should different hunks of matter satisfy 'possibly originally constitutes Albert' to varying degrees. Carrying out these parallels, Forbes should say that '◊Mah_1' is more true than '◊Mah_2', which in turn is more true than '◊Mah_3', and so on. Thus the conditional premises are less than wholly true (since 1 minus the difference in the values of the antecedent and the consequent is less than 1).[11] Thus the argument involves sentences that have more than just the two traditionally recognized truth values and hence the modus ponens inferences it makes are in fact invalid. End of story. End of philosophical story, at any rate.

Now I turn from philosophy proper to the history of recent philosophy. In the paragraph on the extension of the solution (that is, on step 3), I said what I thought Forbes *should* say. What he actually does say is different. Forbes thinks that in [SP] the 'predicate whose application conditions are tolerant' is 'is tall', but he thinks that in [MSP] 'the predicate whose application conditions are tolerant is a predicate expressing the thisness or haecceity of *a*, for which we may simply use the predicate $\xi = a$' (Forbes 1983, p. 239). As we have seen, straightforward substitution into the general form of a sorites paradox should lead Forbes to say that the tolerant predicate is 'possibly originally constitutes Albert', and not, as he has it, 'is identical to Albert'. Forbes's 'substitution error' – whether it really is an error depends on what can be said against making the straightforward substitution – led him to the following concern.

> We turn now to the task of extending the degree-theoretic solution of the sorites paradoxes to the modal [paradox]. There are two obstacles in

[11] I assume that if we started [MSP] with '◊*Mah*' instead of with '◊Mah_1' (and made corresponding adjustments) Forbes would allow that the first premise was wholly true. In any case, Forbes's focus is on the conditional premises.

> the way of such an extension, one technical and one philosophical ... The philosophical difficulty concerns the coherence of the notion of the degree to which an object satisfies such a predicate as $\xi = a$ at a world. In the standard semantics for S5, transworld heirlines of objects are given by transworld identities: the only object which satisfies $\xi = a$ at a world is a. So if there can be degrees of satisfaction of $\xi = a$ at a world w then it looks as if there must be degrees of being identical to a at w. Yet the notion of degrees of identity is incoherent ... Instead, we need to replace standard S5 semantics with some other sort ... The prescient reader will have anticipated that counterpart theory is about to appear on the stage ... The extension of the [counterpart] relation is fixed by considerations of similarity across worlds. Since there is no problem at all about degrees of similarity, degrees of counterparthood are equally straightforward. (Ibid., pp. 247–8)[12]

I will not (here) critically evaluate these remarks of Forbes. Instead I will continue my recounting of history. Forbes's turn to counterpart theory led Salmon to make a number of objections to Forbes's solution to the modal paradox. Salmon's criticisms center on problems he sees with counterpart theory. That is, his criticisms center on what I will call Forbes's *implementation* of his solution rather than on the solution itself. (As will, I hope, become clear soon enough, Forbes need not have taken a stand on the merits of standard versus counterpart theoretic semantics in order to have offered a degree-theoretic solution to the modal paradox; furthermore, it is not the case that, unless vague identity is countenanced, the standard semantics do not have the wherewithal to implement his solution.) Forbes's solution has come to be called the 'counterpart-theoretic solution' (and Salmon's has come to be called the 'intransitive-accessibility solution').[13] This nomenclature has unfortunately led to the obscuring of important philosophical issues that differentiate the solutions of Forbes, Salmon, and Lewis. There is a tendency to see Forbes and Lewis as significantly united (since both advocate versions of counterpart theory), and Salmon as the opponent of both. This, as you will see, I think is a mistake.

Let's pick up the philosophical story again and let it mingle with our historical story. Forbes would be right to say that if he accepts the

---

[12] For anyone curious about it, the technical difficulty concerns the fact that linearly ordered degrees of truth may not be good enough for representing similarity in *multiple* respects. This need not worry us, since we have been concerned with only differences along one dimension, namely original material constitution.

[13] Forbes (1984, p. 176) and Salmon (1986, p. 82) both use this kind of terminology.

standard possible worlds semantics, then in order to be able to say, for example, that the sentence 'It is possible that Albert is originally made from h_2' is less than wholly true, he would have to say that it is less than wholly true that there is a possible world in which Albert is originally made from h_2. Forbes seems to think that saying this will put him in the hopeless position of having to say that identity is vague. And so he is motivated to accept a version of counterpart theory:

> [There is] a vagueness or fuzziness in the limits of the range of sums of wood which possibly constitute [Albert]: there is no sharp distinction between those sums which could, and those which could not, constitute [Albert]. [i] Given that there is no fuzziness in the boundaries of particular sums of wood or in the constitution relation, *it seems that this vagueness must arise from an underlying vagueness in the concept of possibly being identical to [Albert]; [ii] however in standard modal semantics, such vagueness could only be represented by vagueness in [Albert]'s transworld identity condition*, and a solution of the paradox in which we think of identity as vague would be rather unappealing. But it does make sense to think of *similarity* as being vague, in the sense of admitting *degrees* ... Since the counterpart relation is fixed by similarity considerations ... and similarity admits of degrees, the degree-theoretic resolution of non-modal paradoxes ... can be transcribed into the modal logical context. (Forbes 1984, pp. 173–4, my emphasis)

Forbes's thoughts here take some care to work through. What [i] shows us is that he here locates the vagueness in the concept of *possibly* being identical to [Albert] whereas earlier (1983, p. 239) he located the vagueness in the predicate expressing the thisness or haecceity of Albert. But still it seems to me that he has misidentified the predicate that is the analog of 'is tall', which (I remind you) I claimed is 'possibly originally constitutes Albert'. It should be noted that the identity predicate '=' makes no (explicit) appearance in [MP]. What's more [ii] may be false: arguably, vagueness in the predicate 'possibly is identical to Albert' can be represented in the standard semantics by means of a vague accessibility relation. More importantly, vagueness in the predicate that is actually relevant (namely, 'possibly originally constitutes Albert') can be represented in the standard semantics by means of a vague accessibility relation. And, in a more historical note, in the very same article from which the (most recent) block quotation was taken, Forbes recognizes that the standard semantics *can* accommodate his degree-theoretic solution to the modal paradox by 'allowing the accessibility relation to be a relation of degree' (Forbes 1984, p. 179). The idea is simple. If one wants to say, as Forbes does, that it is less than wholly true that it is possible that Albert is originally made from h_2, then the standard semantics makes it a breeze to accommodate the less than absolute truth of that proposition: there's a world, that is less than wholly possible, in which Albert is originally made from h_2. This paraphrase 'locates' the vagueness in the accessibility relation between worlds. And that, after all, is the natural home for the feeling that it is *less than wholly possible* that Albert is originally made from h_2. I say it is the 'natural home' because if one thinks of a possible world as a way things could have been, then to the extent that one thinks that there are ways things *almost* could have been, one should think that there are *almost possible worlds*, that is worlds that are *less than wholly possible* relative to the actual world. But once it is recognized that the standard semantics can accommodate the view that, for example, 'It is possible that Albert is originally made from h_2' is less than wholly true but not wholly false, it should, I think, also be recognized that the motivation that Forbes has given for turning to counterpart theory has been undercut.

The truth, as we have seen, is that Forbes's solution to the modal paradox can be 'implemented' in either standard or counterpart theoretic semantics. To my mind the choice between which of these is the best way to implement the solution is tangential to the issue of what the solution to the paradox is. Forbes's solution to the modal paradox is complete with just these elements: [MP] can legitimately be recast as [MSP]; sorites paradoxes or paradoxes of vagueness arise from the fact that (at least) the conditional premises involved are less than wholly true and from the fact that modus ponens is invalid (in the sense that Forbes defines); and finally [MSP] involves a vague predicate that is relevantly analogous to the predicates in standard sorites paradoxes. End of story. There is no need for Forbes to commit himself to any particular semantics for modal statements. Indeed such a commitment is odd in light of the fact that his official view about modal semantics (even in the 1984 article quoted previously) is the 'reverse translation' view. According to this view, neither the possible worlds translations nor the counterpart theoretic translations of sentences of modal logic mean what they appear to mean (that is, they do not really assert the existence of possible worlds as such); indeed *they have no meaning other than that of the sentences they translate* (Forbes 1985, p. 80). If that were so, there should, it seems, be no relevant difference in the choice of one over the other.

To conclude this presentation of Forbes's views, I want only to stress that I take the issue of the apparatus that he employs to be tangential to the issue of the solution to the paradox. Accordingly, my criticisms below will address only what I consider to be essential to his solution.

3 Presentation of Salmon's solution

Salmon's solution to [MP] is admirably simple: deny that everything that is possibly possible is possible. This allows Salmon to affirm the truth of each of the premises in [MP], to affirm its first conclusion, (C1), but to deny that (C2) follows from (C1).[14]

It is wrong to assume that anything that is possibly possible is possible, Salmon thinks, since that assumption goes against intuition. He offers the following type of example in support of his claim. Let's assume that there is a sharp division between what matter Albert could and what matter Albert could not have originated from.[15] Then, whatever that

---

[14] Salmon credits Chandler (1976) with first suggesting this type of solution. Denying that everything that is possibly possible is possible of course commits one to denying that it is a truth of logic that everything that is possibly possible is possible, and hence commits one to denying the inference from (C1) to (C2). Salmon (1989) argues that even if it turns out as a matter of metaphysics that everything that is possibly possible is possible, it would still not be a truth of logic that everything that is possibly possible is possible, so (C2) would still not follow from (C1). However, (C2) would be obtainable from (C1) together with the additional premise that everything that is possibly possible is possible. See note 4.

[15] The example can be reworked to the same effect if instead of assuming a sharp division, one instead assumes, for example, an interval of vagueness and indeterminacy (see Salmon 1989, p. 5). It is nonetheless an interesting question whether in fact there is a sharp division. Salmon (1986, Appendix) sketched an argument designed to show that there is a sharp cutoff point in the amount of different original matter possible in the construction of an artifact. First, consider the question of whether or not there is a sharp cutoff point in the amount of different matter it is possible to *reconstruct* the same table from. Let $a_1 - a_n$ be a series of different tables, each of which is originally constructed from n molecules. Suppose that, at a later time (say, immediately after original construction), each of these tables is completely dismantled. Suppose that later (say, immediately later) a series of n tables, $a_1' - a_n'$, are built in such a way that a_1' is made from all but one of the molecules from which a_1 was originally made (and is made according to the same plan and so on as a_1 was made); a_2' is made from all but two of the molecules from which a_2 was originally made (and was made from the same plan and so on as a_2 was originally made); and so on through a_n', which is made from all but n of the molecules from which a_n was originally made (that is a_n' is made from matter that is completely different from the matter from which a_n was originally made). Now, since identity does not admit of borderline cases (as Salmon 1981 and elsewhere argues), each statement of the form '$a_i = a_i'$' is either (wholly) true or (wholly) false. Surely a_1 is identical to a_1' and surely a_n

cutoff point may be, it would seem that there is some hunk of matter h_m which is such that it is actually impossible that Albert was originally constructed from it, but which is close enough to being a possible material origin for Albert, that had Albert originated from a certain hunk of matter h_k, which in fact Albert could have originated from, then *it would have been possible* for Albert to have originated from h_m, even though it is not actually possible. In standard Kripke semantics this denial that whatever is possibly possible is possible amounts to denying that the accessibility relation between worlds is transitive.

4 Presentation of Lewis's solution

Like Salmon, Lewis (1986, pp. 243–8) denies that everything that is possibly possible is possible. Thus he can similarly affirm the truth of each of the premises in [MP], affirm its first conclusion, (C1), but reject 'the fatal move' (1986, p. 245) from (C1) to (C2).

But Lewis does all this while maintaining the usual assumption that all worlds are possible relative to each other (and hence that the accessibility relation between worlds is transitive).[16] How can he do this? He rejects the analysis of modality suggested by Kripke semantics (and by commonsense) in favor of his own – the original – version of counterpart theory. According to Lewis, the claim that *it is possibly possible that*

---

is not identical to a_n'. Assuming that for any i, if a_i is identical to a_i' then $a_{(i-1)}$ is identical to $a_{(i-1)}$ and assuming that for any i, if a_i is not identical to a_i' then $a_{(i+1)}$ is not identical to $a_{(i+1)}'$, there must be a sharp cutoff point in what matter a table could be reconstructed from. It seems reasonable that if a table x, which is originally constructed from hunk of matter y, could (not) be *reconstructed* in the specified way from hunk of matter y', then x could (not) have been *originally constructed* from y'. (And here I'm assuming this (or something like it) captures the 'natural assumptions' to which Salmon alludes.) From this it would follow that there is a sharp cutoff point in the matter from which a table could be originally constructed.

16 Lewis (1968) does not provide formal semantics in the usual sense but instead provides a translation scheme. Standardly, a general model for (quantified) modal logic includes (among other things) a set of worlds, a binary relation on that set (the accessibility relation), and a function from worlds to sets of individuals (the individuals that exist at the world). It is natural to think of a Lewis model as adding to this a binary relation on individuals (the counterpart relation). Lewis models would require the accessibility relation to be such that every world is accessible to each world (and hence explicit mention of the relation could be dropped). It is also natural to think of Lewis as doing away with the accessibility relation between worlds altogether.

Albert was originally made from h_m amounts to the claim that there is a (possible) world in which a *counterpart of a counterpart of Albert* is originally made from h_m, whereas the claim that *it is possible that Albert* was originally made from h_m amounts to the claim that there is a (possible) world in which a *counterpart of Albert* is originally made from h_m.

According to Lewis, a counterpart of a counterpart of an individual is not always a counterpart of that individual. In this way, Lewis's theory denies (that it is a logical truth) that whatever is possibly possible is possible.

5 The Salmon–Lewis solution

We've just seen that Lewis and Salmon are in agreement that it is not the case that whatever is possibly possible is possible. Both agree that the inference from (C1) to (C2) in [MP] is illegitimate. Both reject the S5 axiom schema according to which whatever is possibly possible is possible. However, Salmon, it seems, would disagree with my characterization: he calls Lewis 'a friend of S5' and takes him to be a principal objector to his view that S5 is to be rejected as the proper logic for metaphysical modality.[17]

The source of Salmon's surprising epithet is to be found, I suspect, in the differences in the way Salmon and Lewis 'implement' their solution. To repeat, Salmon analyzes '$\Diamond\Diamond Mah_m \rightarrow \Diamond Mah_m$' as the claim that if there is a world that is possible relative to (that is, accessible from) a world that is possible relative to the actual world in which Albert was originally made from h_m then there is a world possible relative to the actual world in which Albert is originally made from h_m. Salmon can coherently deny this conditional since he does not think that all worlds are possible relative to each other. Again, Lewis offers a different analysis: if there is a world in which a counterpart of a counterpart of Albert is

[17] See Salmon (1989, p. 24). Salmon (1986, n. 10 and elsewhere) does point out that Lewis is committed to denying that all instances of $\ulcorner\Diamond\Diamond\phi \rightarrow \Diamond\phi\urcorner$ are true. So it is somewhat mysterious as to why Salmon calls Lewis a friend of S5. To avoid confusion, let me stress that the current issue concerns *propositional* S5: in particular, the issue is whether a particular proposition (that Albert is originally made from h_m) is possibly possible but not possible. It is well known (and Salmon would certainly agree) that Lewis is no friend of *quantified* S5 with identity. (For example, the necessity of identity is a theorem of quantified S5, but it fails in Lewis's counterpart theory.) The sentences we are concerned with do not involve quantifiers over individuals or the identity predicate, though they do contain names for individuals and predicates that apply to those individuals.

originally made from h_m then there is a world in which a counterpart of Albert is originally made from h_m. Lewis can coherently deny this conditional since he does not think that all counterparts of counterparts of an individual are themselves counterparts of the given individual. *If* Lewis accepted the standard analysis of modal talk that is suggested by Kripke semantics, then Salmon's epithet would be appropriate. But since Lewis favors his own analysis in terms of counterpart theory, the epithet is inappropriate. Lewis and Salmon both solve the modal puzzle by rejecting the same axiom schema of S5 (namely, the characteristic axiom schema of S4). In Salmon's 'implementation' this involves saying that the accessibility relation is not transitive; in Lewis's 'implementation' this involves saying that, although the accessibility relation is transitive, the counterpart relation is not. Lewis is no friend of S5.

Lewis offers the following criticism of Salmon:

> There is supposed to be a different defence available. Instead of relying on intransitivity of the counterpart relation to block the fatal move – indeed without assuming counterpart theory at all – we could instead rely on inaccessibility of worlds ... [But] by what right do we ignore worlds that are deemed inaccessible? Accessible or not, they're still worlds. We still believe in them. Why don't they count? (Lewis 1986, p. 246)

Lewis's question is easy enough to answer. Inaccessible worlds don't count, for Salmon, for the very same reason that, for Lewis, counterparts of counterparts don't count: they don't correspond to *possibilities*, but merely possible possibilities. The right by which Salmon ignores the merely possibly possible worlds is the very same right by which Lewis ignores the mere counterparts of counterparts (of the relevant individual).

For all their rhetorical flourish, both Salmon's objection to Lewis and Lewis's objection to Salmon confuse two issues: how to analyze modality and how to solve the paradox. The disagreement that they have about the proper analysis of modality is tangential to the issue that immediately concerns me. I will thus, in this context, for now, speak of the 'Salmon–Lewis Solution' to the modal paradox.

It may be helpful to develop some neutral terminology in which to discuss the Salmon–Lewis Solution. I believe, and so do you, that things could have been different in countless ways. But what does this mean? Ordinary language permits the paraphrase: there are many ways things could have been besides the way they actually are. I believe that things could have been different in countless ways; I believe what is expressed by permissible paraphrases of expressions of what I believe; taking the paraphrase at its face value, I therefore believe in the existence of entities that might be called 'ways things could have been'. I prefer to call them 'possible maximal ways'.[18]

There are other maximal ways (for things to be). There are maximal ways things could not metaphysically have been. That is, there are impossible maximal ways. There are maximal ways things could logically have been. That is, there are logically possible maximal ways. There are maximal ways things could not logically have been. That is, there are logically impossible maximal ways. You get the idea.[19]

One maximal way (hereafter 'm-way') things could be is the m-way things actually are. I prefer to call that possible m-way 'w^*'. (I return to the usual practice of leaving implicit that the possibility here is metaphysical. Also, no harm will result in the current context if we ignore all but the logically possible maximal ways, so we can take those to be the m-ways. I take the metaphysically possible maximal ways and the metaphysically possibly possible maximal ways and so on to be a subset of the logically possible maximal ways.) According to w^*, Albert is originally made from h. It follows from [P] (even though a nominalist about ways would demur) that, according to some possible m-way, Albert is originally made from h_1. (Perhaps the nominalist about ways will not be too upset if I hereafter deny his or her existence. Well, more accurately, if I hereafter stop mentioning that he or she demurs from certain inferences.) It follows from [E] that according to no possible m-way is Albert originally made from h_n. It follows from the fact that [P] is a conceptual truth that there is a possible^n m-way (where 'possible^3 m-way', for example, is short for 'possibly possibly possible m-way') according to which Albert is originally made from h_n. If it follows from the claim that there is a possible^n m-way according to which Albert is originally made from h_n that there is a possible m-way according to which Albert is originally made from h_n, then we have a contradiction. This is our paradox.

[18] Obviously, this paragraph mimics the famous paragraph of Lewis (1973, p. 84). Where I have 'maximal way', Lewis has 'world'. No doubt 'world' is a more elegant way to convey that the ways that concern us are maximal (roughly in the sense of evaluating every single proposition as true or false), but it invites confusing worlds (in the sense of maximal ways) with worlds (in the sense of universes). Besides, my aim was to provide a neutral terminology, and the phrase 'possible world' is problematic for this purpose.

[19] This paragraph expresses ideas that are stated more fully in Salmon (1989).

Salmon and Lewis are united in solving this paradox by holding that the relation of one m-way's being possible relative to another (that is, the accessibility relation between m-ways) is not transitive. Lewis should have no trouble at all understanding why inaccessible m-ways don't count as possible m-ways – in spite of his (at least professed) inability to understand why inaccessible worlds don't count as possible worlds.[20]

6 Discussion of Forbes's solution

In this section I criticize the first and third steps of Forbes's solution, taking them in reverse order. (Criticism of step 2 – his solution to standard sorites paradoxes – is beyond the proper scope of this chapter.[21]) Because I take Forbes's counterpart theoretic 'implementation' of his solution to be inessential to his solution itself, my criticisms do not address problems with counterpart theory. Problems with counterpart theory have been the focus of Salmon's objections to Forbes's solution.

Step 3: the extension of [SP]'s solution to [MSP]

In order for any solution to [SP] that hinges on the claim that the predicate 'is tall' is vague properly to extend to [MSP], it must make sense to think of the allegedly analogous predicate 'possibly originally constitutes Albert' as vague (in the same way). In particular, in the case of Forbes's solution, it must make sense to think of that predicate as being satisfiable to varying degrees. Furthermore, Forbes (1984, p. 176) claims that it is a strength of his solution to [MSP] that each of the conditional premises is treated uniformly in the sense that they are all taken to have the same degree of truth. Forbes maintains that each of the conditional premises of [MSP] is very, very close to being wholly true, but that each falls short of being wholly true, since in each case the antecedent is more true than the consequent.

Taking premise (2) of [MSP] as an example, Forbes maintains that 'it is possible that Albert is originally made from h_1' is more true than 'it is possible that Albert is originally made from h_2'. But this conflicts with intuition, since 'it is possible that Albert is originally made from h_2'

[20] Assuming that Lewis stands by his (1973, p. 84) stipulation to use 'possible worlds' for 'ways things could have been', he apparently has a bit of a problem. (Well, more than a bit.)

[21] Williamson (1994) offers a discussion of the problems with degree theoretic solutions to sorites paradoxes.

seems just as true as 'it is possible that Albert is originally made from h_1'. Surely it is wholly true that Albert could have been originally made from a hunk of matter that is only one molecule different from the hunk of matter from which Albert was actually originally made. And surely it is wholly true that Albert could have been originally made from a hunk of matter that is only two molecules different from the hunk of matter from which Albert was actually originally made.

Although Forbes thinks that it would weaken the dialectical strength of his position, he could respond by abandoning his commitment to saying that *each* conditional premise has the same, very high, truth value: perhaps, he might say, some of them are wholly true, while others are very nearly true.[22] Still, on this view, Forbes is committed to thinking that predicates like 'possibly originally constitutes Albert' are satisfiable to varying degrees. He suggests a test for the appropriateness of degree-theoretic talk about a particular predicate:

> The basic concepts of degree-theoretic semantics are straightforwardly legitimized by the use of vague predicates in the comparative form, for if of two red color patches, one can be redder than another, then the first is red to a greater degree than the other, and so satisfies the predicate 'is red' to a greater degree than the other. (Forbes 1983, p. 242)

Does it make sense to use the comparative form in the case at hand? That is, does it make sense to say that it is more possible for h_1 to constitute Albert originally than it is for, say, $h_{1\text{zillion}}$ to constitute Albert originally? To my mind, it does not, unless that is simply a misleading way of saying that h_1 *could* and $h_{1\text{zillion}}$ *could not* originally constitute Albert (just as saying 'the integer two is more even than the integer three is' would be an extremely misleading way of saying that two is even and three is not). But, to other minds, the comparative may seem to make sense.

Other kinds of possibility admit of degrees, why not metaphysical possibility? We find it natural enough, for example, to say that one

---

22 To my mind this would strengthen Forbes's position, since the position would allow that it is wholly true that Albert could have been originally made from a hunk of matter that was only two molecules different from the hunk of matter from which Albert was actually originally made. Similarly, it would, to my mind, strengthen his solution to the sorites paradox for him to allow that it is wholly true that Kareem Abdul Jabbar is tall (even though some people are taller).

action or set of actions is more permissible (that is, 'morally possible') than another: killing one's father is more morally possible than killing one's father *and* marrying one's mother. Similarly we might say that it is more physically possible for me to jump over my apartment building than to jump over the Empire State Building. Can't we understand degrees of metaphysical possibility along these lines?

My reply has two parts: first, on closer examination, it doesn't seem at all clear that other kinds of possibility do admit of degrees; and second, even if they do, there is good reason to think that metaphysical possibility does not.

It seems to me that, although it may be worse to kill one's father and marry one's mother than it is simply to kill one's father, both sets of actions are wholly morally impermissible (under most circumstances). It is true that, all other things being equal, the latter situation is more like a situation which is wholly permissible than the former is. Nonetheless, both are wholly impermissible. It is also true that, all other things being equal, the latter situation involves the breaking of fewer of the moral laws than does the former. Still, both involve breaking the moral laws and thus both are wholly impermissible. (Analogously, someone who is only one-week pregnant is more like someone who is not pregnant than is someone who is eight-months pregnant, but still both are wholly pregnant.) Moreover, if moral possibility admits of degrees, then we should be able to make sense of some action's being 'kind of (morally) permissible' just as we can make sense of something's being 'kind of red'. Suppose someone asks me if she can (morally speaking) do *x* and I reply, 'You kind of can.' My response seems odd, but we might make sense of it by saying that I mean that she can do *x* and get away with it. But that of course is *not* to say that it is partially morally permissible to do *x*. Or perhaps I mean that it is morally permissible for her to do something similar to *x* – something that would, for example, achieve the goal the person had in mind in doing *x*. But again, this is *not* to say that doing *x* is partially morally permissible. So, I am not convinced that moral possibility does admit of degrees, although I am convinced that some things are morally worse than others. Similar things can be said about physical possibility. So I am dubious of my imagined critic's claim that non-metaphysical forms of possibility admit of degrees.

But, for sake of argument, let me grant that degrees of moral or physical possibility can be cashed out in some way – perhaps in terms of number of violations of laws (assuming these can be individuated in some acceptable way) and degree to which laws are broken. But what could the analog be in the case of metaphysical possibility? Number and degree of 'laws of existence' or 'laws of logic, broadly construed' that are broken? I'm not sure what such laws would be, but whatever they would be, I would think that something could not break them to varying degrees or that something could break one at all. Surely then the default position is that metaphysical possibility does not admit of degrees. And Forbes has offered us no account to make sense of degrees of possibility.[23]

Step 1: the claim that [MSP] and [MP] are equivalent puzzles

Suppose that Forbes is right that 'possibly originally constitutes Albert' is a predicate of degree, and suppose too that he is right about his solution to classical sorites paradoxes. All this helps to solve [MP] *only if* it is correct to regard [MP] and [MSP] as the same puzzle (that is, as logically equivalent puzzles). Intuitively they seem like different puzzles[24] and so far we have seen no reason to question this intuition. Forbes does note, as I mentioned on page 59, that the standardly accepted system of logic for metaphysical modality, S5, allows [MP] to be recast as [MSP]. (S4 also allows the recasting.) That is true, but only because according to S5 (and S4) it is a matter of logic that whatever is possibly possible is possible. But Salmon has provided a counterexample to this. And all that matters (in this context) is that Salmon's counterexample is logically possible. So the dialectical situation is this: the advocate of Forbes's solution must give a reason to think that accessibility (being possible relative to) must be transitive and in so doing provide a reply to Salmon's counterexample.

Forbes does indeed offer an argument for the transitivity of possibility: the argument takes the form of a reductio on the claim that there are contingently impossible worlds (like the world in Salmon's example in which Albert is originally made from h_m). (Just to make sure it is

---

[23] See note 15 for a very different argument against the claim that it is vague as to what matter a given table could be originally constructed from.

[24] I say they intuitively seem like different puzzles because once the premises of [MP] are cashed out in terms of ways for things to be, there is a strong intuition that they are true. Intuitions about the truth value of the premises in [MSP] are not so clear. Of course this difference in intuitions about truth values does not show that the premises in the puzzles are not at bottom equivalent: one could hardly argue that '$(P \& \sim P)$' and '$(\exists x)(\forall y)(Sxy \leftrightarrow \sim Syy)$' are not logically equivalent on the ground that one has firm intuitions that the first is a contradiction, but that one lacks firm intuitions about the second. Nonetheless, these intuitions about the truth values of the premises of [MP] and [MSP] place the burden of proof on the person who would equate the two puzzles.

clear why this reductio is an argument for the transitivity of possibility: a world is contingently impossible iff it is impossible but is not necessarily impossible; that is, a world is contingently impossible iff it is impossible but is possibly possible. So if there are no contingently impossible worlds, then *if a world is impossible then it is not possibly possible*. Contraposing the conditional gives the following conditional: if a world is possibly possible then it is possible.) But, I will show, Forbes's argument is flawed.

Before I give Forbes's argument, it is good to highlight a couple of familiar points. Some necessary truths are conceptual and that fact seems to guarantee their necessity. [P] and [E] are good examples of this. Other necessary truths are not conceptual and in fact require empirical justification. Perhaps the most famous example of this kind of truth is the claim that water is H_2O. One has to discover this truth empirically. One can infer that it is *necessary* that water is H_2O by appealing to the empirical discovery together with the conceptual truth that chemical kinds have their chemical structures necessarily. It is a fairly common view that all empirical necessities are like this in that their justifications appeal to empirical truths together with conceptual necessities.[25]

To make Forbes's argument easy to follow and hence easy to evaluate, I pictorially represent the worlds of Salmon's example below. For each world, I list the salient truths of the world together with the modal statuses of those truths at the world. [E′] is the essentialist claim that is operative in the example. It says that a lot of variation in the original constitution of a material object is not possible.[26]

w^* (the actual world)
[E′] (which is necessary at w^*)
Mah (which is contingent at w^*)
$\sim Mah_m$ (which is necessary at w^*)

w_k (an actually possible world)
[E′] (which is necessary at w_k)

---

[25] For discussions relevant to this view, see Kripke (1971), Salmon (1981), Bealer (1987), and Sidelle (1989).

[26] The difference between h and h_m is a lot; the differences between h and h_k and between h_k and h_m are not a lot. For present purposes this is all the precision we need.

Mah_k (which is contingent at w_k)
$\sim$*Mah_m* (which is contingent at w_k)

w_m (an actually contingently impossible world that is possible relative to w_k)
[E′] (which is necessary at w_m)
Mah_m (which is contingent at w_m)

Now for Forbes's alleged reductio.[27] He asks us to consider a contingently impossible world, like w_m. Then he asks, 'in what could such an impossibility consist? No a priori conceptual truth can fail at it, since it is then not a *possible* [sic] world'. I assume that Forbes meant to say 'possibly possible world' here: *of course* it is not a *possible* world, since it is, *ex hypothesi*, an *impossible* world, albeit only contingently so. So far, so good.

Forbes goes on to ask, 'could some a posteriori necessary truth, necessary at w^* fail at [w_m]?'. Before looking at his reason for the answer he gives to this question, which must be 'no', it is useful to think about what Salmon's example would have us answer. Clearly that answer would be 'yes', since, to take the salient example, '$\sim$*Mah_m*' is necessary at w^* (and hence true at w_k) and false at w_m (where its negation is true).

Forbes's answer to his question is this: 'evidently not: the same a priori conceptual truths hold at every world, and any a posteriori truth T necessary at the actual world is so by being true at the actual world and by some conceptual truth's entailing that T's truth makes it necessary'. This is wrong as I explain in detail below. Forbes concludes, 'thus T holds at any world accessible to the actual world, so the same conceptual truth will make it necessary at such a world over again; hence we never reach a world where some actual impossibility is true'.

It is easy to see what is wrong with Forbes's claim (and with the conclusion that he draws from it) if one takes as one's sample necessary a posteriori truth (that is, as the 'T' in Forbes's answer) that Albert is not originally made from h_m. This claim is true and its necessitation is true. Its necessitation appears to be justified on the basis of empirical truths (that Albert was originally made from h and that h and h_m do not have a lot of matter in common) and a conceptual truth ([E′]). *However*, its necessitation does not follow, as Forbes claims it must, from *its* truth and some conceptual truth *that entails that if it is true then its*

[27] All the quotations in this paragraph are taken from Forbes (1985, p. 237, n. 26).

necessitation is true. Indeed there does not seem to be such a conceptual truth: if it were a conceptual truth that if Albert is not originally made from h_m then necessarily Albert is not originally made from h_m, then surely it would also be a conceptual truth that if Albert is not originally made from h_1 then necessarily Albert is not originally made from h_1; and the latter conditional is false (or at least very nearly so).

And so, although Forbes is right to say that our sample T (namely '~Mah_m') holds at any world accessible from the actual world, this *does not* mean that T is *necessary* at any world accessible from the actual world. He mistakenly thinks that it does because he mistakenly thinks that *T itself* together with some a priori conceptual truth guarantees the necessity of T. What in fact is the case is that *truths other than T* together with the conceptual a priori truth [E′] guarantee the necessity of T: the necessity of T depends crucially on a fact about what Albert *was* (instead of a fact about what Albert *was not*) originally made of together with [E′]. The fact that Albert was originally made from *h* does not hold at w_k (though the fact that Albert was not originally made from h_m does hold there): there Albert was originally made from h_k and that hunk of matter *does* (unlike *h* itself) sufficiently overlap h_m. So Forbes fails to establish that there are no merely contingently impossible worlds. And this means that he fails to show that his recasting of [MP] to [MSP] is legitimate.

7 Conclusion

I conclude simply with an observation. The notion of a possible world (that is, of a maximal way things could have been) that is involved in the Salmon–Lewis solution seems to conflict with the Leibnizian picture of a possible world. According to the Salmon–Lewis solution what is possible depends at least in part on what is actual: had Albert actually been originally made from h_1 instead of *h*, then different worlds would have been possible worlds. Now think of Leibniz's God. He is supposed to find himself presented with a plethora of possible worlds and he is supposed to pick one – the best – to make actual. But what exactly is Leibniz's God supposed to be presented with? It seems peculiar to say that God is presented with only the possible worlds, if which ones are possible depends at least in part on what is actual: when God makes his choice, there is no actual world yet; that is precisely what God is supposed to be deciding. So whatever exactly Leibniz's God is supposed to be presented with, they cannot simply be the metaphysically possible worlds of the Salmon–Lewis solution; that is, they cannot simply be ways things could have been.

8 Postscript: friends and enemies

The issue over which I disagreed with Salmon concerned whether Lewis was a friend of S5. (Bear in mind that it is propositional S5 that is our concern. See note 17.) Salmon claimed that Lewis was a friend of S5. I claimed that Lewis was not a friend of S5. It turns out that Salmon's claim was based in part on the fact that Lewis defended S5 in a seminar co-taught by Lewis and Kripke at Princeton (around 1980) that Salmon attended. Salmon reports (personal communication) that Lewis himself gave a version of the 'oft-used defense of S5 modal logic' that Salmon presents as follows:

> In the metaphysical, unrestricted senses of 'necessary' and 'possible', the characteristic S5 principle that any possible truth is necessarily possible may be easily proved. Suppose *p* is a possible truth, that is, a proposition true in at least one possible world *w*. Then relative to any possible world *w'*, without exception, there is at least one possible world in which *p* is true – namely, *w*. It follows (given our assumption that *p* is possible) that it is necessary that *p* is possible. For in the unrestricted sense of 'possible', one possible world in which *p* is true is all that is required for *p* to be 'possible' relative to any given world *w'*, with no further restriction as to what sort of world *p* is true in or how that world is related to *w'*. (Salmon 1989, p. 10)

So, Lewis in effect defended the claim that any proposition, such that it is possible that it is possible, is possible. (See note 7 on the relationship between the characteristic axiom schemata for S5 and S4.) Yet, as we have seen, he is committed to the claim that the proposition expressed by 'Albert was originally made from h_m' is such that it is possible that it is possible even though it is not possible. On the face of it then, Lewis is committed to a blatant contradiction. This matter is a large topic that cannot be adequately addressed in this postscript. For now, let me retract my claim that Lewis is not a friend of S5: just what constitutes friendship is a delicate issue. However, let me nonetheless affirm the spirit of what I claimed by saying that, with defenders like Lewis, S5 needs no critics.[28]

[28] I thank Stuart Brock, Rebecca Entwisle, Gideon Rosen, Jennifer Saul, Scott Soames, and especially Nathan Salmon for their comments on various versions of this material.

References

Bealer, G. (1987) The Philosophical Limits of Scientific Essentialism. *Philosophical Perspectives*, 1, pp. 289–365.

Chandler, H. (1976) Plantinga and the Contingently Possible. *Analysis*, 36, pp. 106–9.

Chisholm, R.M. (1967) Identity Through Possible Worlds: Some Questions. *Noûs*, 1, pp. 1–8.

Chisholm, R.M. (1976) *Person and Object: A Metaphysical Study*. LaSalle, IL: Open Court.

Forbes, G. (1983) Thisness and Vagueness. *Synthese*, 54, pp. 235–59.

Forbes, G. (1984) Two Solutions to Chisholm's Paradox. *Philosophical Studies*, 46, pp. 171–87.

Forbes, G. (1985) *The Metaphysics of Modality*. Oxford: Clarendon Press.

Forbes, G. (1992) Worlds and States of Affairs: How Similar Can They Be?. In K. Mulligan (ed.) *Language, Truth, and Ontology*. Dordrecht: Kluwer, pp. 118–32.

Kripke, S. (1971) Identity and Necessity. In M. Munitz (ed.) *Identity and Individuation*. (New York: New York University Press), pp. 135–64.

Kripke, S. (1972/1980) Naming and Necessity. In D. Davidson and G. Harman (eds) *Semantics of Natural Language* (Dordrecht: Reidel), pp. 253–355, 763–9; also published as a book, with a substantive preface, as *Naming and Necessity* (Cambridge, MA: Harvard University Press, 1980); all page references are to the book.

Lewis, D. (1968) Counterpart Theory and Quantified Modal Logic. *Journal of Philosophy*, 65, pp. 113–26.

Lewis, D. (1973) *Counterfactuals*. Oxford: Blackwell.

Lewis, D. (1986) *On the Plurality of Worlds*. Oxford: Blackwell.

Loux, M. (1979) *The Possible and the Actual*. Ithaca: Cornell University Press.

Mulligan, K. (ed.) (1992) *Language, Truth, and Ontology*. Dordrecht: Kluwer.

Robertson, T. (1998) Possibilities and the Arguments for Origin Essentialism. *Mind*, 107, pp. 729–49.

Salmon, N. (1979) How Not to Derive Essentialism from the Theory of Reference. *Journal of Philosophy*, 76, pp. 703–25.

Salmon, N. (1981) *Reference and Essence*. Princeton: Princeton University Press.

Salmon, N. (1984a) Fregean Theory and the Four Worlds Paradox: A Reply to David Over, *Philosophical Books*, 25, pp. 7–11.

Salmon, N. (1984b) Impossible Worlds, *Analysis*, 44, pp. 114–17.

Salmon, N. (1986) Modal Paradox: Parts and Counterparts, Points and Counterpoints. *Midwest Studies in Philosophy*, 11, pp. 75–120.

Salmon, N. (1988) Review of D. Lewis's *On the Plurality of Worlds*. *Philosophical Review*, 97, pp. 237–44.

Salmon, N. (1989) The Logic of What Might Have Been. *Philosophical Review*, 98, pp. 3–34.

Sidelle, A. (1989) *Necessity, Essence, and Individuation: A Defense of Conventionalism*. Ithaca: Cornell University Press.

Williamson, T. (1994) *Vagueness*. New York: Routledge.

5
Personal Identity: What's the Problem?*

Nathan Salmon

1 The traditional problem

Saul Kripke is a phenomenon, nothing less, and the discipline of Philosophy is much the better for his contribution to it. My own intellectual development has benefited immeasurably from my association with Kripke. I begin with a pair of quotes from another great contemporary philosopher. Woody Allen said, 'I don't want to achieve immortality through my work; I want to achieve it through not dying'. Like Allen, Kripke will live on through his work long after most of the rest of us are forgotten.

Woody Allen's semi-autobiographical movie, *Stardust Memories*, includes a brief sketch in which Allen's character says the following:

> I've never been able to fall in love. I've never been able to find the perfect woman. There's always something wrong. And then I met Doris. A wonderful woman, great personality. But for some reason, I'm just not turned on sexually by her. Don't ask me why. And then I met Rita. An animal, nasty, mean, trouble. And I love going to bed with her. Though afterward I always wished that I was back with Doris. And then I thought to myself, 'If only I could put Doris's

* This chapter incorporates portions of my 'Trans-World Identification and Stipulation' (Salmon 1996) and is dedicated to the memory of a remarkable woman, Sandy Shaffer. It was delivered (in part) at the University of San Marino International Center for Semiotic and Cognitive Studies Conference on Saul Kripke's Contribution to Philosophy, May 1996; and at the University of Haifa Conference on Naming, Necessity, and More, June 1999. I am grateful to those audiences for their reactions, and to Anthony Brueckner and Jill Yeomans for their astute observations.

> brain in Rita's body. Wouldn't that be wonderful?' And I thought, 'Why not? What the hell, I'm a surgeon.' ... So I performed the operation, and everything went perfectly. I switched their personalities ... I made Rita into a warm, wonderful, charming, sexy, sweet, giving, mature woman. And then I fell in love with Doris.

This little tragedy raises a host of philosophical issues. The central issues concern the irrational nature of human sexual attraction and romantic love, and the often-troubling relationship between the two. The dialogue raises moral issues about the treatment of people as means rather than as ends in themselves, the objectification and victimization of women, and related issues. The passage also concerns the traditional philosophical problem of the identity of a person through change. With profound apologies to the reader, the present chapter is concerned exclusively with personal identity. I shall argue that the traditional philosophical problem dissolves. Recent discussion has tended to focus on the question of 'what matters' in survival, with less attention paid to the original question of what makes someone the very same person even through change. This may because it is widely believed that strict survival – genuine personal *identity* – is not what is fundamentally important and not what ought to concern us. Though I remain doubtful that this has been successfully argued, I shall not discuss the issue here. If I am correct, there is a better reason for dismissing the question of what personal identity consists in.

Others before me have rejected the problem of personal identity (or more generally, the problem of the identity of a thing through change) as a pseudo-problem, on the ground that it presupposes the questionable doctrine that a person is constituted by *stages* (*phases, temporal parts*), which are supposed to be portions of that person's life history.[1] Once this doctrine is rejected, it is argued, it follows immediately that there is no genuine problem about formulating principles of unification that specify which series of person stages constitute genuine persons, as opposed to gerrymandered non-persons. My objection to the alleged problem of personal identity has virtually nothing to do with this one, which seems to me to be wide of the target. I have no quarrel to make against stages or phases. No doubt much of what has been supposed about them is simply wrong, but that is not sufficient reason to doubt

---

[1] For an elegant presentation of the problem of personal identity by means of person stages, see John Perry's introduction, 'The Problem of Personal Identity', to his valuable edited collection (1975, pp. 3–30).

their existence.[2] More important, the typical puzzle cases for personal identity can easily be set out without any appeal, explicit or implicit, to the notion of a person stage (or anything similar). Something different must be said – or at least something more – if the problem, so formulated, is to be rejected as illegitimate.

---

[2] Those who frame the problem of personal identity in terms of person stages tend towards the view that stages are conceptually prior to, or metaphysically more fundamental or real than, the continuants that they constitute through time. They often base their view on Leibniz's Law: *If x is the same thing as y, then x is exactly like y in all respects*. Being a law, this holds for any time *t*. The stage theorist presupposes an alternative, incorrect temporal generalization: For any *pair* of times *t* and *t'*, if *x* is at *t* the same thing that *y* is at *t'*, then *x* is at *t* exactly like *y* is at *t'*. Alternatively (or in addition), some stage theorists misunderstand what it is to have a property at a time *t*. The stage theorist presupposes that to be such-and-such at *t*, for any time *t*, entails being such-and-such *simpliciter* (whereas, in fact, to be such-and-such *simpliciter* is to be such-and-such at the present time). The erroneous temporal over-generalization of Leibniz's Law, and equally the misunderstanding of what it is to have a property at a time, exclude the possibility of genuine change in an enduring object. Each thus raises a pseudo-issue of how, or in what sense, a single thing can be such-and-such at *t* and not be such-and-such at *t'*. The stage theorist's answer is that only part of the thing is such-and-such, while another part is not such-and-such. See Lewis (1986, pp. 202–4) and Johnston and Forbes (1987). Forbes defends an account that I favor of what it is to have a property at a particular time (ibid., pp. 140–2). See Salmon (1986a, pp. 24–43; 1989a). While opposed to Lewis's postulation of stages, Johnston joins Lewis in objecting to the position I take, on the mistaken ground that any time, past or future, is as real as the present. The past *was* real but is so no longer, and the future *will be* real but is not so yet. The present is currently real in a way that the past and the future are not. This truism is unaffected by the context-relativity of the words 'now', 'past', 'present', etc. See Salmon (1987a, pp. 73–90).

Johnston defends an account according to which having a property at *t* is having the property in a certain manner (being such-and-such 'in the *t*-mode', as it were). Though this is virtually derivable as a special case from the account that Johnston joins Lewis in rejecting, Johnston instead takes his account to be superior in allegedly according the past and the future the same ontological status as the present. Johnston's account has the significant disadvantage that it applies only to temporal qualifications of subject-predicate sentences, e.g. 'In 1987, *a* was such-and-such', and does not directly provide an interpretation for sentences like 'It will rain tomorrow', 'In 1987, there was something such that ... it ... ', etc. For those sentences to which his account applies, Johnston ultimately falls back on familiar tense-logical semantics (p. 128). The latter holds that to be such-and-such *simpliciter* is to be such-and-such at the present time, and more generally, that truth *simpliciter* (i.e. in reality) is truth at the present time, whereas Johnston evidently means to reject the very idea of being such-and-such *simpliciter*. Why then not also reject the idea of reality, and replace it with different ways of being real (truth in the *t*-mode, truth in the *t'*-mode, etc.)?

The aspect of the problem that I discuss here is connected to a couple of doctrines recently brought into prominence by Saul Kripke's influential monograph, *Naming and Necessity* (1972). First is the doctrine of *individual essentialism*, according to which some properties of individuals are such that those individuals could not exist without those properties. To put it another way, there are properties that certain individuals have in every possible world in which those individuals exist. Second is Kripke's claim that possible worlds are not discovered like planets but 'stipulated'. In previous work, I have defended the idea that in whatever sense it is correct and useful to recognize possible worlds as entities, it is equally correct and useful to acknowledge that there are also *impossible worlds* (Salmon 1979, pp. 723–4; 1981, pp. 238–40; 1984; 1986b; 1989b; 1993b). My doctrine of impossible worlds has proved controversial, at least partly because it has seemed unclear whether such an apparatus has any philosophical utility. I here apply the doctrine, in a manner that I hope will prove its mettle, to the traditional problem of personal identity. I shall also bring the controversy of haecceitism vs. anti-haecceitism, and the distinction between reducibility and supervenience, to bear on the problem.

To see how the alleged problem of personal identity might be presented without appealing to person stages and principles of unification, one need only look to the non-philosopher who does not know from person stages. Woody Allen's character tells us that he has performed a complex surgical procedure on Doris and Rita, interchanging the brains between their two bodies, and consequently interchanging also what I shall call their 'psychologies' – that is to say, their personality and character traits, their beliefs, attitudes, wishes, hopes, fears, memories, abilities, talents, habits, mannerisms, and the like. The standard philosophical question raised by the incident involving Doris and Rita – *the D/R incident*, as I shall call it – is sometimes framed in terms of how one of the two person stages at some time *t* immediately after the surgery should be related to various person stages prior to the surgery in order for the stages to qualify as stages of a single person. But the question may be framed instead in terms of the identities of the two women to emerge from the surgery. Consider the woman with whom Allen has now fallen in love – she who now occupies what used to be Doris's body but who now has what used to be Rita's brain. Is that woman Doris? Is she Rita? Or is she perhaps someone else – call her 'Dorita' – who was created in the process, while Doris and Rita were destroyed?

At least three philosophical questions must be distinguished here. The issue of whether the woman in question is Doris or Rita, or neither, is *the primary question* about the D/R incident.[3] In addition there is the question of how the correct answer to the primary question is determined. This meta-question is often put by asking for (and very often by demanding) a *criterion*, or *criteria*, that settle the primary question. The question bifurcates into two separate questions, which, although they may call for distinct answers, have often been blurred together. First, there is *the epistemological question* of how, or by what means or evidence, one is supposed to come to know or to discover the answer to the primary question about the D/R incident. Second, and more fundamental, is *the metaphysical question* concerning the correct answer to the primary question, of what makes it the correct answer. In virtue of what fact or facts is it, and not its rivals, the right answer to the primary question? In short, what is it to be the same person? Although each of the three questions has been posed as 'the problem of personal identity', it is the metaphysical question that has the strongest claim to being *the* problem of personal identity, as the phrase is traditionally meant (see Shoemaker 1963, pp. 2–3ff.).

Although the demand for a criterion of personal identity is frequently made, the relevant notion of an identity criterion is usually not made precise. One way of understanding what a personal-identity criterion is that seems to fit much of the literature takes it to be a *trans-temporal link* that connects a person from one time to a person of another and thereby determines that they are the same. More precisely, on this interpretation a *criterion for personal identity* is an ordered triple consisting of a sortal property F and a pair of binary relations R and R', other than personal identity itself, such that it is necessary that for any persons x and y and any times t and t' such that x exists at t and y exists at t', x is the same person at t that y is at t' if there is some F (i.e. something of sort F) to which x bears R at t and to which y bears R' at t'. In most cases, but not all, the intent is better captured by strengthening the 'if' to 'if and only if'. Either way, the particular F is supposed to serve as the link (*via* the relations R and R′) that determines personal identity.[4]

---

[3] The classical discussion of this question is Shoemaker (1963, pp. 23ff.). See also Shoemaker (1959).

[4] The resulting condition for personal identity is the *relative product* of R and the converse of R'. Although the relation of personal identity between x and y is here taken to be a trans-temporal relation, holding between objects across times (more accurately, holding among a quadruple of a person x, a time t, a person y, and a time t'), each of the criterial relations R and R' obtains between objects at a single time. For discussion of an analogous account of cross-world relations, see Salmon (1981, section 13, pp. 116–135). With some ingenuity, other sorts of identity criteria, even criteria for identity at a time (as opposed to identity across time), might also be put into the same general form. For example, the traditional criterion for the identity of sets may be put: $x = y$ iff there is a particular membership m such that x has m and y has m.

A memory-based criterion results by letting F be the sortal *experience token* letting R be the relation of *remembering*, and letting R' be the relation of *experiencing*. According to this criterion, by necessity, x is the same person as an earlier person y if x remembers having some experience token of y's. Here the remembered experience links x to y across time.[5] A body-based criterion, by contrast, results by letting F be the sortal *body*, and both R and R' be the relation of *being the functional owner of* – in this case, the relation u *is the person whose body is* v. According to this criterion, by necessity, x and y are the same person if they are linked by having the same body across time. (The reader is invited to verify whether other criteria that have been proposed can also be put into the same general form involving the existence of a trans-temporal link.)

The ambiguity in the meta-question may be traced to a choice regarding the kind of necessity involved in the notion of a personal-identity criterion. The epistemological meta-question results by taking the necessity to be epistemic. The metaphysical meta-question results by taking the necessity to be alethic rather than epistemic. In the former case, the trans-temporal link is the epistemic basis for the judgment of personal identity over time. In the latter case, the link is the *metaphysical* basis for the *fact* of personal identity. Personal identity would thus *consist in* the existence of an appropriate trans-temporal link.

2 Body-based vs. psychology-based identification

Allen says that he made Rita into the ideal mate he was seeking, and so, naturally, he has fallen in love with Doris. By putting things this way, he is evidently presupposing the body-based criterion for personal identity,

---

[5] This memory-based criterion is not a counter-instance to the observation made in the preceding note that each of the criterial relations R and R' obtains between objects at a single time. The remembering of the experience takes place at a single time when the experience is already past. Although the remembered experience is no longer current, and hence in some sense no longer 'real', the person remembering it enters into a relation with it while remembering it, precisely by remembering it. (Alternatively, one might let F be the sortal *biographical event*, R' be the relation of *being the principal figure involved in* a particular event, and R be the relation of *remembering being the principal figure involved in*.)

The 'if' might be strengthened to 'if and only if' by letting the trans-temporal link be a chronological sequence of ordered pairs of memories and experience tokens, where for each pair, both elements (the memory and the experience token) belong to a single person at a single time and for each successor pair in the sequence, the first element is a memory of the second element of the predecessor pair (with the obvious adjustments for R and R').

according to which the woman who now has what was previously Doris's body is Doris, and the woman who now has what was previously Rita's body is Rita. If Allen had instead presupposed a psychology-based criterion – such as the memory-based or a personality-based criterion – he should have described the outcome of the D/R incident by saying that he has made *Doris* into an ideal mate, but (alas) has fallen in love with *Rita*. Allen puts things as he does not because he is a closet materialist, but because he is a brilliant humorist. For some reason, putting things the other way spoils at least some of the humor of the monologue. This may reflect a natural tendency to identify people by their bodies. This tendency may obtain among most people, evidently including even the cleverest and most philosophical of non-philosophers.

In order not to beg the primary question in setting out the philosophical conundrum, philosophers have invented an artificial terminology better suited to philosophical debate. Philosophers call the person who now has what used to be Rita's brain in what used to be Doris's body 'the Doris-body-person', and we call the person who now has what used to be Doris's brain in what used to be Rita's body 'the Rita-body-person'. We may then pose the question: Is the Rita-body-person Rita, or is she Doris? Allen presupposes that the Rita-body-person is still Rita and the Doris-body-person is still Doris. The artificial terminology allows for a way of putting things that neither presupposes nor excludes any criterion of personal identity. We may say, neutrally, that the Rita-body-person is now an ideal mate, but Allen has fallen in love with the Doris-body-person. The primary question may be posed by asking whether Allen has fallen in love with Doris or Rita. That's not comedy; it's philosophy. The joke has been butchered, but the conundrum has been given life.

The different ways of making the identifications are conceptually at odds. They carry with them different conceptions of the changes that have taken place in Allen's victims. On the psychology-based identifications, Doris and Rita retain their brains intact, and therefore also their psychologies. They have *exchanged bodies*. More accurately, their bodies have been interchanged by Allen. Body swapping would no doubt require a variety of adjustments in one's life, some quite radical. Other than the ensuing psychological adjustments, however, on the psychology-based identifications Doris and Rita remain fundamentally unaltered psychologically. This way of making the identifications is committed to making sense of the alleged phenomenon of re-embodied minds or spirits – or to put it perhaps less tendentiously, of re-embodied persons. (It does not require the possibility of altogether disembodied persons, let alone of persons without brains.) By contrast, on the body-based identification, Doris and Rita retain their bodies while having exchanged brains. Each of their individual psychologies has thereby undergone a radical transformation. Although the two women have the same bodies, they are not at all the same as they used to be. One might even say (as Allen does) that the women have traded personalities. Doris now has the personality that was previously Rita's while Rita now has the personality that was previously Doris's. As persons, they have been psychologically *altered* or *modified.* Rita has been transformed into an ideal mate, and Doris has been modified to such an extent that Allen is now obsessed with thoughts of her. This is a very different interpretation or conceptualization of the changes in Doris and Rita. The psychology-based identifications carry with them the ideology of relocation, Allen's body-based identifications the ideology of transmutation. And, of course, the Dorita hypothesis carries with it the ideology of annihilation.

The two different ways of making the identifications are not merely alternative descriptions differing in conceptual flavor but otherwise equally acceptable. The two conceptualizations are logically incompatible. In effect, they present entirely different scenarios. At least one of them is mistaken. One is a misdescription of the situation. This is proved by the transitivity of identity. On the body-based identification Doris = the Doris-body-person, whereas on the psychology-based identifications Doris = the Rita-body-person. Yet it is clear that the Doris-body-person ≠ the Rita-body-person. Therefore at least one of the criteria gets things wrong. Or again, on the body-based identifications the victims retain their bodies while exchanging psychologies, whereas on the psychology-based criteria the victims retain their psychologies while exchanging bodies. Since it is logically impossible to retain one's body (or one's psychology) while also trading it for another, of necessity one or the other of these accounts of the D/R incident is incorrect. Whichever description is correct (if either is), there is indeed an alternative but equally correct description. For whether it is correct to say of Doris and Rita that they have retained their bodies while switching their psychologies or vice versa, it is equally correct to say that the Doris-body-person has what was previously Doris's body and what was previously Rita's psychology whereas the Rita-body-person has what was previously Rita's body and what was previously Doris's psychology. This is the philosophically neutral way of describing the D/R incident. It is neutral because it is incomplete. It fails to state all the relevant facts. In particular, it does not identify either the Doris-body-person or the Rita-body-person with either Doris or Rita. By design it leaves the identities of the Doris-body-person and the Rita-body-person wide open. To identify is to risk error.

The incompatibility between the two ways of making the identifications will perhaps strike the reader as trivial. That is for the good. The point *is* trivial. But it is often obscured in discussions on the topic – and that is reason enough for me to emphasize it here. It is extremely important to be clear on this point if we are to make any progress toward solving the problem of personal identity.[6]

Allen's joke exploits the body-based identifications. We, however, are not writing comedy; we are doing extremely serious philosophy. And fortunately, though not always easy to do, philosophy is always a good deal easier to do than comedy. Philosophically, the psychology-based identifications seem considerably more plausible than the body-based identifications – not as funny, but more plausible. This is not to say that some psychology-based criterion is correct in general. Even if it is taken as settled that the body-based identifications are clearly incorrect, it is arguable that the person who now has what had been Rita's brain in what had been Doris's body is neither Doris nor Rita but Dorita. Even if the psychology-based identifications are not decidedly vindicated in the D/R incident, the body-based identifications seem decidedly refuted. Moreover, the psychology-based identifications do not seem at all implausible. If the D/R incident presented all there were to the problem of personal identity, we might as well move on to discuss the more intriguing issues raised by the D/R incident. But it does not.

---

[6] Derek Parfit claims (1986, pp. 242–3, 259–60) that the different ways of making the identifications in puzzle cases of personal identity are 'merely different descriptions of the same outcome', while denying that the competing descriptions are incompatible. His argument assumes that if facts of one kind (e.g. personal identity) are reducible to those of another (psychological and/or bodily continuities), hence not 'further facts', then the latter are compatible with utterly different ways of fixing the former. (He also evidently assumes that the former are therefore a matter of decision.) On the contrary, it is only if there is *no* reduction, i.e. only if there is independence between the two kinds of facts, that facts of one kind are compatible with different ways of fixing the other.

Bernard Williams (1970; 1973, pp. 52–5) presents a rich account of the conceptual distinctions between the two different ways of making the identifications in a case like the D/R incident. He notes that a description of the incident in completely neutral terms seems to lead naturally to the psychology-based identifications, but he also says of the situation given by the body-based description that it is in fact the same incident 'differently presented'. Unlike Parfit, Williams explicitly adds that the two 'presentations' thus lead to contrary conclusions (1973, p. 61). Indeed, Williams sees the incompatibility of these otherwise plausible presentations of the incident as producing a philosophical quandary.

3 The problem redux

Suppose that instead of transplanting brains, Allen had made use of the BW device. Although it is sometimes referred to as 'the brain washer', the initials 'BW' actually refer to the device's inventor, Bernard Williams. As Williams describes the device, it extracts 'information' from a person's brain – or, as we might put it nowadays, it encodes the operating system, memory, and all stored data and software (no actual hardware is removed), and stores the digitally encoded information. Once the brain is repaired, the device is set in the reverse mode, whereby it copies the encoded information back into the brain, restoring the brain to exactly the same state it was in when the information was extracted.[7] The BW device is especially useful when removing a brain tumor that is located perilously close to brain areas intricately tied to certain higher cognitive phenomena (including certain abilities, long-term memories, vocabulary, and capacity for speech, sense of humor, and various other aspects of a personality). On one or two occasions, the BW device successfully extracted information from a dying brain and replaced it in an artificial brain that had been surgically implanted in place of the old one. The BW device also has the capability simply to render the brain a *tabula rasa*. If the information had been correctly extracted and stored, the washed brain can be restored to its former glory. Although the prospect has been condemned as unethical by extremists, it is theoretically possible using two BW devices simultaneously to interchange all of the information of two brains.

Suppose Allen had done exactly that to Doris and Rita. Let us call the original D/R incident 'D/R-1' and this new scenario 'D/R-2'. We may pose our three questions with regard to D/R-2: Which way of making the identifications, if either, is right in D/R-2? How is one supposed to settle the primary question? Finally, whichever way of making the identifications is correct, by virtue of what facts is it, rather than the alternative way, the right way?

D/R-2 seems to make our problem of personal identity less tractable than it first seemed. For now the body-based identifications do not seem as implausible. Interestingly, they may even seem more plausible

---

[7] Williams (1973, p. 47). Parfit's (1986, pp. 199–201) 'Branch-Line Case of the Teletransporter' is a variant of the BW device. The essential feature of the BW device is that it is mind altering. Any thought-experimental mind-altering device (such as hypnosis, brain disease, drugs, brain washing techniques, direct brain manipulation, or some designer combination thereof) suits my present purpose to the extent that it is conceptually possible for the device to replicate someone else's psychology.

in this case than the psychology-based identifications. Anyone who does not find them so is urged to reread Williams's discussion, in which he deftly uses a puzzle case like D/R-2 to argue that one cannot legitimately dismiss the body-based criterion as cavalierly as one might be inclined to do.[8] Intuitive support for the body-based identifications is provided by supposing that one's own brain were drastically altered through a BW device, and considering how one views the further prospect of the resulting person's being painfully tortured. Perhaps Allen's body-based identifications are the right ones after all. The two meta-questions become more pressing.

The very fact that our intuitions may diverge between D/R-1 and D/R-2 is itself an extremely important aspect of the problem. Presented in the right light, D/R-1 and D/R-2 bring our intuitions into direct conflict, thereby creating an especially perplexing conceptual difficulty. The tension between the intuitions that are operative in D/R-1 and D/R-2 shows that the problem of personal identity is not so easily laid to rest.

If D/R-1 stacks the deck in favor of psychology-based criteria and D/R-2 stacks the deck in favor of the body-based criterion, we can make

[8] Williams argues that a neutral 'presentation' of cases like D/R-1 and D/R-2 leads to the psychology-based identifications, whereas a specially designed alternative presentation leads to the opposite identifications. He evidently concludes that the case for psychology-based identifications is deeply inconclusive (see note 7). In noting the conceptual differences between the alternative presentations, Williams emphasizes two aspects that are prominent in his own presentations: First, in presenting the scenario in neutral terms the victims are referred to using the third person, whereas the body-based scenario is presented as addressed to one of the victims using the second-person pronoun (and as understood by the victim using the first person); and second, in presenting the body-based scenario, Williams makes little mention of the other victim. Williams creates the impression that these differences are crucial to the philosophical issues. These differences, however, are largely stylistic, reflecting different perspectives that Williams chose, perhaps at least in part, for dramatic effect. He could have provided a body-based presentation using the third-person perspective, or a neutral presentation using the second person (and even the first person, as by 'the my-body-person'), and still raise the principal philosophical questions on that basis. A more significant difference is given by the very fact that the body-based presentation explicitly includes particular identifications. By contrast with Williams, I believe that the proper lesson of his investigation is that the psychological evidence in favor of the psychology-based identifications – which is the focus in Williams's neutral description – has no force, since the very same psychological reactions would arise in Doris and Rita even if the body-based identifications prevailed. (Compare Kripke's (1972, pp. 107–8) 'schmidentity' argument strategy elaborated on in Kripke (1977, pp. 16–18).)

our problem even more intractable by considering a case that does not stack the deck at all. In D/R-3, something mysterious happened to Doris and Rita while they slept, with the result that the Doris-body-person awoke with what was previously Rita's psychology and the Rita-body-person awoke with what was previously Doris's psychology. Allen did not interchange their brains. He did not apply BW devices to exchange information between their brains. He did not do anything to them. Someone else – or something else – did. Perhaps it was the fruition of a curse against their ancestors in ancient Egypt. Perhaps space creatures zapped them with alien rays. Perhaps it was the magic fulfillment of a mutual wish to trade places. Never mind what it was. Allen has fallen in love with the Doris-body-person. But who is that?

Consider now the primary question and the two meta-questions concerning D/R-3. Our intuitions seem to offer decidedly less assistance in this case than they did before. Whatever conviction one may have had when considering D/R-1 that Doris and Rita have exchanged bodies is considerably weakened. The opposite intuitions tapped by D/R-2 now seem equally legitimate. And conversely, whatever conviction one may have had when considering D/R-2 that Doris and Rita have retained their bodies while becoming psychologically altered is also considerably weakened, in light of the equal legitimacy of the intuitions tapped in D/R-1. Concerning D/R-3, both intuitions seem equally legitimate, or equally illegitimate. There seems to be little to recommend the psychology-based criteria over the body-based criterion, or vice versa. The metaphysical meta-question concerning D/R-3 in some sense represents the traditional problem of personal identity in its purest and least tractable form.

Some philosophers maintain that there is no determinate, objective fact of the matter (independently of any decision we may make about the case) as to whether the Doris-body-person is identical with Doris or Rita, or neither. This position, however, is not a viable option. Let us name the Doris-body-person 'Doris-bod'. There is a fact of the matter concerning whether Doris-bod is identical with Doris-bod. The fact that Doris-bod is Doris-bod is an instance of a law of logic. If there is no objective fact of the matter as to whether Doris is Doris-bod, then that yields one respect (at least) in which Doris differs from Doris-bod. For on this hypothesis, Doris-bod has the feature that there is a fact as to whether she is Doris-bod while Doris lacks this feature. But if Doris and Doris-bod are not exactly alike in every respect – if they differ in any respect whatsoever – it follows by Leibniz's Law that they are distinct persons. (Or if one prefers, it follows by the contrapositive of Leibniz's

Law – see note 2 above.) And if they are distinct, then there is a determinate, objective fact of the matter after all as to whether they are identical. The same argument may be made concerning Rita and Doris-bod. As desperate as the Dorita hypothesis seems, one may be inclined at this point to run with it.[9]

---

[9] Parfit takes the position that there is no determinate, objective fact of the matter in some of the puzzle cases of personal identity. See for example Parfit (1971; 1986, pp. 236–43). The motion is seconded by Johnston (1989, pp. 371–3, 393; 1992, p. 603). (Curiously, Parfit also says that in puzzle cases of personal identity, different ways of making the identifications are 'different descriptions of the same outcome', and furthermore that for reasons of symmetry, the best description of the standard fission case has it that the original person is distinct from each of the two subsequent people. Each of these claims seems incompatible with Parfit's doctrine of indeterminate identity, as well as with each other. See note 7 above.) I urged a version of the proof just given against Parfit in Salmon (1981, pp. 242–6). Philosophers who embrace, or otherwise defend, the logical possibility of indeterminate identity have gone to extreme lengths to ward off the counter-proof. Typically, they have responded by accepting that the objects in question (in our case, Doris and Doris-bod) differ from each other in the respect cited while rejecting the Leibniz's-Law inference from '*a* and *b* are not exactly alike' to '*a* and *b* are not the same thing', on the ground that the conclusion may lack truth value even when the premise is true. Parfit (1986, pp. 240–1) endorses such a response. The response, however, requires a fundamentally counter-intuitive departure from classical reasoning. For it should be agreed that, of necessity, any *one* thing has every property it has, without exception. It follows by classical reasoning that if Doris lacks some property that Doris-bod has, then they cannot be *one* person. But if they are not one person, then they are two. (They are certainly not one and one-half persons, for example. See Salmon (1997).) (*Homework exercise*: Formalize and derive the preceding argument. What inference rules and/or logical axioms are involved in the derivation? Notice also my use of the plural form '*objects* in question' and of the phrase 'differ from each *other*' in stating the typical response to the original proof. Is this usage consistent with the position stated thereby? If not, is there a coherent way to state the position, in its full generality?) Parfit says furthermore that even if the proof that there is always a fact of the matter is correct, it only shows that in those cases in which there is no fact of the matter, it is incumbent upon us, if we wish to avoid incoherence, to create a fact by making a decision about the case at hand. This betrays a serious misunderstanding of the proof – and indeed, I believe, a fundamental confusion concerning such things as facts, decisions, and incoherence. The proof demonstrates that there is *already* a fact of the matter, quite independently of any decisions one may wish to make. In addition, a slight variation of the argument shows that it is quite impossible to make a pair of things identical (or distinct) by decision. Doris and Doris-bod are already what they are, and no decision on anyone's part can possibly affect their status with regard to the question of identity.

4 Haecceitism and reductionism

D/R-1, D/R-2, and D/R-3 are distinct possibilities. Technically, though, they are not genuine, full-fledged possible worlds. Possible worlds are

---

Johnston argues instead that even if the notion of personal identity (the notion of *same person*) is taken to be strict numerical identity restricted to persons, and even if strict identity is determinate for every pair of objects, there are nevertheless cases in which it is indeterminate whether *a* is the same person as *b* owing to an ambiguity in the word 'person'. His position appears to be that there are (at least) two distinct kinds, or notions, of a person – let us call these person_1 and person_2 – such that, in such cases, each of *a* and *b* is a person_1 and also a person_2, but because the two kinds differ in the identity conditions they specify for their members, *a* is (determinately) the same person_1 as *b* yet not the same person_2 (so that neither is essentially a person_2). This position, however, implies that $a = b$ and $a \neq b$. (The same inconsistency occurs in Johnston (1987, p. 76). See also Johnston and Forbes (1987, p. 123). Although Johnston opposes the Cartesian-dualist position that persons exist 'separately' from their bodies, his view that kinds specify identity conditions for their members, with different kinds specifying differing conditions, leads him to a position even more radical than the dualism he rejects: that we are not organisms, or indeed biological life forms of any kind.) A consistent variant would be this: *a* is both a person_1 and a person_2 at a time t_1, *b* is the same person_1 at a later time t_2 that *a* is at t_1, but *b* is *not* a person_2 at t_2 and consequently not the same person_2 at t_2 that *a* is at t_1. Since Johnston concedes that personal identity is strict identity restricted to persons, this alternative position reduces to the following: *a* is both a person_1 and a person_2 at t_1, whereas *a* is only a person_1 and no longer a person_2 at t_2. Whatever this prospect may mean for our ordinary concept of a person, it does not warrant the dramatic conclusion that the notion of personal identity is indeterminate for *a*. The alleged ambiguity may render some confusion over the issue of whether *a* is still a 'person', but there is no lingering issue, and there should be no problem, concerning whether the thing at t_2 (whether or not it is still a person) is still the *same thing*, and if so, what makes it so. In the usual puzzle cases of the traditional problem of personal identity (including Johnston's favored puzzle case of fission), there is typically no serious question about the status of any of the relevant individuals as persons. Instead it is *given* that the principal individuals in question are persons. Typically, *a* is stipulated to be a person (man, woman) by hypothesis, while *b* is given descriptively as 'the *person* who emerges from such-and-such a process' (e.g. as 'the *a*-body-*person*', or as 'the *man* who now has the left hemisphere of what was previously *a*'s brain', etc.). The primary question concerns *a* 's identity with, or distinctness from, *b* – not whether *b* is a person at t_2, or whether the erstwhile person *a* (whose identity with *b* is in question) is still a person at t_2. Indeed, the prospect that *a* is determinately no longer a person at t_2 (and for that reason alone, not the same person as *b*) is typically ignored altogether. (See note 23. Curiously, even Johnston does not consider this prospect in his cataloguing of potential solutions to the problem.)

fully specific with respect to all questions of fact, down to the finest of details. There are numerous alternative conceptions of what a possible world is. (Not all of these need be thought of as competing conceptions.) The conception I favor is that of a maximally specific scenario that might have obtained (see Salmon 1989b). On this conception (and on suitably closely related conceptions), each of the puzzle-case scenarios is the intersection of an infinite plurality of possible worlds, i.e. a constituent 'mini-world', or sub-scenario, common to each. Each of the three puzzle-cases may be regarded as representing a distinct class of worlds. D/R-1, for example, represents the class of worlds in which Allen performs brain transplants with the result that the Rita-body-person is now an ideal mate and Allen has fallen in love with the Doris-body-person. The primary question for each of these scenarios is which identifications obtain in the worlds represented by that scenario.

Viewing the puzzle cases as representing classes of worlds, there appears to be some kinship between the problem of personal identity and another identity problem of contemporary philosophy: *the problem of trans-world identification*, i.e. the problem of identifying individuals in different possible worlds. Consider the possibility of Richard Nixon having continued as United States President for the duration of his second term in office. We may ask: Would the Democrats have regained the presidency, as they did in the actual world? Would they have nominated Jimmy Carter? And so on. But before we can answer, a philosopher interrupts. What determines whether the President in the possible world under discussion is Nixon? How can we know that it is Nixon rather than someone else who resembles Nixon in a variety of important respects, except for having finished out his presidency rather than resigning in disgrace? And furthermore, what does being Nixon consist in for someone in another possible world? In short, what is the *criterion*, or *criteria*, of trans-world identity that settles the question of whether someone in another possible world is Nixon? In a celebrated critique, Kripke has exposed the alleged problem of trans-world identity as a pseudo-problem (1972, pp. 15–20, 42–53, 76–7). He counters that possible worlds are not like independently existing planets with features to be investigated: '"possible worlds" are *stipulated*, not *discovered* by powerful telescopes. There is no reason why we cannot *stipulate* that, in talking about what would have happened to Nixon in a certain counterfactual situation, we are talking about what would have happened to *him*' (ibid., p. 44).

Kripke's contention that possible worlds are 'stipulated' has been seriously misunderstood.[10] Many philosophers take it as a thesis about the ontological and/or epistemological status of possible worlds, about how they came into being and how we come to know of them. They see Kripke as a *modal conceptualist*, who believes that possible worlds are somehow created by us with the properties that we assign to them (a position analogous in certain respects to constructivism about mathematical entities). Readers have thought that Kripke holds that we are the masters of metaphysical modality, in the sense that it is entirely for us to decide, by 'stipulation', what is metaphysically possible and what is not. These are serious misinterpretations. Kripke's observation that 'possible worlds are not discovered but stipulated' is simply his endorsement of a version of the doctrine that David Kaplan calls *haecceitism*. The *haecceity* of an individual *x* is the property of being identical with *x*, i.e. the property of being *that very individual*. Kaplan defines haecceitism as the doctrine that:

> we can meaningfully ask whether a possible individual that exists in one possible world also exists in another without taking into account the attributes and behavior of the individuals that exist in the one world and making a comparison with the attributes and behavior of the individuals that exist in the other world ... [the] doctrine that holds that it does make sense to ask – without reference to common attributes and behavior – whether *this* is the same individual in another possible world, that individuals can be extended in logical space (i.e. through possible worlds) in much the way we commonly regard them as being extended in physical space and time, and that a common 'thisness' may underlie extreme dissimilarity or distinct thisnesses may underlie great resemblance. (Kaplan, 1975, pp. 722–3)

---

10 A dramatic case in point is Allen Hazen (1979). Hazen asserts (pp. 334–5) that when Kripke says that possible worlds are stipulated rather than discovered, what he means, in part, may be explained by saying that a possible world is a combination of a purely qualitatively specified world together with a particular stipulated choice among various similarity correspondences or mappings (which need not be one–one) between individuals in other worlds and individuals of the qualitatively specified world. Hazen thinks of the similarity correspondences as schemes that represent an individual in some other world by means of a selected counterpart in the qualitatively given world. Hazen's entire apparatus is decidedly anti-Kripkean. Kripke adamantly insists that possible worlds need not be purely qualitatively specified, and that the very same individuals may exist in different possible worlds rather than being represented in another world by 'counterparts' in that world.

Despite the usual gloss on Kaplan's explanations, the central doctrine of haecceitism is not concerned primarily with the identification of individuals in distinct possible worlds – although the doctrine does have important consequences concerning cross-world identifications. The central doctrine primarily concerns an issue of *legitimacy*. It concerns the question of whether it is 'meaningful' to stipulate the facts about particular individuals in particular possible worlds, including such facts as that the individual with such-and-such properties in a given world *w* is a particular individual *a*, or is not the particular individual *a*, as the case may be. Haecceitism holds that it is perfectly legitimate, when introducing a possible world for consideration and discussion, to specify the world explicitly in terms of facts directly concerning particular individuals, designating those individuals directly by name if one chooses to.

An extreme version of the doctrine – *extreme haecceitism*, as I shall call it – combines haecceitism in the preceding sense with a further doctrine: that facts concerning the particular individual *a* are in some relevant sense primitive, not reducible to any more general facts, such as that the individual with such-and-such properties is thus-and-so. Extreme haecceitism holds that it is legitimate to stipulate facts concerning particular individuals in a world, identifying those individuals by name, precisely *because* such facts about a world are held to be *separate* facts that are not fixed by, and cannot be logically inferred from, facts that do not specify which individuals are involved. I shall use the term 'reductionism' for the opposing doctrine that any such facts about a world *w* as that the individual with such-and-such properties is *a*, or is not *a*, if indeed such facts exist, are reducible to such qualitative facts as that the individual with such-and-such properties in world *w* is the individual with so-and-so properties in world *w′* (where the so-and-so properties are similar, or closely related, to the such-and-such properties).

Unfortunately, it is unclear what it means to say that facts of one kind are *reducible* to facts of another – or using alternative terminologies, that facts of the first kind 'consist in', or are 'nothing over and above', facts of the second kind, or that facts of the one kind are 'grounded in', 'derived from', 'based upon', 'constructed out of', or 'constituted by' facts of the other kind. The central idea seems to be that any fact of the first kind is a *logical* or *conceptual* consequence of facts of the second kind. An example would help enormously here. But there are precious few, if any, uncontroversial examples. One example from the philosophy of language may do. On Frege's philosophy of semantics, the referential (denotative, designative) facts concerning a language are reducible to other sorts of facts – in particular to intensional-semantic facts about what the sense of an expression is together with extra-linguistic facts about what a given sense *metaphysically determines*. To illustrate, the English noun 'water', in its use as a name for the familiar liquid, semantically expresses a certain concept (or property) *c* as its English sense, perhaps *the colorless, odorless, potable liquid found (with varying amounts of impurities) in lakes, rivers, and streams.*[11] This is a fact in the theory of meaning – a fact concerning the semantics of sense – and not a fact in the theory of reference. The concept *c*, in turn, metaphysically determines the chemical compound H_2O, in the sense that the compound exactly fits *c* and (let us suppose) no other substance does. This fact is completely independent of language. It is a straightforward logical consequence of these two – the meaning fact and the metaphysical fact – that there is some concept or other such that the word 'water' expresses that concept as its English sense and that concept in turn determines H_2O. The latter, according to a Fregean philosophy of semantics, just *is* the fact that 'water' refers in English to H_2O. This fact is thus partly semantic and partly metaphysical in nature.[12] In this sense, the fact that the English noun 'water' refers to H_2O is 'nothing over and above' (consists in, is grounded in, is derived from, etc.) the two facts that the English noun 'water' expresses *c* and that *c* determines H_2O.[13]

---

[11] I use the word 'concept' here in the same sense as Alonzo Church, which is decidedly distinct from that of Frege's artificial use of the German *Begriff*.

[12] In the terminology and conceptual apparatus of Salmon (1993a), the fact in question is (according to Frege's theory of it) a fact of *applied* rather than *pure* semantics, since it involves some extra-linguistic metaphysics.

[13] The notion of reducibility involved here will be clarified further in Section 6 below. An alternative notion of reducibility results by replacing the relation of logical consequence with the notion (metaphor?) of part-whole constitution. We may say that a fact *f* is *mereologically reducible* to a class of facts *c* if *f* is literally composed, without remainder, of the elements of *c*. Thus a mereologically complex fact is mereologically reducible to its constituent sub-facts. This notion is suggested by a more literal construal of the terminology of one fact being nothing over and above, or consisting in, etc., a plurality of other facts. The notion presupposes a picture of compound facts as complex wholes resulting from an assemblage of other facts. This picture raises baffling questions about the relationship between mereological reducibility and the logical or conceptual notion of reducibility explicated in the text. On Frege's meta-semantical theory, is the fact that the English word 'water' refers to H_2O mereologically reducible to other facts? In particular, does it mereologically reduce to the pair of facts that 'water' expresses *c* and that *c* metaphysically determines H_2O? Is it supposed to be obvious that it does? Suppose 'water' had expressed a different concept in English, but one which also determines H_2O. Would the fact that 'water' refers in English to H_2O then be a different fact, consisting of different sub-facts?

A doctrine more extreme than simple reductionism opposes simple haecceitism. *Anti-haecceitism* is the doctrine that in introducing a possible world for consideration and discussion, one may not legitimately specify facts while mentioning the individuals involved by name (or by something similar, such as by a demonstrative uttered while pointing to an actual individual). Instead, one may specify only the general, qualitative sorts of facts to which the facts concerning a particular individual (if there are any such facts) are reducible according to reductionism. Specifying the facts concerning a particular individual *a*, explicitly identifying *a* by name, is regarded as a form of cheating – or rather, it is held to be meaningless. Some anti-haecceitists go so far as to reject the very existence of such facts about a world as that the individual with such-and-such properties is, or is not, the very individual *a*. They hold that one may not legitimately specify such facts in giving a possible world for the simple reason that there are no such facts to be specified. This view might be called 'extreme anti-haecceitism'. Less extreme anti-haecceitists embrace reductionism, holding that while there are facts directly concerning specific individuals, they are reducible to general facts to the effect that the individual with such-and-such properties is, or is not, the individual with so-and-so properties. Extreme haecceitism, in contrast to anti-haecceitism, and in sharp contrast to extreme anti-haecceitism, holds that the former facts are *further* facts over and above general facts, not reducible to or constructed out of the latter. Along with the general facts, these separate facts concerning specific individuals are held to be built into the very fabric of the possible worlds themselves.

Little or no notice has been made in the extant literature on haecceitism of the distinction between the moderate and extreme versions of

---

Let us say that the proposition that such-and-such, if it is true, *corresponds to* the fact that such-and-such. On some theories, this relation of correspondence is simply identity restricted to true propositions. Suppose that a proposition *p* corresponds to a mereologically reducible fact *f*, and that propositions q_1, q_2, q_3, ... correspond to the sub-facts to which *f* mereologically reduces. Is *p* then logically equivalent to the conjunction (q_1 & q_2 & q_3 & ...)? Or is *p* merely a logical consequence of the conjunction? Or might the two even be logically independent?

Lacking answers to these and other questions, I shall rely in the text primarily on the conceptual notion of reducibility that invokes logical consequence rather than the part–whole relation. It may be useful, however, to bear in mind the possibility that a particular author may instead mean the mereological notion, or something else. Where appropriate, one should distinguish between mereological reductionism and conceptual reductionism (the notion explicated in the text), as I shall do in some notes below.

these various doctrines. I have endeavored to make my usage correspond as closely as possible to established usage of the terms 'haecceitism' and 'anti-haecceitism'. That is why I have introduced the special terms, 'extreme haecceitism' and 'reductionism', for the opposing doctrines concerning the question of reducibility (which is less often the primary focus), and a third term, 'extreme anti-haecceitism', for what may be the most controversial of the doctrines. Extreme haecceitism and reductionism are the exact denials of one another. Extreme haecceitism, therefore, might also be called 'anti-reductionism'. One may consistently combine haecceitism (*simpliciter*) with reductionism by holding that it is legitimate to introduce a possible world for consideration by stipulating which facts concerning particular individuals obtain in the world, even though such facts are reducible to, or nothing over and above, other sorts of facts. (It is possible that Kripke takes this position. See note 19.)

The various versions of haecceitism and anti-haecceitism are perhaps best formulated by invoking a concept from the theory of propositions, that of a *singular proposition*. A singular proposition is a proposition in which at least one individual or object that the proposition is about occurs directly as a constituent, and the proposition is about that individual by virtue of directly including it, rather than a concept by which the individual is represented (determined, denoted). In introducing the terminology of 'singular propositions', Kaplan equates haecceitism with the acceptance of singular propositions (1975, pp. 724–5). More accurately, haecceitism is the doctrine that one may legitimately cite singular propositions in specifying the propositions that are true in a possible world introduced for discussion. Extreme haecceitism is the stronger doctrine that the truth values of any and all manner of singular propositions are among the primitive, brute facts about which propositions are true and which are false in a given possible world. If one conceives of possible worlds as maximal compossible sets of propositions, then haecceitism holds that possible worlds include singular propositions among their elements in addition to non-singular, or general, propositions, and extreme haecceitism holds that the entire subset of non-singular propositions included in a world to the effect that the *F* is such-and-such, for particular properties *F*, logically entails no singular proposition to the effect that *x* is such-and-such. Reductionism holds that the subset of singular propositions, assuming one countenances such propositions at all, is fixed by the subset of non-singular propositions. Anti-haecceitism (*simpliciter*) holds that possible worlds include *only* general propositions to begin with, leaving open the question of the truth values of any singular propositions, and extreme anti-haecceitism denies that there are any singular propositions to be concerned about.

Kaplan points out that one should strictly speak of haecceitism, anti-haecceitism, and their variants as relativized to a particular kind of entity *K*, as for example, *anti-haecceitism with regard to concrete things*, *reductionism with regard to social institutions*, etc. Reductionism with regard to political nations, for example, is the often-cited doctrine that facts involving political nations are reducible to other sorts of facts, such as the actions and histories of particular persons. Extreme haecceitism regarding political nations is the denial of this alleged reducibility. Haecceitism with regard to a kind *K* is logically independent of haecceitism with regard to any logically independent kind *K′*. One may consistently combine haecceitism regarding human bodies with anti-haecceitism regarding persons, for example, by holding that it is legitimate to specify which bodies exist in introducing a possible world for consideration but not to specify which persons exist in that world.

The astute reader will have noticed that I have described the various versions and variants of haecceitism and anti-haecceitism without mentioning the alleged problem of trans-world identification, focusing instead on the role of facts concerning specific individuals in presenting a possible world. How does the trans-world identity problem come in? On anti-haecceitism regarding individuals, possible worlds do not include specific individuals themselves. Instead they provide a structure and framework, given purely qualitatively, in which individuals are represented by means of individual concepts. It is not labeled which individual a given individual concept represents. For the anti-haecceitist, then, there is a special problem about how the individuals thus represented in distinct possible worlds are to be identified with, or distinguished from, one another. If identification is your game, some assembly is required. And all one has to go on are the individual concepts that represent the individuals. One thus needs criteria of trans-world identity. There is no like problem for the haecceitist, since facts concerning specific individuals may be given directly in specifying the possible worlds under discussion. This is what Kripke means when he says that a possible world need not be given purely qualitatively. Haecceitism holds that facts concerning the haecceities – or in more ordinary parlance, the identities – of specific individuals may be taken as given in introducing a possible world for consideration, and extreme haecceitism holds that all facts concerning specific individuals are directly settled by the internal make-up of the possible worlds themselves. Possible worlds come already equipped with identification labels for the individuals that exist in them. No assembly is required, no identity criteria needed.

Kripke's assertion that possible worlds are not discovered but stipulated is a somewhat less felicitous way of stating what I take to be the central doctrine of haecceitism *simpliciter*, or a closely related doctrine. Criteria for trans-world identity are to be replaced by stipulations. In fact, in this respect possible worlds are no different from anything else that might come under discussion. Suppose I say, 'Some cities have monuments made of marble,' as a prelude to saying something about some or all such cities. It would be silly (at best) for someone to object that while there are indeed marble monuments in *this* city (the city we are in), I must justify my claim that the monuments in the other cities I have in mind are really made of marble – instead of, say, some other material that was fashioned to look the way marble looks around here. I am discussing cities with marble monuments. I do not have to specify the relevant class of cities purely qualitatively and then provide a criterion for inter-city identity of material. I simply select the class of cities that I wish to discuss by specifying that they have monuments made of ... , well, *marble*. Kripke contrasts possible worlds, which he says are stipulated, with planets, which are discovered. This may have given the wrong impression. Even independently existing planets may be stipulated in the sense that Kripke intends. One astronomer says to another, 'There are undoubtedly thousands of planets that, like Earth, have significant amounts of oxygen in their atmospheres. What is the temperature range for such a planet?' Suppose a philosopher who has been eavesdropping interrupts, 'Not so fast. How do you know, and what makes it true, that the atmospheric gas on the planet in question is oxygen, rather than some other element that superficially resembles oxygen? After all, you're not on that planet; you're in no position to send up a weather balloon or to conduct other atmospheric experiments. Are you supposing that, say, atomic number provides a criterion for interplanetary identity of elements? If so, why atomic number? Why not some other feature, like that of having its source in the particular portion of ancient post-Big-Bang material from which our Earth-bound oxygen was originally formed?' A reaction by the astronomers of eye-rolling annoyance would be completely justified. The astronomer simply *stipulated* that he was discussing planets that have significant amounts of oxygen in their atmospheres. Even if interplanetary identity criteria for elements are readily available, our astronomer is under no obligation to specify the planets he has in mind purely qualitatively and then ensure that they contain significant amounts of oxygen by providing the available criteria. It is in this sense that even planets are 'stipulated'. When Kripke says that we do not discover but stipulate possible worlds, he is not making a special claim about their peculiar ontological or epistemological status, or about our peculiar status vis-à-vis possible worlds. Nor is he claiming that we decree what is possible and what is not. Instead what he means is that the question of which class of possible worlds is under discussion (and in particular the question of which individuals exist in those worlds) is like the matter of which class of entities of any sort is under discussion – whether they be animals, vegetables, minerals, sticks, stones, or even planets. It is a matter that is entirely open to, and may be entirely governed by, the stipulations of the discussants. The possibility of simply stipulating which individuals are involved renders trans-world identity criteria unnecessary.

5 The triumph of haecceitism

Does the debate about haecceitism have any bearing on the problem of personal identity? The problems of trans-world identification and of personal identity differ from each other in at least one relevant respect. The personal-identity puzzle cases begin with the stipulation that Doris and Rita are present in each. There is no question of identifying the Doris of D/R-1 with the Doris of D/R-2 or the Doris of D/R-3. For one thing, we are given that it is the same Doris in each scenario. For another, that does not help. We are not attempting to identify individuals across possible worlds. Instead we are attempting to identify individuals within a possible world (or within each of the possible worlds represented by the scenario under discussion). Kripke's observation about the stipulatory character of cross-world identifications appears to offer little help.

This appearance is deceptive. We are attempting to determine the identity (haecceity) of the Doris-body-person in D/R-1. This may be thought of as an attempt to identify an individual in an arbitrary possible world w of type D/R-1 with an individual of a possible world w', where the former is given qualitatively by means of the individual concept *the woman who now occupies such-and-such body*, and the latter is given directly, i.e. haecceitally, as either Doris or Rita. It happens that $w = w'$. This may be regarded as a special limiting case of the problem of trans-world identification in which the worlds in question are identical. Seen in this light, it emerges that the issue of reductionism and the controversy between haecceitism and anti-haecceitism are relevant to the problem of personal identity.

One point about the traditional problem of personal identity is perhaps obvious to anyone familiar with the topic. The problem presupposes a version of reductionism regarding persons. It is safe to say that nearly all writers on the topic of personal identity are reductionists. Nearly everything in the literature on the topic simply assumes reductionism regarding persons without mentioning it as such.

It is therefore ironic that reductionism regarding persons entails the Dorita hypothesis. This is shown by a variation of the proof given in Section 3 that, for any pair of objects *x* and *y*, there is a determinate, objective fact of the matter as to whether $x = y$. Consider D/R-1. Let us name the Doris-body-person in D/R-1 'Doris-bod$_1$'. Suppose first, for the sake of argument, that Doris-bod$_1$ is Rita rather than Doris. Reductionists who make this identification claim that the fact that Doris-bod$_1$ = Rita is grounded in the fact that Doris-bod$_1$, and no one else, now has exactly such-and-such a psychology, which used to be Rita's psychology before the brain transplant. If this hypothesis is correct, then it yields one respect in which Doris-bod$_1$ differs from Rita. For the fact that Rita = Rita is a fact of logic, grounded in her existence perhaps but not in facts about her psychological history. Rita therefore lacks Doris-bod$_1$'s property that the fact that she is Rita is reducible to her psychological history. Conversely, Doris-bod$_1$ lacks Rita's property that the fact that she is Rita is independent of psychological features of Doris-bod$_1$'s biography. Either way, it follows by Leibniz's Law that Rita ≠ Doris-bod$_1$, contradicting our hypothesis. But the alternative hypothesis that Doris-bod$_1$ = Doris is subject to refutation by an exactly analogous argument, employing reducibility to facts about Doris-bod$_1$'s bodily history in lieu of reducibility to facts about her psychological history. Either way, whether it is judged that Doris-bod$_1$ is Rita or Doris, the reductionist is driven, or at least committed, to giving up that judgment. And this leads to the Dorita hypothesis. An exactly similar argument may be made in connection with D/R-2 and D/R-3.

This is an uncomfortable result for reductionists. Insofar as the Dorita hypothesis is regarded as implausible with regard to any of the puzzle-case scenarios, so too, to the same extent, is the reductionist assumption that personal identity is grounded in such matters as psychological or bodily continuity. Assuming that one or the other of the rival hypotheses is correct, the thesis that the haecceity of Doris-bod$_1$ is metaphysically reducible to other facts – facts about her psychological, or alternatively facts about her bodily, history – is thereby disproved.

In fact, a version of extreme haecceitism (anti-reductionism) is susceptible of a variation of the same proof. Suppose, for a *reductio*, that there is an object *x* from a possible world *w* and an object *y* from a possible world *w'* such that the fact that $x = y$ is reducible to (or consists in, is nothing over and above, is derived from, etc.) general facts about *x* in *w* and *y* in *w′*. Their identity might be reducible, for example, to *x*'s bearing the relation *R* in *w* to the same *F* to which *y* bears *R′* in *w′*, for appropriate intra-world relations *R* and *R′* and an appropriate cross-world sortal *F*. It is evident, by contrast, that the fact that $x = x$ is not similarly reducible to general facts about *x* in *w* or in *w′*. For the fact that $x = x$ is a fact of logic. If it is grounded in any other fact at all, it is grounded only in *x*'s existence (in *w* or in *w′*). But then *x* differs from *y* in at least one respect. For *x* lacks *y*'s feature that its identity with *x* is grounded in general (cross-world) facts about *x* and it. Conversely, *y* lacks *x*'s feature that its identity with *x* is a primitive fact, not grounded in any general facts about *x* other than its existence. Either way, it follows by Leibniz's Law that *x* and *y* are different objects, contradicting the hypothesis that they are identical.[14]

Can we simply *stipulate* that the Doris-body-person in D/R-1 is, say, Rita? Haecceitism regarding persons implies an affirmative answer. And indeed on extreme haecceitism regarding persons, the matter of whether the Doris-body-person is Doris or Rita *should* be stipulated, since the identity (haecceity) of the Doris-body-person is a *further* fact, not reducible to such qualitative facts as that the Doris-body-person now has such-and-such a psychology (formerly characteristic of Rita). If we can simply stipulate that the Doris-body-person is Rita, then we should be equally free to stipulate instead that the Doris-body-person is Doris. Again, haecceitism regarding persons implies that this is indeed so. Of course, the Doris-body-person cannot be both Doris and Rita. But we are not considering making both stipulations simultaneously. We are considering selecting one of them. And why not?

There is no particular reason why not. We *can* legitimately do this. As we have seen, the particular scenario D/R-1 represents a class of worlds. That class, it turns out, is diverse. The primary question concerning D/R-1 presupposes that in each of the worlds represented by that scenario, the identifications go the same way. This presupposition is erroneous. In some of the worlds represented by D/R-1, the Doris-body-person is Rita. In others of those worlds, the Doris-body-person is Doris. It is illegitimate to ask whether the Doris-body-person in D/R-1 is Doris or Rita. This is a matter to be settled by a stipulation concerning which worlds of the D/R-1 type are under discussion. We may say, 'Consider a world of type

---

[14] See Salmon (1987b). For a variety of controversial, but similarly proved, philosophical theses concerning identity, see the Appendix to Salmon (1986b, pp. 110–14, especially T6 and T7).

D/R-1 in which Allen performs brain transplants on Doris and Rita with the result that they have exchanged bodies. In any such world, Allen thereby made Doris into an ideal mate, but fell in love with Rita.' We may also say, 'Consider another world of type D/R-1, different from the last one, in which again Allen performs brain transplants on Doris and Rita, only in this case their individual consciousnesses remain with their bodies, so that they have exchanged their brains and their psychologies. In any world of this alternative sort, Allen thereby made Rita into an ideal mate, but fell in love with Doris.' Given extreme haecceitism, both sorts of worlds – both of these scenarios – are equally legitimate. They are equally legitimate *qua* scenarios. Neither is incoherent.

When a philosopher poses the D/R-1 scenario (or the D/R-2 or the D/R-3 scenario), and asks whether the Doris-body-person is Doris or Rita, and how this is supposed to be determined, the extreme haecceitist response – what I believe to be the correct response – goes something like this: You tell us who the Doris-body-person is. Until you do, you have not provided a scenario that is specified fully enough to settle the question. In response to your meta-question(s), it is not for us to *determine* which way the identifications go. It is up to you to *stipulate* which class of scenarios you have in mind. As stated, your questions presuppose that the identifications automatically go the same way for all scenarios of the relevant type. Since the identifications you seek are not reducible to the facts you have given us, that presupposition is false. Until you make the necessary stipulations, your primary question is unanswerable in principle. And once you make the necessary stipulations, the answer is then trivial (Salmon 1981, pp. 242–3).

6 Bifurcation of the traditional problem

Given haecceitism regarding persons, or at least given its extreme cousin, the traditional problem of personal identity does not get off the ground. Yet an alternative version of the problem obstinately remains. Imagine that Allen actually *does* perform the operation on Doris and Rita. Imagine this really happening. Imagine that Allen really does – right here and now – implant what had been Doris's brain in what had been Rita's body and conversely. The Rita-body-person is now an ideal mate. Allen has fallen in love with the Doris-body-person. Who now has Allen fallen in love with?

This is not in any way a matter to be settled by stipulation. Surely there already is some fact of the matter concerning the Doris-body-person's identity. And it is not subject to our control what that fact is. If she is Rita, that is not at all a result of my (or of our) stipulating that this should be so. No one has made any such stipulation, nor would it have the slightest effect on things if one did. Instead the Doris-body-person's identity with Rita – the fact that Doris and Rita have exchanged bodies – seems to be somehow a result of the way the surgery was performed, somehow a result of the fact that the Doris-body-person now has what used to be Rita's brain and consequently also what used to be Rita's psychology. The whole business of identity criteria being replaced by Kripkean stipulations seems beside the point, if not completely wide of the mark.

One may feel uneasy about the idea of going beyond mere consideration of the possibility of a given situation, and instead imagining it to be actual. We know it is not actual. Why pretend that it is?

For a simple reason. The point is to mobilize intuitions concerning what *would* be the case if D/R-1 *had* occurred. If, counterfactually, Allen had performed brain transplants on Doris and Rita, then there would be a resulting fact as to whether the Doris-body-person was Rita or Doris, and that fact would not be a matter of our stipulating what is so. Kripke's observation that 'possible worlds are stipulated', properly understood, is simply a recognition of the fact that in considering certain possibilities, we are free to stipulate which possibilities we have in mind by specifying which individuals are involved in them. As we have already seen, it is not a thesis to the effect that what is possible with respect to those individuals is subject to our decision. Nor is it a thesis to the effect that we decide what *would* be the case under certain counterfactual circumstances. There is already a fact of the matter, independently of us, as to who the Doris-body-person would be if D/R-1 had occurred.

Let us suppose again that the Doris-body-person would be Rita. If this hypothesis is correct, it appears to be a direct result of the fact that the Doris-body-person has what was previously Rita's brain with Rita's psychology relatively intact. Insofar as it is true that if D/R-1 had occurred, the Doris-body-person would be Rita, something significantly stronger is equally true. It is not as if the D/R-1 scenario might have had different results. If the Doris-body-person would have been Rita had D/R-1 occurred, then it is in fact metaphysically *impossible* for D/R-1 to occur with the Doris-body-person being Doris, or anyone else other than Rita. In a word, it is *necessary* that the Doris-body-person in D/R-1 is Rita.

Earlier I said that the class of worlds represented by the D/R-1 scenario was diverse, that there are possible worlds in which the D/R-1 scenario is realized and the Doris-body-person is Rita and other worlds in which the D/R-1 scenario is realized and the Doris-body-person is Doris. Now I am saying that the latter outcome is impossible, that there are no possible worlds in which the Doris-body-person is Doris. I seem to have contradicted myself.

I have not. It is at this juncture that I invoke impossible worlds. Haecceitism does not entail that it is in some way for us to decide what is, and what is not, metaphysically possible. Even extreme haecceitism does not entail this. Haecceitism simply holds that in introducing a world for consideration and discussion, we are free to stipulate the facts that obtain in the world. Depending on what we stipulate, the world, or worlds, we so introduce may turn out to be impossible rather than possible. This is so even if it was our intent to stipulate a possible world. We decide which individuals exist and what properties they have in the world we wish to consider, but metaphysics decides, under its own authority, whether such a world is possible or impossible. The latter issue is completely out of our hands. There are indeed D/R-1 worlds in which the Doris-body-person is Rita, and there are indeed other D/R-1 worlds in which the Doris-body-person is Doris. For that matter, there are D/R-1 worlds in which the Doris-body-person is Madonna (altered to have Rita's psychology), and still other D/R-1 worlds in which the Doris-body-person is Ethel Merman resurrected (and psychologically altered). This is a consequence of extreme haecceitism. The question of the Doris-body-person's haecceity – the question of who the Doris-body-person is – is not to be found among, and does not reduce to or consist in, the facts that are given in the D/R-1 scenario. There are many different ways for the identifications to go. But most of those ways are quite impossible. In all of the genuinely *possible* D/R-1 worlds, the Doris-body-person is Rita. This is fixed by law but not by legislation. It is fixed by metaphysical law.

It emerges from this analysis that there are two very different ways of interpreting the problem of personal identity, depending on whether reductionism is presupposed. A puzzle case like D/R-1 is first set out, and the primary question and the two meta-questions then posed. If the questions are put forward under the presupposition of reductionism, it is assumed that one has been given all the facts that are required for deciding the primary question, taken as a question about *all* the worlds represented by the puzzle-case scenario, possible and impossible. One may restrict one's focus to possible worlds, but there is no need to do so. The same answer will obtain for the impossible worlds as well, or at least for the logically consistent ones. For the reductionist, so-called criteria of identity are reductionist analyses or definitions of what it is for a pair of individuals at different times or in different worlds to be identical – or at least analytic sufficient conditions for cross-circumstantial identity. The metaphysical meta-question is concerned with the presupposed reduction of personal-identity facts to facts about psychologies or about bodies. It is, in effect, a demand to be given a reductionist analysis for personal identity through change. We may call this *the reductionist problem of personal identity*. It is the orthodox or canonical form of the problem.[15] As an extreme haecceitist, I reject this alleged problem as bogus (along with the alleged problem of trans-world identification).

If the primary question and the two meta-questions are put forward without presupposing reductionism, one is then presumably being asked to confine one's attention to genuinely possible worlds. In those *possible* worlds in which D/R-1 (or D/R-2 or D/R-3) is realized, who is the Doris-body-person? In particular, if D/R-1 *were* realized, who *would* the Doris-body-person be? This question is perfectly legitimate. The facts of that case are sufficient to zero in on one metaphysically necessary outcome. That is to say, even if the Doris-body-person's identity (haecceity) is not *reducible* to the sorts of facts that one is given in D/R-1, the Doris-body-person's identity does *supervene modally* on exactly such facts. For present purposes, the relevant notion of supervenience may be defined as follows:

> Properties of kind *K* *modally supervene on* properties of kind $K' =_{\text{def}}$. It is metaphysically necessary that for any class *c* of *K*-properties and for any class *c′* of *K′*-properties, if there is something whose *K*-properties are exactly those in *c* and whose *K′*-properties are exactly those in *c′*, then it is metaphysically necessary that anything whose *K′*-properties are exactly those in *c′* is such that its (his/her) *K*-properties are exactly those in *c*.

---

15 I have borrowed the terms 'reductionism' and 'further facts' from Parfit (1986, p. 255), who explicitly calls himself a 'reductionist' in rejecting the idea that identity facts are further facts. Williams defends his setting out the problem of personal identity by means of the BW device thus: 'Such a process may, perhaps, be forever impossible, but it does not seem to present any purely logical or conceptual difficulty' (1973, p. 79). The exact intent of these remarks is perhaps unclear, but on one natural interpretation, Williams is prepared to allow for the prospect (putting the matter in terms of my apparatus) that all of the logically or conceptually possible worlds in which the D/R-2 scenario occurs are metaphysically impossible. Never mind; there is still supposed to be a problem. On this interpretation, the resulting 'problem of personal identity' is a problem only on the assumption of reductionism.

Thus, to say that *K*-properties modally supervene on *K'*-properties is to say that which *K*-properties a thing has is metaphysically necessitated by which *K'*-properties it has. For example, to say that a person's psychology modally supervenes on his/her brain and its physical states is to say that a complete accounting of the facts concerning a person's brain and its physical states leaves room for only one possible outcome concerning his/her psychology, in the sense that it would be metaphysically impossible for the person's brain to be in exactly those physical states while the person has a different psychology (even one that is only slightly different). What I am claiming here is that the Doris-body-person's haecceity modally supervenes on, but is not reducible to, exactly the sorts of biographical facts given in D/R-1.[16]

One may define a notion of reducibility by means of a simple adjustment in the above definition of supervenience, changing the metaphysical modalities to *conceptual* (or properly *logical*) modalities. It may be assumed here that conceptual necessity entails metaphysical necessity but not vice versa. What is conceptually necessary is true in every conceptually possible world, including such worlds as are metaphysically impossible. To say, then, that properties of kind *K* are *conceptually reducible to* properties of kind *K'* is to say that it is conceptually (or logically) necessary that for any class *c* of *K*-properties and for any class *c'* of *K'*-properties, if there is something whose *K*-properties are exactly those in *c* and whose *K'*-properties are exactly those in *c'*, then it is conceptually (logically) necessary that anything whose *K'*-properties are exactly

[16] Jaegwon Kim (1984) defines some non-equivalent notions of supervenience. The notion defined in the text corresponds to Kim's favored notion of *strong supervenience* (where the modality involved is metaphysical modality). (The definition probably ought to be restricted, to avoid unwanted collapse, to kinds *K'* that include properties something might have and kinds *K* that include properties something might not have. An analogous definition, with an analogous restriction, may be given for the notion of *K*-facts supervening on *K'*-facts. An analogous restriction applies to the definitions of reducibility given below.)

If I am correct, recognition of the distinction between supervenience and reducibility is crucial if we are to make significant progress toward solving the traditional problem of personal identity. The reductionist regarding personal identity typically supposes that the haecceity of the Doris-body-person ought to be not merely supervenient on the sorts of facts about her that are given in D/R-3, but reducible to them. The weaker doctrine that personal identity modally supervenes on, but is not reducible to, such biographical features of a person as his/her psychological or bodily history may be what Parfit means when he speaks of what he calls *the further fact view* (1986, p. 210). (Presently I shall deny that the haecceity of the Doris-body-person even modally supervenes on the facts given in D/R-3.)

those in *c′* is such that its (his/her) *K*-properties are exactly those in *c*. The idea here is that which *K*-properties a thing has is a conceptual or logical consequence of which *K′*-properties it has. For example, on Frege's meta-semantical theory, the referential semantics for a language is reducible to the language's intensional semantics (i.e. its semantics of sense) together with some metaphysics, in that the referential properties of a language are reducible to the language's sense properties taken together with the extra-linguistic matter of what objects are determined by those senses. Given that conceptual necessity entails metaphysical necessity but not vice versa, it follows that conceptual reducibility entails modal supervenience but not vice versa.[17] A claim to the effect that *K*-properties supervene on *K′*-properties therefore normally carries the implicature that *K*-properties are *not* reducible to *K′*-properties. And indeed, when philosophers explicitly advocate a supervenience thesis, they often explicitly contrast that thesis with the corresponding reducibility thesis, which they reject, or at least decline to endorse. I am doing exactly that here.

On the modal-supervenience interpretation of the problem of personal identity, the two meta-questions about 'criteria for personal identity' are distinct. The metaphysical question is the deeper of the two – or at least, the more metaphysical. It is a demand for a metaphysical principle, or principles, that entail the answer to the primary question. It is, in effect, a demand for an individual person *a*'s *essence*, in the sense of a property such that it is metaphysically necessary that someone has the property if and only if he or she is the very individual *a* and no other. Or perhaps it is a demand merely for a modally *sufficient* property for *a*'s haecceity, i.e. a property such that, necessarily, anyone with that property is the very individual *a* and no other. Or at the very least, it is a request for an *essential* property of *a*, i.e. a property that *a* has necessarily. The sought-after modal property must be adequate to the task of answering the primary question, interpreted now as a question about genuinely possible worlds in which the puzzle-case scenario obtains. This is *the essentialist problem of personal identity*, to be distinguished from the reductionist problem. The essentialist problem does not presuppose that the sort of fact sought in answer to the primary question is reducible to, or is nothing over and above, facts of some other sort. The problem is perfectly compatible with the extreme haecceitist thesis that

---

[17] Given a certain kind of mereological essentialism, it follows that mereological reducibility of the sort described in note 13 likewise entails modal supervenience but not vice versa.

identity facts are further facts. Even by the extreme haecceitist's lights, it may be seen as a legitimate, and non-trivial, philosophical problem.[18]

We have seen that modal supervenience differs from reducibility (in one sense) over the type of modality involved. The two interpretations of the problem of personal identity carry with them correspondingly different notions of necessity that are involved in the explication given in Section 1 of the concept of a criterion of personal identity. We said that a criterion of personal identity was a triple consisting of a sortal property F and a pair of binary relations R and R', other than personal identity itself, such that it is somehow necessary that x is the same person at t that y is at t' if (or perhaps iff) there is some trans-temporal link of sort F to which x bears R at t and to which y bears R' at t'. A purely epistemological criterion emerges by taking the necessity involved to be epistemic, e.g. knowability a priori, or perhaps the weaker notion: *given what we know, it must be that* (i.e. the dual of epistemic possibility: *for all we know, it may be that*). This would answer the epistemological meta-question. The essentialist problem of personal identity takes the necessity involved to be metaphysical necessity, i.e. truth in all metaphysically possible worlds. The reductionist problem of personal identity takes the necessity involved to be truth in all logically possible worlds, whether metaphysically possible or metaphysically impossible. (The phrase 'criterion of identity' may not be entirely appropriate on the essentialist interpretation of the problem, since it

---

[18] Kripke (1972, pp. 50–3) describes a version of the problem of trans-world identification that he finds legitimate, adding explicitly (p. 51) that there is a similarly legitimate problem concerning identity over time. The alleged problem is concerned with identifying physical objects in different possible worlds given only the facts concerning the relevant molecules (or other, more basic components). Insofar as Kripke is distinguishing between a pseudo-problem of cross-circumstantial identification that presupposes reductionism with a genuine problem that instead presupposes mere modal supervenience, I am here echoing his sentiments specifically in regard to the traditional problem of personal identity. The textual evidence inconclusively suggests, however, that Kripke's remarks concern the reductionist problem (which I dismiss as bogus), as opposed to the extreme-haecceitist/essentialist problem. See Salmon (1996).

It is possible that Kripke endorses a mereological reductionism of the sort described in note 13 above, and that his problem of trans-world identification presupposes this kind of reductionism rather than conceptual reductionism. Although Kripke advocates haecceitism in its moderate form, discussions I have had with him (subsequent to the appearance of *Naming and Necessity*) make me doubtful whether he is prepared to hold, as I do, that haecceities are separate from, or facts over and above, such facts about individuals as their molecular composition (though he may be). Compare Kripke (1972, p. 51) and Salmon (1989b, p. 20).

seems to carry with it in connotation an acceptance of the reductionist construal. But I shall continue to use it.)

The literature on personal identity has suffered from a failure to distinguish sharply between the reductionist and the essentialist interpretations of the problem. Philosopher *A* provisionally proposes a solution that is (or that at least might be) appropriate to the essentialist problem, only to have it dismissed by philosopher *B*, noting that the proposed criterion does not work for every conceivable case, and thus construing it as a non-solution to the reductionist problem. It even happens sometimes that *A* and *B* themselves bear the relation of personal identity.[19] When the distinction between the two interpretations is not emphasized, there is also the opposite danger that a haecceitist who rejects the (*sic.*) problem of personal identity as unreasonably demanding, construing it reductionistically, will miss the significance of the essentialist problem.

7 A proposal regarding the essentialist problem

Let us reconsider the primary question and the metaphysical meta-question concerning D/R-1, interpreted now as concerning the class of

[19] I take Johnston (1987) to be an example of the converse situation. Johnston sees the problem of personal identity in the standard reductionist way. (His reductionism regarding persons is evidenced by his emphasis on conceptual possibility and conceptual necessity (Johnston 1989), and by his use of such phrases as 'that in which personal identity consists' (Johnston 1987) and 'the core relations that actually constitute personal identity' (Johnston 1992). Unlike the typical reductionist, though, Johnston does not claim that the haecceity of the Doris-body-person is reducible to the sorts of facts given in D/R-3. See note 17 above.) Frustrated by an alleged conflict of intuitions regarding scenarios like D/R-2 and by the failure of previous attempts to solve the problem of personal identity, Johnston concludes, erroneously in my view, that the standard philosophical methodology of putting hypothetical cases to the test of intuition is somehow misguided. He argues that one should address the metaphysical meta-question instead with an eye to the epistemological meta-question. This procedure may make sense from the reductionist standpoint, since whatever else identity facts are, they are knowable. Johnston opts for a solution to the metaphysical meta-question which, while it may be appropriate for the essentialist problem, would be proved mistaken from the reductionist standpoint by the questioned method of testing cases against intuition. Johnston's failure to distinguish between the reductionist and essentialist interpretations of the problem is further evidenced by his complaint that, according to the challenged methodology, 'the supposition that I could survive my body's petrification implies that the relations that tie me to my body are contingent' (1987, p. 71). The phrase 'supposition that I could' here means conceptual possibility, while 'contingent' evidently means metaphysical contingency. Johnston also conflates reducibility and mere supervenience (1992, pp. 590–1). See also Johnston (1989, p. 381).

possible worlds (excluding the impossible worlds) incorporating that scenario. At the end of Section 2, it seemed as though the psychology-based identifications were correct – or at least that the body-based identifications were clearly incorrect. We may now go further. It is evident that, necessarily, in D/R-1 the psychology-based identifications are indeed correct. There are D/R-1 worlds in which the Doris-body-person is Doris, but such worlds are one and all impossible. In every *possible* world in which D/R-1 occurs, Doris and Rita have simply traded bodies (apart from their brains). To this extent, our original intuitions about this case are correct.

It does not follow that some psychology-based criterion for personal identity (such as the memory-based criterion) yields a correct answer to our metaphysical meta-question, interpreted on the essentialist scheme. Psychology-based criteria are not the only criteria according to which Doris and Rita have exchanged bodies in D/R-1. A brain-based criterion would issue the same identifications. A brain-based criterion usually echoes the psychology-based criteria in the identifications it makes, but there is divergence in cases of brain damage. If a person's brain is damaged to an extent that significantly affects his/her psychology – such as by significantly altering his/her personality and/or memories of past events – corresponding psychology-based criteria deem the resulting person to be numerically distinct from the person prior to the brain damage. If the brain nevertheless continues to function sufficiently to produce consciousness and a psychology adequate for being a person, the brain-based criterion judges the resulting person to be literally and numerically the same as the person before the damage – only now not the same as he/she used to be.

Given what science informs us about the importance of the brain to consciousness, there does not seem to be much room for debate. The brain-based criterion, construed as an essentialist criterion for personal identity, is intrinsically more plausible than either the body-based or the psychology-based criteria. I am not my body. But neither am I my psychology *as such* – my thoughts, my personality, my memories, my beliefs. I am more closely bound to my *consciousness* than to any of these other things. Not to my 'stream of consciousness', mind you – the flow of thoughts, feelings, sensations, experiences, etc. – but the consciousness itself, the arena through which the flow flows. I may not be strictly identical with my consciousness. I continue to exist even through periods of unconsciousness (e.g. when asleep), even if not through all such periods. But there seems to be some connection between my consciousness and myself that is more intimate than that between my body and myself.[20] The brain is the organ that produces consciousness. Perhaps no one can say exactly how the brain does it. It may be that, at some sufficiently deep level of understanding, it is *impossible* to know how the brain does it. But somehow the brain does it, and that is something we do know. This knowledge provides forceful intuitive support for a brain-based essentialist criterion for personal identity.

The body-based and psychology-based criteria each yield the same identifications in D/R-2 as they did in D/R-1. But the brain-based criterion has a special problem with D/R-2. Here the Doris-body-person has what was previously Doris's brain as well as what was previously Doris's body, but her brain now holds the information that was extracted from Rita's brain. Even if one has decided to make the identifications by attending to the brains rather than to the bodies or the psychologies, one still has to decide whether the person's identity goes with the brain itself or instead with the information held within the brain. In D/R-2 these two come apart. The brain-*qua*-organ-based criterion is obtained by letting the sortal *F* in our explication of a personal-identity criterion be *brain* and letting both *R* and *R′* be the relation of *being the functional owner of* – which in this case may be taken to be the relation *u is the person whose brain is v*. The brain-information-based criterion is obtained instead by letting the sortal *F* be *brain-information* (operating system and RAM, etc.) and letting both *R* and *R′* be the relation: *u is a person whose brain holds exactly the information v*. According to the brain-*qua*-organ-based criterion, *x* is the same person as *y* if they have the same brain across time. According to the brain-information-based criterion, *x* is the same person as *y* if their brains store the same information across time. The brain-*qua*-organ-based criterion goes with the body-based criterion in D/R-2, the brain-information-based criterion with the psychology-based criteria.

Williams says that the primary advantage of setting out the problem of personal identity by means of the BW device rather than by means of brain transplants comes from the fact that D/R-2 is less radical than D/R-1 in the way it secures the condition that the Doris-body-person is appropriately connected to Rita so that the Doris-body-person's apparent memories of Rita's past are not automatically disqualified from being genuine memories. This remark of Williams strongly suggests – and indeed much of the literature on personal identity assumes – that

---

[20] The identification of a person with a consciousness, as opposed to a stream of consciousness, probably lies behind Descartes's proof of his own existence via his '*cogito ergo sum*'. Ironically, it also lies behind Hume's denial of his own existence.

the identifications should come out exactly the same in both D/R-1 and D/R-2. (See note 9 above.) But it is at least potentially a mistake to assume this at the outset, without any argument or further ado. This is especially true since D/R-2 forcefully challenges the psychology-based criteria that seem so fitting when considering only D/R-1. It is logically possible, for example, that although the Doris-body-person is Rita in D/R-1, the Doris-body-person is instead Doris in D/R-2. This would have the consequence that the Doris-body-person of D/R-1 is numerically distinct from the Doris-body-person of D/R-2. But this is a logical possibility.[21]

I believe this logical possibility is philosophical reality. The primary question not only about D/R-1, but equally about D/R-2, when interpreted on the essentialist scheme, is legitimate. In any genuinely possible D/R-1 world, the Doris-body-person is Rita, owing to the fact that the Doris-body-person in D/R-1 has what had been Rita's brain, still functioning in a normal manner. By contrast, in any possible D/R-2 world the Doris-body-person is Doris. And this is a result of the fact that the Doris-body-person in D/R-2 has what had been Doris's brain, still functioning in a normal manner. One noteworthy feature of the brain-*qua*-organ criterion – and an important argument in its favor – is that it discriminates between D/R-1 and D/R-2. It does indeed seem possible for a person to be given a different body by transplanting his/her brain into it. And it seems equally possible for a person to have his/her psychology radically altered by inducing substantial changes in his/her brain. Indeed, it is not an uncommon occurrence for someone's psychology to become significantly altered with brain damage. What seems impossible is for a person to take possession of a new body merely by having his/her psychology replicated in the new body's brain while his/her old brain is destroyed, or for a person's psychology to be modified by transplanting someone else's brain, with its ready-made psychology, into his/her body. Of the several personal-identity criteria considered so far, the brain-*qua*-organ-based criterion is the only one that captures all of these intuitions. If one views the essentialist problem of personal identity as a multi-partied election, then at this stage of the campaign at least, given our current state of knowledge, the

---

21 The expressions 'the Doris-body-person' and 'the Rita-body-person' are definite descriptions (where a *Doris-body-person* is defined as being a person who now occupies what was Doris's body before the relevant procedure). There is therefore nothing about their semantics, as such, that requires them to be rigid designators, in the sense of Kripke.

brain-*qua*-organ-based criterion probably deserves one's vote. One thing seems clear: the rival criteria do not.

The solution I favor for the essentialist problem of personal identity is to look neither to the body nor to the psychology, but to the organ of consciousness: the brain. I tentatively submit a pair of modal principles concerning persons and their brains. As a first approximation, consider the following essentialist principle:

> Necessarily, for any person *P* and any person-brain *B*, if *B* is *P*'s brain at some time *t* (i.e. if *P*'s consciousness is produced at *t* by *B*, etc.), then necessarily, for any time *t'* at which *P* is not brain-dead, *P*'s brain at *t'* is *B*, so that if *P* is conscious at *t'*, his/her consciousness is produced at *t'* by *B*.

The idea is that a person's brain is an essential property of the person, in the sense that as long as he or she is not brain-dead, his or her brain must be *that very brain* and no other. A different person-brain (for example, an artificial brain), no matter how extensively it replicates a person's original brain, cannot take the place of the original brain for that person. If the new brain produces consciousness, it is not that person's consciousness. Let us call this principle *the essentiality of one's brain*. The principle does not entail that a person's brain cannot undergo change. A person's brain might become damaged or undergo various surgical improvements (e.g. removal of tumors). The principle does not even deny that parts of a brain might be replaced with artificial components. What the principle entails is that whatever changes a brain undergoes, it must remain the same, numerically identical brain if its functional owner is to remain the same, numerically identical person. Replacement of a functional brain is homicide.

Kripke and others have proposed other essentialist principles concerning individuals, e.g. that the original material out of which an artifact was constructed is an essential feature of the artifact, and that any natural kind (e.g. the species) to which a creature belongs is an essential feature of the creature. As with these other principles, the essentiality of one's brain is a posteriori. It is subject to falsification and adjustment by the empirical facts. And as with other a posteriori essentialist principles, there is some more general, a priori essentialist principle from which the essentiality of one's brain is obtained. This may be the principle that if there is a single organ that is responsible for a person's consciousness, then it is essential to the person that he/she has that very one (and not, for instance, a transplanted organ of the same type), or at least that his/her original organ of consciousness be the very same one. The essentiality of one's brain derives its aposteriority from the supplementary observation that the organ of consciousness among persons is the brain. The latter observation is subject to falsification, e.g. by the improbable empirical discovery of a person lacking a brain.

The general principle itself is also subject to revision through critical inquiry, perhaps even through empirical findings. Philosophers ponder the prospect of fission, whereby a single person is divided into two people by bisecting his/her brain and transplanting one or both of the brain-halves into a brainless body. It may be that anything that might be reasonably called a *person* must, as a matter of actual physiology, have more than one-half of an ordinary brain (see Robinson 1988). The loss of a smaller portion of one's brain might in some cases be regarded as damage that the brain survives – that is, as the brain's losing a part without thereby ceasing to exist as a functional brain. But if it should turn out that (as is frequently supposed in the relevant literature) enough of a person's psychology and consciousness can be retained with only one-half (or even somewhat less) of a brain, we may decide to replace the principle of the essentiality of one's brain with a weaker principle of *the essentiality of some sufficient portion or other of one's brain*. According to this essentialist principle, a person could survive the destruction of his/her brain by retaining a sufficiently functional portion. An essentialist version of the fission problem might then arise.[22] There may be even more recherché possibilities. It is difficult to conjecture about what the limitations are. Perhaps gradual bionicization is a real possibility. Perhaps

[22] The fission problem is analogous in some respects to a similar problem concerning artifacts, as illustrated by the famous Ship of Theseus. The former problem, interpreted on the essentialist scheme, may be amenable to an analogue of the solution I proposed to the latter (Salmon, pp. 219–29). There are alternative solutions to the fission problem which are not usually considered but which, if sound, would save the principle of the essentiality of one's brain. One is the claim that what survives the removal of a brain hemisphere is not the original person, but only what had been a part of that person and what is now a full-fledged (though perhaps impaired) person in his/her own right. In this case, the two persons who emerge from fission were formerly not persons at all, but two halves of the original person, who was destroyed. A variant of this solution holds that the original person continues to exist even after the fission, but only as the scattered aggregate of two separate persons, and therefore not itself a person. The fission would in that case constitute a radical metamorphosis whereby what had been a person is transformed from a solo act into a duo. On both of these solutions, any person who loses one of his/her brain's hemispheres is distinct from the person (or from each of the persons) who emerges from the procedure with only the remaining hemisphere. Both of these prospects are worthy of more serious attention.

different brain functions, including different aspects of consciousness, can be gradually taken over by different artificial devices, making the brain itself dispensable, thus requiring further modification in the essentiality of one's brain. But suppose the discarded brain were refurbished. Who would its functional owner be?[23]

If it is assumed that Doris and Rita continue to exist in both D/R-1 and D/R-2 after the relevant procedure, then the essentiality of one's brain answers the primary questions, as interpreted on the essentialist scheme. Given Doris's and Rita's survival, the principle entails that they have exchanged bodies in D/R-1 and have exchanged psychologies in D/R-2. In both cases they retain their individual brains. Indeed, according to the principle, they *must* retain their individual brains if they are to survive the relevant procedure, whether it is a brain transplant or a BW-exchange. This suggests a complementary essentialist principle:

> Necessarily, for any person-brain *B* and any person *P*, if *B* is *P*'s brain at some time *t*, then necessarily, for any time *t'* at which *B* is functioning roughly normally, the person whose brain at *t'* is *B* is *P*, so that if *B* is producing consciousness at *t'*, the consciousness produced is *P*'s.

The idea is that a brain's functional owner is an essential property of the brain, in the sense that, as long as the brain is functioning in a substantially normal manner (allowing for some malfunctioning due to brain damage, etc.), the brain's functional owner must be *that very person* and no other. (It is assumed that necessarily, for any time *t*, any person-brain that is functioning substantially normally has exactly one functional owner at *t*, i.e. there is exactly one person whose brain it is at *t*.) No matter how much the psychology may have been altered – due to brain washing, under the influence of drugs or religious fanaticism, etc. – if the same brain is still producing consciousness in a more-or-less normal manner, it is the same person, even if he/she has been psychologically deeply altered in the process. We may call this principle *the essentiality of a brain's ownership*.[24]

---

[23] One carefully guarded variation of the principle in the text is the following. Necessarily, for any person *P* and any person-brain *B*, if *B* is *P*'s brain at some time *t*, then necessarily, for any later time *t'* at which *P* is not brain-dead and such that *P* has a functioning brain throughout the period from *t* to *t'*, *P*'s brain at *t'* is a portion of *B*.

[24] By the definition of supervenience given in Section 6, if one's haecceity modally supervenes on the original ownership of one's current brain, it follows that for any person *x*, no one other than *x* can possibly currently have what was originally *x*'s brain. This is, in effect, the principle of the essentiality of a brain's ownership.

Seen in one light, the twin principles of the essentiality of one's brain and the essentiality of a brain's ownership are the same but for a different focus. The two principles may be combined into a single principle of *the essentiality of brain ownership*:

> Necessarily, for any person *P* and any person-brain *B*, if *B* is *P*'s brain at some time *t*, then necessarily, for any time *t'* at which either *P* is not brain-dead or *B* is functioning substantially normally, *P* is the person whose brain at *t'* is *B*.

A couple of points bear repeating here. First, the issue of whether this principle is correct is one that is appropriately settled partly by reference to empirical facts and partly by philosophical inquiry. Second, whether it is the essentiality of brain ownership or some alternative essentialist principle that is supported by empirical facts and philosophical analysis, the resulting 'criterion' for personal identity solves the essentialist problem, not the reductionist problem. The necessity involved in any brain-based criterion cannot be conceptual or logical necessity. It is manifestly not conceptually or logically necessary (e.g. it is clearly not an analytic truth) that persons have brains at all, let alone that a person has the same brain as long as he/she has the capacity for consciousness. Just as it is logically possible for a tin man to lack a heart yet live, it is likewise logically possible for a brainless scarecrow to be magically conscious, even impressively clever.[25]

---

[25] See Wiggins (1967, p. 55). Williams evidently denies the principle of the essentiality of one's brain. He asserts that 'it seems pretty clear that under these circumstances [in which the BW device is used to copy information extracted from one brain into another] a person could be counted the same if this were done to him, and in the process he were given a new brain ... here we have personal identity without the same brain, though of course we have identity of the rest of the body to hold onto' (1973, p. 80). Parfit (1986) argues similarly (see note 8) that retaining some or all of one's brain is not what fundamentally 'matters' in survival. Although Williams may be a reductionist (see note 15), his claim here is framed using the subjunctive construction 'if this *were* done to him', suggesting, perhaps, that if it is metaphysically possible to extract and restore brain information, then it is also metaphysically possible for someone to be given a new brain. Williams might be interpreted here as denying even the essentiality of a portion of one's brain. (As a reductionist, however, Williams would be forced to regard personal identity in such a case as consisting in something else – hence the remark about the identity of the rest of the body as something to 'hold onto'.)

John Perry (1978, p. 47) suggests a principle similar to the essentiality of one's brain and proceeds to criticize it. Perry is also a reductionist regarding persons (see, for example, pp. 21–2), and his criticisms suggest that his intended target is a principle supporting a brain-based criterion of personal identity as a solution to the reductionist problem.

An essentialist principle is a principle of modal intolerance; it imposes limitations on the variety of genuinely possible worlds. The essentiality of brain ownership does not concern impossible worlds. I am not proposing that a person's identity is *reducible* to (or that it is nothing over and above, consists in, follows from, is grounded in, derived from, etc.) facts about brains and their former owners. I maintain that the matter of the haecceity of a person given qualitatively as *the person who now functionally owns brain B* is a further fact. The traditional, canonical form of the problem of personal identity is correctly solved by rejecting it as a spurious pseudo-problem. One is free to stipulate that one is considering worlds in which the person who now has what used to be *a*'s brain is not *a* but someone else. There is a price to be paid for doing so: the worlds under consideration will be metaphysically impossible worlds. But there is absolutely no problem with that.[26]

---

[26] The combined principle of the essentiality of brain ownership is similar to what Parfit (1986, p. 204) calls *the physical criterion* (although the latter is actually a principle of the essentiality of unique ownership of some sufficient portion or other of a brain). The thesis I am proposing is significantly different from the view of Thomas Nagel (1986). Nagel is at least tempted to identify a person with his/her brain, while denying that the connection is a priori. On his view, the sentence 'Jones = Jones's brain', and likewise the sentence 'Jones = *B*' where '*B*' names Jones's brain, express necessary a posteriori truths. I am claiming that though a person and his/her brain are not identical, they are essentially related to each other by functional ownership. On my view, the sentence 'Jones's brain = *B*' – or more cautiously, the sentence 'If Jones has a functioning brain, then it is a portion of *B*' – expresses a necessary a posteriori truth, whereas Nagel's allegedly necessary a posteriori sentences are not even true.

On the other hand, Nagel describes the identification of person and brain as a 'mild exaggeration' (p. 40). Nagel's actual view may thus be closer to the view defended here. Parfit reports (1986, pp. 289–93, 468–77), that in then unpublished work (possibly a draft of Chapter 3 of *The View From Nowhere*), Nagel rejects the extreme haecceitist thesis that the identity of a person, given qualitatively, is a further fact about the person given thus. Nagel reportedly defends a brain-*qua*-organ-based criterion as a solution to the meta-question for a reductionist problem of personal identity. It is possible, however, that he endorses a mereological reductionism of the sort described in note 13. Being an extreme haecceitist, I reject the traditional reductionist problem of personal identity as a pseudo-problem. I similarly reject the idea that the identity of the person having a particular brain is mereologically reducible to facts about the brain. Whatever force Parfit's objections may have against Nagel's reported view, they carry little or no weight against my proposed essentialist principles. Another account having important points of contact with the account presented here is that in Unger (1990, p. 42) – with the significant difference that he declines to endorse any non-trivial essentialism of the sort that is central to the present view.

8 A fuller proposal

The twin principles of the essentiality of one's brain and the essentiality of a brain's ownership yield answers to the metaphysical meta-question on the essentialist version of the problem of personal identity. They also yield answers to the primary questions about D/R-1 and D/R-2, interpreted on the essentialist scheme, different answers to each. Scenario D/R-3 is another matter. The essentialist principles seem not to help at all in settling the primary question about D/R-3 – even when interpreting it as a question about the genuinely possible worlds represented by the scenario. We are not told whether the changes that have taken place in D/R-3 are the result of brain transplants, or information extraction by means of a BW device, or alien rays, or magic (if such is possible), or something else. The body-based and the psychology-based criteria go about their business in D/R-3 just as they do in D/R-1 and D/R-2, making the same identifications in all three scenarios. But the brain-*qua*-organ criterion comes up short in D/R-3. The criterion is not up to the task of answering the primary question about the most puzzling of puzzle cases, interpreted on the essentialist scheme. There seems to be nothing in this neutral scenario for the criterion to take hold of.

There is something. The brain-*qua*-organ criterion discriminates between D/R-1 and D/R-2, making opposite identifications in each. That in itself, I have argued, is an important feature of the criterion. And it is a feature that the criterion brings with it to D/R-3. D/R-3 is neutral regarding the sort of facts in virtue of which D/R-1 and D/R-2 differ from each other. The reason the brain-*qua*-organ criterion is unable to settle the primary question in D/R-3 is that D/R-3 is silent where D/R-1 and D/R-2 are specific. D/R-3 fails to specify the sort of facts that the brain-*qua*-organ criterion needs in order to identify the post-switch body-persons. If D/R-3 is brought about by brain transplants performed by alien surgeons, then the identifications go the same way as in D/R-1. If D/R-3 is brought about instead through an alien version of the BW device, then the identifications go the same way as in D/R-2. Some facts or other of this sort must obtain in any scenario that realizes D/R-3. Yet D/R-3 fails to specify what they are.

The difficulty encountered in the attempt to answer the primary question creates the impression that one is confronting a deep philosophical conundrum for which the brain-*qua*-organ criterion's effectiveness breaks down and is seen to be inadequate. But the difficulty (indeed impossibility) of answering the primary question about D/R-3 is not due to a defect in the brain-*qua*-organ criterion. It is due to a defect in the scenario. It is under-specified, and for that very reason the brain-*qua*-organ criterion yields no answer to the primary question. In truth, D/R-3 is not so much a particular puzzle-case scenario for the essentialist problem of personal identity as it is a generic *category* or *classification* of puzzle cases. It represents a *class* or *type* of genuinely possible scenarios. In some possible scenarios of that type, Doris and Rita exchange bodies while retaining their brains, and consequently also their psychologies. In other possible scenarios *of the very same type*, Doris and Rita exchange their psychologies while retaining their bodies, including their brains. In some possible D/R-3 scenarios the Doris-body-person is Doris; in other possible D/R-3 scenarios the Doris-body-person is Rita. The reason the best criterion yet considered does not yield a single, unequivocal answer to the primary question, interpreted on the essentialist scheme, when asked of D/R-3 itself, is that no answer is correct for all such cases. Any criterion that provides a single answer for all genuinely possible puzzle cases of that type is *ipso facto* mistaken. This would include both the body-based and the entire array of psychology-based criteria.[27]

This is true to a lesser extent about D/R-1 and D/R-2 as well. D/R-1 and D/R-2 are also under-specified, indeed in infinitely many respects. D/R-1 fails to specify, for example, the details of the surgical procedure that Allen performs on his victims. And D/R-2 does not specify very much at all about how the marvelous BW device works. The Doris/Rita incidents are not so much particular puzzle-case scenarios for the essentialist problem of personal identity as they are *types* of puzzle cases. But there is an important difference between D/R-1 and D/R-2 on the one hand, and D/R-3 on the other. Arguably, all possible D/R-1 cases yield the same identifications, and all possible D/R-2 cases also yield the same identifications, exactly opposite to those of D/R-1 cases. The class of genuinely possible worlds represented by D/R-1 is a uniform class in regard to the relevant identifications. Similarly for the class of genuinely possible worlds represented by D/R-2. D/R-3, by contrast, defines a remarkably mixed bag. D/R-3 fails to specify the very sorts of facts upon which the answer to the primary question supervenes – to wit, the matter of whether the Doris-body-person's consciousness is being produced by what had been Doris's brain or by what had been Rita's. The class of genuinely possible worlds represented by D/R-3 remains diverse, in the same way as the class of all worlds, possible and impossible, represented by either D/R-1 or D/R-2. The primary question

---

27 For related discussion, see Salmon (1981, pp. 242–6).

about D/R-3, even when interpreted on the essentialist scheme, is thus a 'wife-beating' question. It remains unanswerable because of its false presupposition that the answer modally supervenes on facts concerning psychologies and/or bodies.

References

Hazen, Allen (1979) Counterpart-theoretic Semantics for Modal Logic. *Journal of Philosophy* 76, 6: 319–38.

Johnston, Mark (1987) Human Beings. *Journal of Philosophy* 84, 2: 59–83.

Johnston, Mark (1989) Fission and the Facts. In J. Tomberlin (ed.) *Philosophical Perspectives, 3: Philosophy of Mind and Action Theory*. Atascadero, CA: Ridgeview, 369–97.

Johnston, Mark (1992) Reasons and Reductionism. *The Philosophical Review*, 101, 3: 589–618.

Johnston, Mark and Graeme Forbes (1987) Is There a Problem about Persistence? *Proceedings of the Aristotelian Society*, supplementary vol. 61: 107–55.

Kaplan, David (1975) How to Russell a Frege-Church. *Journal of Philosophy* 72: 716–29.

Kim, Jaegwon (1984) Concepts of Supervenience. *Philosophy and Phenomenological Research* 65: 257–70.

Kripke, Saul (1972) *Naming and Necessity*. Cambridge, MA: Harvard University Press.

Kripke, Saul (1977) Speaker's Reference and Semantic Reference. In P. French, T. Uehling, and H. Wettstein (eds) *Contemporary Perspectives in the Philosophy of Language*. Minneapolis: University of Minnesota Press, 6–27.

Lewis, David (1986) *On the Plurality of Worlds*. Oxford: Basil Blackwell.

Nagel, Thomas (1986) *The View From Nowhere*. Oxford: Oxford University Press.

Parfit, Derek (1971) Personal Identity. *The Philosophical Review* 80: 3–27.

Parfit, Derek (1986) *Reasons and Persons*. Oxford: Oxford University Press.

Perry, John (ed.) (1975) *Personal Identity*. Berkeley: University of California.

Perry, John (1978) *A Dialogue on Personal Identity and Immortality*. Indianapolis: Hackett.

Robinson, John (1988) Personal Identity and Survival. *Journal of Philosophy* 85: 319–28.

Salmon, Nathan (1979) How *Not* to Derive Essentialism from the Theory of Reference. *Journal of Philosophy* 76, 12: 703–25.

Salmon, Nathan (1981) *Reference and Essence*. Princeton: Princeton University Press; (2005) expanded edition, Amherst, NY. Prometheus Books.

Salmon, Nathan (1984) Impossible Worlds. *Analysis* 44, 3: 114–17;

Salmon, Nathan (1986a) *Frege's Puzzle*. Atascadero, CA: Ridgeview.

Salmon, Nathan (1986b) Modal Paradox: Parts and Counterparts, Points and Counterpoints. In P. French, T. Uehling, and H. Wettstein (eds) *Midwest Studies in Philosophy XI: Studies in Essentialism*. Minneapolis: University of Minnesota Press, 75–120; reprinted in Salmon (2005), 273–344.

Salmon, Nathan (1987a) Existence. In J. Tomberlin (ed.) *Philosophical Perspectives, 1*. Atascadero, CA: Ridgeview, 49–108.

Salmon, Nathan (1987b) The Fact that $x = y$. *Philosophia* (Israel) 17, 4: 517–18.

Salmon, Nathan (1989a) Tense and Singular Propositions. In J. Almog, J. Perry, and H. Wettstein (eds) *Themes from Kaplan*. Oxford: Oxford University Press, 331–92.
Salmon, Nathan (1989b) The Logic of What Might Have Been. *The Philosophical Review* 98, 1: 3–34.
Salmon, Nathan (1993a) Analyticity and Apriority. In J. Tomberlin (ed.) *Philosophical Perspectives, 7: Logic and Language*. Atascadero, CA: Ridgeview, 125–33.
Salmon, Nathan (1993b) This Side of Paradox, *Philosophical Topics* 21: 187–97.
Salmon, Nathan (1996) Trans-World Identification and Stipulation. *Philosophical Studies*, 84, pp. 203–23; reprinted in Salmon (2005), 345–75.
Salmon, Nathan (1997) Wholes, Parts, and Numbers. In J. Tomberlin (ed.) *Philosophical Perspectives, 11*. Atascadero, CA: Ridgeview.
Shoemaker, Sydney S. (1959) Personal Identity and Memory. *Journal of Philosophy*, 56: 868–82; reprinted in Perry (1975) op. cit.
Shoemaker, Sydney S. (1963) *Self-Knowledge and Self-Identity*. Ithaca: Cornell University Press.
Unger, Peter (1990) *Identity, Consciousness, and Value*. Oxford: Oxford University Press.
Wiggins, David (1967) *Identity and Spatio-Temporal* Continuity. Oxford: Basil Blackwell.
Williams, Bernard (1970) The Self and the Future. *The Philosophical Review* 79, 2.
Williams, Bernard (1973) *Problems of the Self*. Cambridge: Cambridge University Press.

Part III
Meaning

6
A Fregean Look at Kripke's Modal Notion of Meaning

Gilead Bar-Elli

In *Naming and Necessity* (*NN*) Kripke criticizes Frege for conflating two notions of meaning (or sense),[1] one is meaning proper, the other is the way reference is determined (p. 59). More precisely, he argues that Frege conflated the question of how the meaning of a word is given or determined with the question of how its reference is determined. The criterial mark of meaning-determination, according to Kripke, is a statement of synonymy: if we give the sense of '*a*' by means of '*b*', then the two expressions must be synonymous. The criterial mark of reference-determination is knowledge, typically a priori, of the truth of their identity: if the reference of '*a*' is given by '*b*', then we know a priori that *a* is *b*. Kripke then argues that Frege's conceptions both of meaning-determination and of reference-determination were wrong, and proposes an alternative picture of reference-determination.

I shall discuss some details of Kripke's arguments in the last part of this chapter. In the meantime I wish to point out, in very general terms, that the main flaw Kripke finds in Frege's conception is that it is what we may call 'over-cognitive': Frege, according to Kripke, mistakenly construes the reference of a term as being determined by beliefs or conditions allegedly known to the speaker. Frege then compounds mistakes by identifying this with the meaning or sense of the term. Much of this attack on the Fregean cognitive conception of meaning is couched in terms of a detailed critique of a descriptive theory of the sense of (proper) names, which is the ostensive target of most of Kripke's arguments. The tacit assumption is evidently that a cognitive conception is manifested in a descriptive theory (the sense) of names.

---

[1] 'Meaning' has often been used as a translation of Frege's *Bedeutung*. Kripke sometimes uses it as akin to Frege's *Sinn*. I shall do the same.

The relationships between a cognitive conception of sense and the descriptive theory of names are rather elusive. Many theorists assume (with Kripke) that the latter is implied by, or is part of, the former. They also assume that this was Frege's view. *NN* can be read rather narrowly as launching an attack on the descriptive theory of names, which Kripke ascribes to Frege. This, of course, is important enough, independently of whether the attribution of the descriptive view to Frege is correct. (I shall come back to this in the last part of the chapter.) On this reading Kripke's arguments against the descriptive conception of names are, I believe, quite compelling. However, *NN* can be read more ambitiously as an attack on any cognitivist conception of meaning and of reference-determination. It is, I believe, on this more ambitious reading that *NN* has been justly regarded as one of the most important landmarks in the philosophy of language, as cutting deep into the basic conceptions in terms of which we construe the notions of meaning and reference-determination. It is mainly with the ambitious reading that I shall be concerned here. On this reading Frege's actual view deserves careful examination, for it, or a particular interpretation of it, is widely conceived as one of the most important versions of a cognitive conception of meaning. However, as will be spelled out later, I believe it is, or at least suggests, an important version of a cognitive conception of meaning, which is not committed to the descriptive theory Kripke attacks.

The alternative Kripke proposes for reference-determination is couched, accordingly, in terms of two non-cognitive factors: (a) causal relations between speakers and between them and objects or situations in the real world; and (b) intentions of co-referring – intentions on the part of a speaker to retain the reference of previous links in the causal chain by which the name has passed on to him or her. Reference, according to Kripke, is determined not by any piece of knowledge or by beliefs available to the speaker, but by a certain kind of semantical intention[2]

---

[2] The exact nature of this intention raises some problems. One of them, pertinent to our present concerns, is whether this intention is constrained by epistemic considerations – whether one can form such an intention, on a specific occasion, contrary to one's firm existential beliefs. One may well argue that given certain beliefs and epistemic conditions, the appropriate intention may be unavailable to the speaker, and that his or her use of a name will thus become spurious. I heard from a Kabbalist long stories about Bilar, the king of devils. Since I don't believe there are such creatures, it seems to me that I cannot form the appropriate intention (to refer to whatever the Kabbalist was referring to), even if, contrary to my convictions, it turns out that there are devils and they have a king, and the Kabbalist did refer to something.

and by causal factors in the actual situations in which a speaker utters the term and by which he or she has mastered its use.

In this wide conception of *NN*, it is one of the main origins of the externalist position, according to which the meanings of various linguistic expressions, such as proper names and terms for natural kinds, are essentially related to things in the actual world, without which they cannot be grasped. This view, whose hold in philosophy of language and philosophy of mind has strengthened over recent generations, is not opposed, I believe, to Frege's view. On the contrary, it is in full harmony with Frege's view that the sense of a term is a way its reference is given to us, which forms a particular supervenience relation between sense and reference. From this perspective Frege should be regarded also as one of the founding originators of the externalist position.[3]

One may wonder whether this causal theory of reference-determination has not gone too far in its non-cognitive orientation, for the notions of reference and reference-determination should serve in a theory of meaning whose ultimate goal is to account for our use of words in our language. The causal chain, of which the speaker need not be, and usually is not, aware, may lead to a referent he doesn't know, and of which he hasn't even dreamt; it may lead to something utterly and categorically incompatible with whatever he intended to say. In fact it may lead to nothing at all. This may be entirely unknown to the speaker, and hence hardly affect his use of the terms involved. If the picture of reference-determination is thus detached from anything that is within the cognitive horizons of the speaker, how can it provide for an account of his use of these words?[4] For this reason, it seems to me particularly desirable to construe a version of Kripke's causal chain theory as characterizing one mode in which a reference is given to us within the bounds of a cognitive conception of sense. I shall not go here into details, but rather remain at a general level, arguing that the alleged contrast between this theory and Frege's cognitive conception are over-stated.

A quite common retort here (possibly held by Kripke himself) is that semantics and theories of reference should be separated from the cognitive aspects of our use of language. These aspects are of course important but they should be dealt with in other terms and by separate theories.[5]

---

[3] I have expanded on this in Bar-Elli (2009, chs 3, 7, 8, 10).

[4] Related points have been widely discussed in the literature. See, for instance, Dummett (1973, pp. 146–51; 1981, pp. 182–6). I shall not go into this here.

[5] See, for instance, Salmon (1981, ch. 1) and Wettstein (1986).

I believe that such a move undermines one of Frege's greatest insights: that a theory of thought, in its wide sense, cannot be thus detached from a theory of meaning; it is dependent on it and constrained by it. Again, the issues involved are very wide and intricate, and I shall not go into them here.

In the first part of what follows I shall describe what may be called Kripke's modal conception of meaning, which I regard to be a novel and important notion of meaning. This, along with the non-cognitive attitude towards meaning and reference-determination sketched above, form, perhaps, the most significant contribution to the conception of meaning in this celebrated monograph. It may appear that the modal notion of meaning is a feature of the non-cognitive approach to meaning. The relationship between these two central doctrines is, however, more complicated than might at first sight appear, and I suggest that the modal conception is not, in itself, opposed to the cognitive conception, and can be incorporated in it. In the last part of this chapter I shall examine Kripke's arguments against Frege's (cognitive) conception of sense from a Fregean perspective. I shall try to show that the modal conception of meaning in itself does not suffice for discarding Frege's cognitive conception of sense and of reference-determination. A Fregean cognitive conception of meaning may be, therefore, compatible with something like the modal conception of meaning – or so I shall argue.

I mean to focus here on *NN* exclusively, but I cannot avoid mentioning an interesting link between this non-cognitive trend in *NN* and the view Kripke suggests, in Wittgenstein's name, in his later book on Wittgenstein. For, on the picture suggested in *NN*, objective reference is effected (and secured) not by conscious states of the speaker (like his beliefs) on the one hand, nor by a direct (cognitive) relation he has to the world, on the other hand, but, basically, by his belonging to a speech community. It is this belonging to a speech community, implied by both (a) and (b) above, which secures the objective reference of the speaker's words. *NN* may seem to be worlds apart from the book on Wittgenstein, and as far as I know Kripke has not suggested a connection between them, but this seems to me to be an important link between these celebrated monographs. (See, however, 'Speaker's Reference and Semantic Reference' (SRSR), note 20.)

Kripke's modal notion of meaning

Although much of Kripke's discussion in *NN* is concerned with reference-determination, there is a novel and distinctly non-Fregean conception of meaning proposed in *NN*. Kripke is surprisingly sparse on this.[6] The notion of the meaning (sense) of a name is hardly mentioned in *NN* except for the above critical remarks about conflating synonymy and reference-determination.

Indeed, he is so sparse on the subject that many scholars ascribe to him the view that proper names have no meaning (sense) (Dummett and Salmon are notable examples). Although some formulations of Kripke's may support such a view, I believe that ascribing it to him is wrong or, at least, overstated. In fact, the theses that proper names are rigid designators, that they are not synonymous with descriptions, as well as the thesis about the way their actual reference is determined (the causal chain theory), are all theses about their meaning or sense (cf. *NN*, pp. 33, 39, 55, 56, 57, 59; we shall come back to this). In another place, Kripke elaborates a bit more on the notion of the meaning of words:

> The notion of what words can mean in the language is semantical: it is given by the conventions of our language. What they mean, on a given occasion is determined, on a given occasion, by these conventions, together with the intentions of the speaker and various contextual features ... If a speaker has a designator in his idiolect, certain conventions of his idiolect (given various facts about the world) determine the referent in the idiolect: that I call the *semantic referent* of the designator. (SRSR, p. 14)

(He is clear in this paper that by 'semantic' he means 'truth-conditional'.)

Kripke is usually credited with advancing an effective critique of what he regards to be the Fregean conception of how reference is determined. He is also credited with proposing an alternative picture of the determination of the reference of proper names. He hardly deals in *NN* with the question of what reference is, what the very ascription of a reference to a word amounts to, and may be regarded as accepting the essentials of the Fregean answer to this question, namely, that the reference of a term is its contribution to determining the truth-value of sentences containing it.[7]

---

[6] Surprisingly, 'meaning' does not appear in the index of the book, though 'theory of meaning' occurs under other entries, such as 'description theory of proper names'.

[7] In Bar-Elli (1996, ch. 5) I expanded on the distinction between 'the essential problem' of what meaning (reference or sense) is, namely what the very ascription of meaning to a word amounts to, and 'the determination problem' of how the meaning of a word (or a word of a particular kind) is determined. I proposed the distinction in accounting for the relationships between the context principle and compositionality.

Kripke is then credited with making the distinction mentioned above between reference-determination and meaning-determination and with pointing out the Fregean conflation of these. On many of these points Kripke was criticized by Fregean scholars of misrepresenting Frege's views, which, when properly understood, allow, with slight modifications, for most of Kripke's right observations. I have voiced doubts of this sort myself, but I won't go into these here.

But beyond all these I think that Kripke suggested in *NN* a novel, distinctly non-Fregean conception of meaning, a conception that underlies the main tenor of argument of that work, which I would call *a modal conception of meaning*. Let me quote from the Preface to *NN*:

> Consider:
> (1) Aristotle was fond of dogs.
> A proper understanding of this statement involves an understanding both of the (extensionally correct) conditions under which it is in fact true, *and* of the conditions under which a counterfactual course of history, resembling the actual course in some respects but not in others, would be correctly (partially) described by (1). (*NN*, p. 6)

This is couched in terms of understanding, not of meaning. But I think we should not persist in making the distinction, and assume that these two are correlative notions. Again, in explaining the notion (or rule) of rigidity, Kripke says that it is

> the rule that there is a single individual and a single property such that, with respect to every counterfactual situation, the truth conditions of the proposition are the possession of the property by that individual, in that situation. (*NN*, p. 10)

This is a conception of meaning and understanding that dominates the course of argument in *NN*. It is, I believe, a novel one and distinct from a simple truth-conditional view of meaning. On this view the meaning of a sentence like (1) is stated by the conditions (in the actual world) in which it is true and those in which it is false. We don't have to consider its truth conditions in counterfactual situations or possible courses of the world, as in Kripke's conception. Granting its novelty, what is its basis? Why should one, in order to understand a statement, consider its truth conditions in counterfactual situations, and know which counterfactual course of history would be correctly described by it? Kripke evidently thinks that this is not a stipulation concerning an artificial notion of meaning (in the formal semantics of systems of modal logic), but an explicative condition required by our intuitive notion of understanding. Kripke would agree, I suppose, with the view, championed by Dummett and ascribed by him to Frege, that the notion of meaning concerned should serve in an explanation of understanding. But unlike Frege (and Dummett), he thinks that this notion of meaning is *intrinsically modal*, in that the mastery and understanding of simple sentences involve understanding their truth conditions in counterfactual situations.

In thus saying that this notion is intrinsically modal I do not mean to imply that we are concerned here with the notion of the meaning of sentences involving modal operators, or with their role or meaning within complex sentences involving modal operators. Kripke is clear on this, and he emphasizes the point again in the Preface to *NN* (pp. 11–12), where he also accuses Dummett of misunderstanding this point.[8] The doctrine of rigidity, he says, 'is a doctrine about the truth conditions, with respect to counterfactual situations, of (the propositions expressed by) all sentences, including simple sentences' (*NN*, p. 12). So, in understanding a simple sentence, we have to know its truth conditions *simpliciter* and its truth conditions with respect to counterfactual situations. I mention here what Kripke regards as a misunderstanding on Dummett's part in order to sharpen the novelty of this modal conception of meaning, which is probably what escaped Dummett. Relying on the conventional (i.e. non-modal) conception of meaning, Dummett naturally construed Kripke's insistence on the modal factor in understanding the meaning of a term as understanding the meaning of modal sentences containing it.[9] But this, on Kripke's view, is a mistake. Understanding the truth conditions of a sentence in a counterfactual situation is required, on Kripke's conception, for understanding any sentence, including simple ones (sentences without operators, modal or otherwise), with no view to their possible role in modal complexes. In order to understand a simple

[8] Dummett probably remained unconvinced, for he repeats virtually the same point, ignoring Kripke's remarks, in Dummett (1981, p. 184); and later in 1991, p. 48).

[9] I state this with hesitation, for in later writings Dummett seems to endorse the modal notion of meaning. See for instance 'Could There Be Unicorns?' in Dummett (1993, p. 335): 'Any thesis about the meaning or reference of a word must draw its substance from how we use it or should use it in hypothetical circumstances' (cf. pp. 340–1). Whether 'hypothetical' includes 'counterfactual' is unclear.

(non-modal) sentence like (1) one should know not only its actual truth conditions, but also its truth conditions in a counterfactual course of history (a course, for instance, where Aristotle was not a philosopher, and had never seen dogs). And it is precisely these truth conditions in counterfactual situations which render the meaning of (1) different from that, for example, of its Russellian analysis (*NN*, p. 9).

It is reasonable to understand this modal conception of meaning in a strong way according to which one should know the truth conditions of (1) in any counterfactual course of history relevant to the sentence (under some specification of relevance here). Thus, all counterfactual situations which differ from the actual ones concerning Aristotle, and all counterfactual situations which differ from the actual ones concerning dogs (for instance, a situation in which dogs are huge animals tearing to pieces whatever they can get hold of), should be relevant to understanding (1).

One may question my emphasizing the novelty of this conception, for it obviously has its roots in the notion of interpretation in formal semantics and model theory, and as Kripke himself remarked, some of his observations sprang from work in the semantics of modal logic (*NN*, p. 3). It was moreover brought into philosophy, one may argue, by philosophers like Carnap, who proposed a modal notion of meaning, for example in *Meaning and Necessity*. But I believe that as a requirement of our general, intuitive conceptions of meaning and of understanding simple (non-modal) sentences in natural language, it is novel.

This conception has a strong intuitive appeal. One may still wonder about its philosophical basis. What are the general principles governing the notion of meaning and its role in a theory of understanding that warrant this conception?

Our previous remarks seem to suffice for rejecting one possible answer to this query, namely, that the modal conception of meaning is based on the role of words in modal contexts. In understanding a name like 'Aristotle' we should know how to evaluate modal contexts in which it occurs. The justification for that might be derived from Frege's context principle: if the meaning of a word is its systematic contribution to all sentences in which it occurs, modal sentences should be considered as well as others. But this, from a Fregean point of view, is a weak defense, and I don't think it plays any role in Kripke's view either. It is weak because, given Frege's compositional conception and his clear hostility to holistic views, it is clear that the meaning of a simple sentence is prior to and independent of the meaning of a complex sentence containing it. Except for operators forming complex sentences, the meaning of a word (e.g. a name) is therefore primarily its contribution to simple (atomic) sentences containing it. Hence, the context principle does not provide a justification for the modal conception in the manner suggested.

Alternatively, the modal conception of meaning may have its ultimate grounds in a view Wittgenstein proposed in the *Tractatus* to the effect that understanding a sentence should be construed as independent of the facts, or of knowing the truth of any sentence (cf. 2.0211–2.0212). This is one of the central theses of the *Tractatus*, which Wittgenstein later explicitly rejected. It is unclear to me whether Kripke would want to base his modal conception of meaning (and understanding) on it, but it seems to me a promising avenue.

Up to here I have suggested that *NN* proposes an important and novel conception of meaning, according to which understanding a sentence, any sentence, involves understanding not only its actual truth conditions, but also its truth conditions in any 'relevant' counterfactual situation. It may seem quite natural to regard this modal conception as a feature of the non-cognitive attitude towards reference-determination, which, as I said before, dominates *NN*. For in holding that understanding a sentence involves knowing its truth conditions in counterfactual situations, one is in fact saying that it is independent of the facts we know (for instance, of what we know of Aristotle or dogs). And this may be taken as showing that a cognitive conception of meaning is flawed.

I suggest, however, that this temptation should be resisted. A cognitive conception should not be thus reduced to knowledge of facts: senses and the ways things are given to us are cognitive factors that are not reducible to facts and their knowledge. Moreover, our ability to assess truth conditions in counterfactual situations presumes, and is completely dependent on, our understanding their descriptions, which is itself in the realm of sense and is constrained by the ways things are given to us. Hence, it is not evident that a cognitive conception, in this broad (Fregean) sense, is incompatible with the modal notion of meaning. In the next section I shall examine some of Kripke's specific arguments against the Fregean conception. The point of this examination is not only to see whether Kripke's presentation is faithful to this or that feature of Frege's views, but to demonstrate at what turns Frege's cognitive conception can accord with the modal notion of meaning, by dissociating itself from Kripke's version of the descriptive theory. Hence, Kripke's (convincing) critique of the description theory should not discard a cognitive conception like Frege's.

Kripke's challenge from a Fregean perspective

Let us consider a typical example of the kind of arguments advanced in *NN* against the Fregean conception of the meaning of a name.[10] Consider a simple sentence like (1) 'Aristotle was fond of dogs'. The argument is based on a line of thought consisting in the following main steps:

1. *The descriptive claim*: the sense of a name like 'Aristotle' is given by a description, say 'The greatest philosopher who studied under Plato'.
2. *The synonymy assumption*: a name and its sense-giving description are synonymous – have the same sense.
3. *The Kripkean counterfactual move*: imagine a counterfactual situation in which Aristotle never studied under Plato, and Antisthenes was Plato's only student.
4. *The reference question*: to whom does 'Aristotle' refer in that counterfactual situation? – Obviously, to Aristotle, not to Antisthenes.
5. *The meaning claim*: the meaning of (1) determines also its truth conditions in the counterfactual situation described (and the meaning of 'Aristotle' should be construed accordingly). (cf. *NN*, p. 30; Salmon 1981, pp. 29–30.)[11]

This is by now almost a standard move against the Fregean conception, and it is widely considered to be conclusive. But is it? The argument seems to rely on some assumptions, which are worth spelling out:

Assumption (a): the meaning of a sentence is couched in terms of truth conditions.

Assumption (b): in general (perhaps always), the sense of a name is given by a description.

---

[10] Kripke has other arguments, which I shall not discuss here. About one – an epistemic argument – I shall remark upon later on.

[11] A typical example of Kripke's argument on this point is the following. 'If "Aristotle" meant *the man who taught Alexander the Great*, then saying "Aristotle was a teacher of Alexander the Great" would be a mere tautology. But surely it isn't; it expresses … something we could discover to be false' (*NN*, p. 30). One peculiarity of this passage is the use of italics here: why doesn't Kripke put the italicized expression in quotation marks, as he does with 'Aristotle'? If to say that 'A' means the same as 'B' is to state a synonymy, to state that the two expressions have the same meaning, then both expressions should be mentioned – not used. Kripke perhaps uses the italics here as a means for mentioning the meaning of the italicized expression (as suggested to me by Jonathan Berg). But then we still lack an argument that this is the only way of giving the meaning of 'A', without which the synonymy claim doesn't follow.

Assumption (c): if 'm' gives the meaning (sense) of 'n', they are synonymous – have the same sense.

Assumption (d): if two expressions are synonymous they have the same reference in all possible worlds ('sense determines reference').

Assumption (e): sense is 'conceptual' – it is basically a set of properties (or conditions), the satisfaction of which is sufficient and necessary for determining the reference.

Assumption (f): the modal conception of meaning: understanding a sentence involves knowing its truth conditions in counterfactual situations, and understanding a term is knowing its use in such situations.

I would like to make some comments on these assumptions from a Fregean perspective. The issues are rather intricate and I must be very brief. Let me repeat, however, that the following is written on the assumption of the ambitious reading of *NN*, according to which it is intended as an attack on a cognitive conception of the meaning of names, and not merely on a descriptive theory of names.

Assumption (a): sense and truth conditions

According to a widespread conception, stemming from Frege, meaning is given in terms of truth. According to a strong version of this conception, the meaning of a sentence is its truth conditions. The meaning of other, sub-sentential expressions is their systematic contribution to the meaning of all, or at least a distinguished class, of the sentences in which they occur. This picture is often ascribed to Frege, who is even acclaimed as being its inventor. Ascribing the general picture to Frege is, I believe, right, but ascribing to him the strong version is wrong, but this is not vital for assessing Kripke's argument. Kripke's argument need not rely on this strong version and all it needs is the weaker claim that sentences differing in truth conditions also differ in sense.

The term 'meaning' is notoriously ambiguous between Frege's late sense (*Sinn*) and reference (*Bedeutung*). The aforementioned conception applies, of course, to meaning in the sense of sense. However, Frege, to my knowledge, never speaks of the sense of a sentence as its truth conditions. By this I don't wish to deny the centrality of the notion of truth in his conception of meaning (and of logic), but this in itself does not mean that the sense of a sentence *is* its truth conditions. In *Begriffsschrift* (1999 [1879]) Frege did not yet have the systematic sense/reference distinction and spoke in terms of an undifferentiated notion of content (*Inhalt*). The notion of truth was hardly used at all.

Frege there explained his logical operators and logically compound sentences in terms of affirmation (*Bejahung*) and denial (*Verneinung*) of sentences and their possible combinations. Likewise, truth was not used in his later unpublished 'Boole's Logical Formula-language ...' of 1882. However, the analogues of the affirmation–denial table in 'Boole's Logical Calculus ...' of 1880 are couched in terms of truth, in something like the modern truth tables (Frege 1979, p. 11). The notion of truth and its centrality in logic and semantics comes to prominence in his subsequent writings, but, again, not in a way that warrants equating the sense of a sentence with its truth conditions. He usually talks of the sense of a sentence as the thought it expresses ('On Sinn and Bedeutung' (SB) and many subsequent writings), where thought is taken as a primitive, undefinable, and irreducible notion, on a par with truth. This is particularly true of the sense of simple sentences. The closest Frege comes to the general truth-conditions conception of the sense of a sentence is in section 32 of *The Basic Laws of* Arithmetic:

> Every such name of a truth-value expresses a sense, a thought. Namely, by our stipulations it is determined under what conditions the name denotes the True. The sense of this name – the thought – is the thought that these conditions are fulfilled.

There is, however, a marked difference between saying that the sense of a sentence is its truth conditions, and saying, with Frege, that it is the thought that its truth conditions are fulfilled. The most obvious difference is that truth conditions are often construed extensionally: two sentences that are true in exactly the same conditions then have the same truth conditions. On this view, the way the truth conditions are given to us, the way we conceive of them, is of no moment. This is evidently not true of Frege's conception, where the senses of two sentences may be radically different even when they have the same truth conditions. Tautologies are clear examples; statements of identity, as argued in SB, are others.[12] Frege's formulation in terms of the thought that the truth conditions are fulfilled is evidently not open to this charge, for such thoughts may be different even when the truth conditions concerned are extensionally the same.

In distinction to many alternative approaches, the Fregean conception is 'modest', or non-reductive in its orientation. Sense is explained

12 See Bar-Elli (1996, e.g. pp. 172–3). The gist of this conception is already stated in Section 8 of *Begriffsschrift*, as argued in Bar-Elli (2006).

as the thought that the truth conditions are satisfied. Thought and its intrinsic opacity or perspectiveness are ineliminable. There can be two different thoughts, with respect to the same truth conditions, that these truth conditions are satisfied. Hence, though sense is couched in terms of truth conditions, Frege would reject the thesis that the sense of a sentence is its truth conditions. However, as stated above, this is not vital for Kripke's argument.

Assumption (b): the descriptive claim

This is a central and a very widespread assumption, but its ascription to Frege has been (rightly) rejected by many Frege scholars.[13] I shall therefore not go into it in detail here. This is true of the descriptive theory (of the sense of proper names) in general. It is more emphatically true of a particular strong version of it. The idea of this version is that the description involved is, ultimately, 'pure' or 'completely universal' in that it does not include names or indexicals like pronouns and demonstratives. Ascribing the general descriptive view to Frege has a very slim basis in a note in SB (Note B, Frege 1997, p. 153) in which Frege gives an example of a case in which two persons can use the same name (with the same reference) in two different senses. When read in context, this note says nothing like the general descriptive claim. It is implausible that if Frege meant the descriptive claim in this general way he would leave such a central doctrine only to what can be implied by a note. But even there the descriptions in the examples Frege gives are not 'pure'.

In general, Frege speaks of the sense of a name as a way its reference is presented or given to us, or as a constituent of a thought. The former is the principal way he introduces sense in SB; it recurs, for instance in his 1918 article 'Der Gedanke' (65–6, 333, in Frege 1997) and in his correspondence (Frege 1980, e.g., p. 80). The latter occurs mainly in *The Basic Laws of Arithmetic*. There is no reason to suppose that this way can be expressed by such a 'pure' description. Fregean sense is often described (mainly by Dummett and many following him) as a 'route to the reference', or a way of determining the reference of a term. This has only a slim basis in Frege, and has a different orientation and overtones from Frege's characterization. Frege's notion of sense – a way something is given to us – is epistemic: it is, as it were, directed from the world to us (as linguistic creatures). The Dummettean characterization has a semantical orientation and goes, as it were, in the opposite direction – from us (or our language) to the world.

---

13 Beginning perhaps already with Dummett (1973, e.g. pp. 110, 135). See also, e.g., Burge (1979, p. 224ff.).

Moreover, the descriptive theory, as a particular version of the 'route to the reference' conception, has often been conceived in terms of satisfaction – the described object is the one satisfying the description. Satisfying is then construed in terms of a concept applying to (being true of) an object. The relationship between sense (of a name) and reference (object) is therefore construed in this conception in terms of properties or concepts applying to the object – in terms of predication. As an explication of Frege's view this is definitely wrong (see Assumption (e) below). He was explicit that the relationship of sense to reference is not predicative but entirely different.[14] I therefore think that there are good reasons to claim that Frege would reject (b).

Assumption (c): sense-determination and synonymy

This assumption is not less problematic from a Fregean perspective. In discussing meaning-determination Kripke assumes that the only way one could 'give' or determine the meaning (sense) of an expression is by using a synonymous one. Kripke often talks this way and passes smoothly from meaning-determination to synonymy determination as if they were the same. This is a possible and quite widespread conception, but from a Fregean perspective it does not seem to be correct.

The sense of a name is, for Frege, a way its reference is given to us. It is not clear what 'giving the sense' of an expression, as it occurs in (b), means here. The clear exception to this is the very special case of giving a stipulative definition (what Frege calls in 'Logic in Mathematics' (1979, p. 212) a 'constructive (*abauende*) definition'), where an expression which was senseless ('not in use') is given sense by stipulating a definition. This is a case in which 'giving the sense' of an expression is clear; and it is a case in which such a procedure results in stating a synonymy – after stipulating the definition the two expressions have the same sense. But this is a very special case, which is rare outside of mathematics and logic, and even there it cannot apply to all terms. In the case of many words (names) in a natural language, one does not 'give' the sense of an expression by another. Rather, the sense is expressed by using the term to refer to its reference. And even when the sense may be suggested by another expression, as in what Frege calls the 'analytical (*zerlegende*) definition', the picture is much more complicated, and they are not synonymous. The criterion of

[14] I expanded on this and on a related mistake of regarding senses as objects in Bar-Elli (2009, chs 3 and 9).

synonymy for Frege is that it must be self-evident, which is rarely, and with respect to proper names almost never, the case. Even his main logical definitions of the central arithmetical notions of the natural numbers, of the concept of number or of following in a series were not regarded by Frege as self-evident, or as resulting in synonymous expressions. 'Analytical definitions', or explications, of terms in use, are in general not synonymous to these terms (Frege, 1979, pp. 208–12, in particular 210).[15]

One can, for example, 'give' the meaning (sense) of a name by a particular way of stating what its reference is. Dummett presented Frege's view in a similar manner, using Wittgenstein's distinction between saying and showing. Alternatively, one can explain the meaning of a term, in a Wittgensteinean spirit, by describing the way it is used, or by giving examples of its application, etc. Another approach, perhaps less Fregean and more Davidsonian in spirit, was argued by J. McDowell (1977), and there are others. All these seem to be compatible with Frege's basic doctrines about sense. And they are all uncommitted to the synonymy condition. Hence, it is very doubtful whether Frege could accept Assumption (c); I think he should not.

Assumption (d): reference in possible worlds

Frege, of course, did not think of sense in terms of possible worlds or counterfactual situations, and it is hard to know what he would say on this. But insofar as this thesis expresses the Fregean doctrine that sense determines reference – a sense has determinate reference in each possible world (waiving aside for the moment indexicals, which pose a special problem) – it is quite Fregean in spirit.

Assumption (e): sense as a property

This assumption is again objectionable from a Fregean perspective. Properties, for Frege, are concepts – the references of predicates: 'I call the concepts under which an object falls its properties' ('Concept and Object' in Frege 1997, p. 189). Therefore, clearly, a sense is not a property (concept) or a set of properties. A sense of a name is a way in which its reference is presented or given to us, and Frege was very clear and persistent in distinguishing it from properties of the referent (object).

---

[15] I have expanded on Frege's notion of analytical (*zerlegende*) definition in Bar-Elli (2014) and in more detail in Bar-Elli (2013).

It is also misleading to think of the sense of a term as a condition, the satisfaction of which determines the reference:

> Now it is easy to become unclear about this by confounding the division into concepts and objects with the distinction between sense and meaning (reference), so that we run together sense and concept on the one hand and meaning (reference) and object on the other. (Frege 1979, p. 118; cf. SB (1997, p. 158); 1979, p. 194; letter to Husserl 24 May 1891, (1997, p. 149)).

Frege's conception of sense was intrinsically intentionalistic. A sense is not a mediating entity between a term and its reference – it is a way in which the reference is given, a way that is intrinsically connected to its reference. Frege's conception of reference is, in this light, direct; it is not mediated by a conceptual condition that the reference has to satisfy.[16]

Assumption (f): the modal conception of meaning

I have already suggested that although Frege did not speak of meaning in modal terms of possible worlds and counterfactuals, such a view can be incorporated quite naturally in his cognitivistic conception of meaning.

We thus see that the argument against Frege's conception of meaning is inconclusive, from a Fregean point of view, independently of the modal conception of meaning. In other words, a Fregean may accept this modal conception of meaning, without accepting the argument in its entirety – he may have enough degrees of freedom to incorporate the modal conception of meaning within the general principles of his theory of sense.

Kripke advances another main argument against the descriptive theory, and claims that the theory is wrong not only with regard to the meaning (sense) of names but also with regard to the determination of their reference. This kind of argument is exemplified in detail mainly in the second lecture of NN, and has often been referred to in the literature as 'the epistemic argument'. The descriptive theory allegedly claims that the reference of a name is determined by a description – 'the so and so' – even though the description need not be giving the meaning (sense) of the name, i.e. the name and the description are not supposed to be synonymous. Kripke advances two arguments against the theory.

(i) It is rarely, if ever, the case that a speaker knows or believes a description, which individuates the referent of a given name. Thus very few

[16] I have elaborated on this conception of sense and on its implications in Bar-Elli (1996, esp. chs 1 and 7).

users of 'Einstein' know or believe individuative descriptions about him (see e.g. *NN*, pp. 80–2). Hence, their competent use of the name cannot be conditioned on such knowledge.

(ii) It is a fortiori not the case that even if the identity between a name and a description is in fact true, it is known a priori, as one could expect it to be if the referent of the name were determined by the description (see e.g. *NN*, pp. 87–90). In other words, even if the description in fact applies to the referent of the name, we can easily conceive that it might turn out not to be so. And even if we strongly believe such an identity, we can easily imagine ourselves to be proved, after all, wrong.

There are two remarks I wish to make about these arguments, and, since I am concerned in this chapter mainly with the notion of meaning (not of reference) I shall be very brief here. First, few people, I believe, would deny (i). It is usually handled by some version of what Putnam called 'the division of linguistic labor' (and to which Kripke himself hints at in *NN*). But this seems to suggest that when the speech community is considered as a whole, and when we consider the meaning of a name in a language, not in this or that idiolect, Kripke's counter-examples lose much of their force. For in the community at large some identifying descriptions of the reference are known.

As to (ii), why should we know a priori of a description that it is true of a referent?[17] Well, if the description fixes the referent (as the reference of a term), then it seems we should know a priori that it is true of the referent. If this were the standard or typical way a reference is given or is being 'fixed', the argument would have much force. When considered as a thesis against Frege's view, much depends here on how one understands 'sense' or 'way of being given' or 'a mode of presentation' (all translations of Frege's *Art des Gegebenseins* and correlated expressions) in these contexts. Many scholars, including notably Dummett, construe this notion as 'a way of determining the referent', or 'a route to the reference', something like a sort of algorithm that one can follow to get to the referent. A descriptive theory of reference-determination fits in quite naturally here. In some very special contexts this picture of sense may be adequate and present Frege's views fairly, but, as noted above, as a general picture of the senses of names, and of the Fregean notion

[17] I leave here aside the difference between the notion of apriority assumed by Kripke (which may be quite the standard one today) and Frege's notion, which has to do only with justification or justifiability (I have expanded on this in Bar-Elli 2010).

of 'mode of presentation', it is, I believe, wrong and misleading. A mode of presentation of an object, a way it presents itself to us, as understood by Frege, need not lend itself to a non-circular descriptive articulation. Debarred of this picture, there is no reason to expect a non-circular description to be a priori true of the referent. So here again, strong as the Kripkean arguments may be against a descriptive theory, conjoined with the above algorithmic picture of 'determining the reference', they lose much of their force when directed against a cognitive approach, which is dissociated from these, as I believe Frege's view was.

To sum up, although its ultimate philosophical grounds may be unclear, *NN* makes a strong case for an important, and quite novel, modal feature of the notion of meaning. But this conception, in itself, doesn't tell against the basic principles of Frege's notion of sense. Rather, it can be incorporated within the framework of these principles. As noted in the beginning, *NN* may be read narrowly, as launching an attack on the descriptive conception of names. This of course is important enough, and from this perspective the question of whether Frege actually held such a position is of minor significance. *NN* may be read, however, more broadly as having a more ambitious aim: to discard any cognitive conception of meaning and of reference-determination. It is under this more ambitious reading that *NN* is rightly regarded as a landmark in the philosophy of language, and this, I believe, is the way many people have read it. For people (like myself), who believe that Frege founded and paved a way for a viable cognitive conception of meaning, an argument against such a conception cannot disregard Frege's actual views (even if amended here and there). If the arguments in *NN* are not directed against them as they are, their sting against a cognitive conception of sense is somewhat blunted.

This may hold well, however, also apart of this or that aspect of Frege's actual views. For assessing the cogency of Kripke's arguments on the ambitious reading of *NN*, it is enough if a sort of cognitive, non-descriptive conception of sense and of reference-determination is viable, by being based, for example on the notion of a way of being given (for objects and other types of referents). For any such view the Kripkean arguments may remain effective against a descriptive conception of sense and of reference-determination, but much less so against the other sort of cognitive approach to these notions.

References

Bar-Elli, G. (1996) *The Sense of Reference: Intentionality in Frege*. Berlin and New York: De Gruyter.

Bar-Elli, G. (2006) Identity in Frege's *Begriffsschrift*. *Canadian Journal of Philosophy* 36.

Bar-Elli, G. (2009) *The Fathers of Analytic Philosophy, vol. 1: Frege: Logic, Meaning, Intentionality* (in Hebrew). Jerusalem: Goryn.

Bar-Elli, G. (2010) Analyticity and Justification in Frege. *Erkenntnis* 73.

Bar-Elli, G. (2013) Philosophical Constraints on Analytic Definitions in Frege. Unpublished MS.

Bar-Elli, G. (2014) Three Kantian Strands in Frege's View of Arithmetic. *The Journal of the History of Analytic Philosophy* 2.

Burge, T. (1979) Sinning Against Frege. *Philosophical Review* 88; reprinted in his *Truth, Thought and Reason*. Oxford: Oxford University Press, 2005.

Carnap, R. (1956) *Meaning and Necessity*. Chicago: University of Chicago Press.

Dummett, M. (1973) *Frege: The Philosophy of Language*. London: Duckworth.

Dummett, M. (1981) *The Interpretation of Frege*. London: Duckworth.

Dummett, M. (1991) *The Logical Basis of Metaphysics*. Cambridge: Harvard University Press.

Dummett, M. (1993) *The Seas of Language*. Oxford: Oxford University Press.

Frege, G. (1999 [1879]) *Begriffsschrift*. In J. van Heijenoort (ed.) *From Frege to Goedel*. Cambridge: Harvard University Press.

Frege, G. (1964) *The Basic Laws of Arithmetic*, trans. M. Furth. Berkeley: University of California Press.

Frege, G. (1979) *Gottlob Frege: Posthumous Writings*, trans. P. Long and R. White, eds H. Hermes, F. Kambartel, and F. Kaulbach. Oxford: Basil Blackwell.

Frege, G. (1980) *Philosophical and Mathematical Correspondence* (tr. H. Kaal), Chicago: Chicago University Press.

Frege, G. (1997) *The Frege Reader*, ed. M. Beaney. Oxford: Blackwell.

Kripke, S. (1979) Speaker's Reference and Semantic Reference (SRSR). In P. French, T.E. Uehling and H.K. Wettstein (eds) *Contemporary Perspectives in the Philosophy of Language*. Minneapolis: University of Minnesota Press, 6–28.

Kripke, S. (1980) *Naming and Necessity* (NN). Cambridge: Harvard University Press.

Kripke, S. (1982) *Wittgenstein on Rule Following and Private Language*. Oxford: Blackwell.

McDowell, J. (1977) On the Sense and Reference of Proper Names. *Mind* 86: 159–85. Reprinted in M. Platts (ed.) *Reference, Truth and Reality*. London: Routledge.

Salmon, N. (1981) *Reference and Essence*. Princeton: Princeton University Press.

Wettstein, H. (1986) Has Semantics Rested On a Mistake? *Journal of Philosophy* 83: 185–209.

Wittgenstein, L. (1971) *Tractatus Logico-Philosophicus*, trans. D. Pears and B. McGuinness. London: Routledge.

7

Semantics in the Twilight Zone

Jonathan Berg

In 'A Puzzle about Belief' Saul Kripke tells the tale of Pierre, whose pronouncements regarding his urban likes and dislikes have become legendary. But the final conclusion of Kripke's paper seems to remain widely unknown, misunderstood, or neglected. In the last paragraph of the paper Kripke concludes that the case of Pierre 'lies in an area where our normal apparatus for the ascription of belief is placed under the greatest strain and may even break down'. This is the area David Kaplan has dubbed 'the Twilight Zone'. In this chapter I shall try to clarify what the Twilight Zone is, how we get into it, and what we should do about it.

I shall begin by briefly reviewing the main argument of 'A Puzzle about Belief' in order to clarify just which of Kripke's conclusions it is that I wish to discuss. Then, after extricating some assumptions about belief attributions on which Kripke seems to rely, I shall go on to show how these particular assumptions about belief attributions may be derived from entirely general considerations about natural language. Turning next to how one might react to the general type of phenomena being considered, I will argue for the preferability of trying to push back the bounds of the Twilight Zone. I shall then describe two ways in which this might be done, and finally I shall briefly show how this discussion might bear on the semantics of belief.

A standard interpretation of 'A Puzzle about Belief'

In order to highlight what I think has not been sufficiently appreciated in Kripke's paper, I shall first review what I take to be the standard interpretation of it. According to this interpretation, Kripke is objecting to the traditional rejection, by *reductio ad absurdum*, of the Principle of Substitutivity. The principle may be formulated thus:

Principle of Substitutivity (SUB):
Codesignative proper names are interchangeable *salva veritate*.

And the traditional *reductio* argument against it may be formulated thus:

Traditional rejection of SUB by *reductio ad absurdum*:
1. Suppose SUB is true.
2. Then if Jones thinks Cicero is bald, then since Cicero is Tully, Jones must think Tully is bald.
3. But Jones might think Cicero is bald without thinking Tully is bald.
4. So SUB must be false. QED

Kripke objects that this *reductio* is not valid, since more is supposed than just SUB. In particular, the third premise seems to rely on this supposition:

Principle of Disquotation (DISQ):
If a normal English speaker, on reflection, sincerely assents to 'p', then he believes that p.

So, since the *reductio* relies on supposing more than just SUB, it does not show that SUB is false; it could just as well be a *reductio* of DISQ – especially since DISQ yields a contradiction even without SUB (as illustrated by the case of Pierre).

This interpretation – which I take to be more or less standard – is a reasonable one, as far as it goes; but it does not go quite far enough. That it is reasonable as far as it goes is born out by this concluding remark of Kripke's:

> We repeat our conclusions: Philosophers have often, basing themselves on Jones' and similar cases, supposed that it goes virtually without saying that belief contexts are not 'Shakespearean'. I think that, at present, such a definite conclusion is unwarranted. (1979, p. 160)

But the continuation of the very same passage suggests that the standard interpretation does not go far enough:

> Rather Jones' case, like Pierre's, lies in an area where our normal apparatus for the ascription of belief is placed under the greatest strain and may even break down. (Ibid.)

It is one thing to say that the traditional grounds for rejecting SUB are inadequate, and that they cut at least as well against DISQ. It is quite another to say that certain cases of belief ascription lie in a semantically anomalous area where our normal apparatus for the ascription of belief may well just break down. Although this latter claim does not appear in the central parts of the paper (and may not have always been explicit in earlier oral versions), it figures prominently in the paper's concluding pages, not only in the passage cited but in the following as well:

> The situation of the puzzle seems to lead to a breakdown of our normal practices of attributing belief and even of indirect quotation. (Ibid., p. 155)

> It is wrong to blame unpalatable conclusions about Jones on substitutivity. The reason does not lie in any specific fallacy in the argument but rather in the nature of the realm being entered. Jones's case is just like Pierre's: both are in an area where our normal practices of attributing belief, based on the principles of disquotation and translation or on similar principles, are questionable. (Ibid., p. 157)

> When we enter into the area exemplified by Jones and Pierre, we enter into an area where our normal practices of interpretation and attribution of belief are subjected to the greatest possible strain, perhaps to the point of breakdown. (Ibid., p. 158)

It is Kripke's conclusion about the breakdown of normal practices of belief ascription that I think has been insufficiently appreciated and which I would like to examine more closely.

Kripke's view of the Twilight Zone

Kripke provides several characterizations of the Twilight Zone (*de re*, of course) as a place in which:

(i) There is a breakdown of our normal practices of attributing belief;
(ii) Our normal practices of attributing belief, based on the principles of disquotation and translation or on similar principles, are questionable;
(iii) Our normal practices of interpretation and attribution of belief are subjected to the greatest possible strain, perhaps to the point of breakdown;

(iv) Our normal apparatus for the ascription of belief is placed under the greatest strain and may even break down.

These formulations seem to rely on three underlying assumptions about belief attributions, which I would like to spell out. First, there is an assumption about normal practice:

> **Assumption 1:**
> We have normal ways of using the word 'believes' and its synonyms and cognates, and normally there is no problem in doing so.

For example, normal use of the word 'believes' is described in part by DISQ. A more general principle which Kripke applies to belief attributions is this:

> **Principle of Translation (TRANS):**
> If a sentence of one language expresses a truth in that language, then any translation of it into any other language also expresses a truth (in that language). (Ibid., p. 139)

Since TRANS applies to all sentences, it describes in particular normal usage of sentences containing the word 'believes'.

Another assumption underlying Kripke's characterizations of the Twilight Zone concerns the possibility of strain:

> **Assumption 2:**
> Using these words ('believes', etc.) in the normal ways (in accordance with DISQ, TRANS, etc.) may be difficult in unusual cases.

The difficulty in applying DISQ universally is well-known. Even after laboring to shore it up against counter-examples, Kripke readily concedes that the principle may well be in need of still further qualifications. And as Kripke notes, even such an innocuous norm of usage as TRANS runs into trouble (as in the case of 'This sentence is in English').

The final assumption I would like to make explicit is about normal practices breaking down:

> **Assumption 3:**
> In some unusual cases, these practices (in accordance with DISQ, etc.) might not be feasible – there might not be any way at all to use these words ('believes', etc.) in these ways.

This, of course, is what seems to happen in the case of Pierre; and these are the cases comprising the Twilight Zone.

A broader view of the Twilight Zone

The picture of the Twilight Zone as it emerges in 'A Puzzle about Belief' concerns only the word 'believes' and its synonyms and cognates; and it emerges only by observation in the particular case of Pierre (and Peter). But given some plausible assumptions about the semantics of natural language, what happens in the case of Pierre can be seen as a particular instance of a general phenomenon pervading natural language. And the existence of this general phenomenon, which Kripke's puzzle so ingeniously illustrates, can be derived on the basis of completely general considerations about meaning and use. So, whereas Kripke arrives at a circumscribed Twilight Zone by means of a bottom-up approach, I would like to show how a top-down approach can lead us to a very far-reaching Twilight Zone.

I shall begin with a couple of empirical facts, which may be presented as a view of semantics:

> **Extrapolation-Based Semantics (EBS):**
> How we use words and what they mean depend on how they have normally been used.

There are two threads to this line, one psycholinguistic and the other lexicographical. The psycholinguistic point is that we go about using words by extrapolating from typical cases. In deciding whether to use a particular word on a particular occasion, we are guided by our past experience with the word, trying to carry on in accordance with those uses of the word we have experienced that we take as paradigmatic (normal, typical, exemplary, classic). Of all the times I have heard (or seen) a word used, there are some that I take as paradigmatic – as opposed to borderline cases, nonliteral uses, errors, etc.[1] It is on the basis of these that I judge whether the word is the right one to use in a new case.

The other thread of EBS is lexicographical: claims about what particular expressions mean in particular natural languages are claims about

---

[1] I use the word 'paradigmatic' in the ordinary sense, as roughly synonymous with 'typical', 'normal', exemplary', etc. This is to be distinguished from whatever technical senses the word has acquired in psychological theory.

standard linguistic practice among the speakers of that language. That is, a word means what it means in a particular language in virtue of how the speakers of that language normally use it. The word 'chair', for instance, has the English meaning it has because it has been the custom among English speakers to use it with regard to chairs; had the word 'chair' normally been used with regard to tables rather than chairs, it would have had an entirely different meaning (i.e. the meaning that the word 'table' now has).

If we accept EBS – which seems hard to deny – we may derive three general principles, of which the three aforementioned assumptions underlying Kripke's characterizations of the Twilight Zone are specific instances:

> **Principle of Normal Practice:**
> We have normal ways of using words (exemplified by uncontroversial, paradigm cases), and normally (in cases not too dissimilar from paradigm cases) there is no problem in doing so.
>
> **Principle of Strain:**
> As cases diverge from the paradigmatic, it may be difficult to use the words in the normal way – i.e. it may be unclear how to extrapolate from the most normal cases to less normal cases.
>
> **Principle of Breakdown:**
> In sufficiently unusual cases there is no natural (coherent, principled, straightforward) way to extrapolate from usual cases.

A classic formulation of the principles of EBS is provided by Wittgenstein:

> It is only in normal cases that the use of a word is clearly prescribed; we know, are in no doubt, what to say in this or that case. The more abnormal the case, the more doubtful it becomes what we are to say. And if things were quite different from what they actually are – if there were for instance no characteristic expression of pain, of fear, of joy; if rule became exception and exception rule; or if both became phenomena of roughly equal frequency – this would make our normal language-games lose their point. (1958, §142)

For example, consider the word 'chair'. As the Principle of Normal Practice predicts, we have normal ways of using the word 'chair', and normally there is no problem using the word in these ways. Just as

DISQ describes normal usage of 'believes', we can formulate principles describing normal usage of 'chair', e.g.:

> **Principle of Shape (SHAPE):**
> If something looks like this it is a chair:

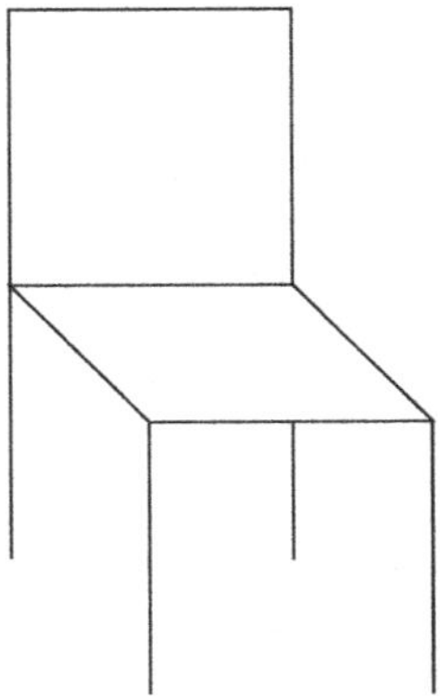

> (That is (?), if something is shaped like two adjacent faces of a cube, along with the four parallel edges of the cube on the other side of one of those faces that are perpendicular to that face, it is a chair.)

(As with DISQ one might take the biconditional of this as the Strengthened Principle of Shape.) However, as predicted by the Principle of Strain, SHAPE is not as easily applied to chairs that are less paradigmatically chair-shaped. When we are dealing with chairs that verge on being stools, chairs that verge on being benches, pedestal chairs, or other unusually shaped chairs, our normal practice of ascribing chairhood on the basis of SHAPE is subjected to strain. And then, as predicted by the Principle of Breakdown, there seem to be some extreme cases to which there is no way at all to extrapolate from the usual cases of chairhood. For instance, although chairs are usually the right size for one person to sit on, there could be perfectly chair-shaped objects that are extremely large or extremely small – the size of a building, say, or the size of a pea. Would these objects be chairs? It is doubtful whether there is any simple, correct answer to this question. And even if there were, it seems one could always concoct cases even more bizarre – as does Wittgenstein:

> I say 'There is a chair'. What if I go up to it, meaning to fetch it, and it suddenly disappears from sight? – 'So it wasn't a chair, but some kind of

> illusion.' – But in a few moments we see it again and are able to touch it and so on. – 'So the chair was there after all and its disappearance was some kind of illusion.' – But suppose that after a time it disappears again – or seems to disappear. What are we to say now? (1958, §80)

Such an object, oscillating in and out of existence, is neither clearly a chair nor clearly the mere illusion of a chair; the principles that normally guide our use of the word 'chair' are of little use here. Just as Kripke says of the belief puzzles that they 'are in an area where our normal practices of attributing belief, based on the principles of disquotation and translation or on similar principles, are questionable' (1979, p. 157), so too we see that the chair puzzles are in an area where our normal practices of attributing chairhood, based on the Principle of Shape or on similar principles, are questionable.

Thus, from the perspective of EBS it quickly becomes evident that the Twilight Zone is not peculiar to Kripke's puzzle about belief. Rather, Kripke's puzzle is an instance of a general phenomenon to be expected in connection with many (if not all) expressions of natural language; for we find ourselves in the Twilight Zone whenever any word is used in unusual enough circumstances. Semantic breakdown is inevitable, in that our normal practices with regard to the use of any word (more or less) are bound to become questionable, if not altogether inapplicable, at some point of deviation from normal circumstances.

Coping with breakdown

How should we deal with the semantic breakdown awaiting us in the Twilight Zone? I would like to consider three kinds of responses.

First, if you think the Twilight Zone affects only selected, expendable expressions, you might simply choose to leave them out of your semantic theory. This seems to be an approach that Quine has advocated:

> The notion of knowing or believing who or what someone or something is, is utterly dependent on context . . . Of itself the notion is empty . . . Our renunciation must extend to all *de re* belief, and similarly, no doubt, for the other propositional attitudes . . . I see the verb 'believe' even in its *de dicto* use as varying in meaningfulness from sentence to sentence. (1977, p. 273)

Faced with breakdown phenomena for a particular expression – such as the verb 'believe' (or the adverb 'necessarily') – one might conclude that it simply has no coherent semantics – and hence no place in one's semantic theory. This is no problem for a theorist whose logico-semantical objective is 'to distill the essence of scientific discourse' (Quine 1955, p. 235) – assuming there are enough other expressions that do *not* suffer from semantic breakdown (so that the distillation process will leave enough for the requisite 'vehicle of austere scientific theory' (1987, p. 159)). But as I have argued above, such an assumption is not tenable; the Twilight Zone is not limited to incidental, exotic cases, but rather pervades the semantics of natural language.

Alternatively, if you think semantic theory cannot cope with any semantic breakdown at all, then when the Twilight Zone looms ahead, you might decide to give up on semantics altogether. This position has been suggested by Stephen Schiffer:

> I have proposed that, if natural languages have compositional truth theories, then the hidden-indexical theory is the correct account of the accommodation of belief ascriptions in them. I have also offered some reason for thinking the hidden-indexical theory is false. If it is both conditionally correct and false, then it follows that natural languages do not have compositional truth theories. (1992, p. 519)

If the semantic theory of a language must determine the truth-conditions of every sentence of the language, then if any sentence of the language lacks fully determinate truth-conditions, the language can have no semantic theory. And sentences lacking determinate truth-conditions – in the form of semantic breakdown – is exactly what we find in the Twilight Zone. So one might take the discovery of the Twilight Zone as proof of the impossibility of semantics.

Such a rejection of semantics in response to the Twilight Zone is based on the assumption that the semantic theory of a language must determine the truth-conditions of every sentence of the language. But how reasonable is this assumption? Specifically, how reasonable is it to suppose that the semantic theory of a natural language cannot tolerate any semantic breakdown in the language? Preposterous as it is to think that a semantic theory might apply where semantics breaks down, it does not follow that there is no place for semantic theories at all. Instead of demanding of a semantic theory that it apply to every single sentence of the language in every single circumstance, we might more modestly expect it to apply only to those sentences and circumstances where semantics does *not* break down. Indeed, this more modest view of the constraints on semantic theories would appear to be a consequence of EBS. For according to the Principle of Normal Practice, there are at least *some* ways of using words in at least *some* cases that are regular enough to bear a coherent semantic theory; whereas according to the Principle of Breakdown, there are also some cases where the semantic theory that normally works breaks down.

So, instead of reacting to the semantic breakdown of an expression by denying that there is any coherent semantic theory for the language containing it, or even by denying just that there is any coherent semantic theory for that expression, one might try to make the best of a tough situation by seeking a semantic theory that goes as far as possible – a coherent theory for a maximal fragment of the language, including at least all the normal cases. For we aim in the semantics of natural language to formulate precise theories of imprecise phenomena. This qualitative difference between our semantic theories and their objects is forcefully marked by Carnap:

> A language, as, e.g., English, is a system of activities or, rather of habits, i.e., dispositions to certain activities, serving mainly for the purposes of communication and of co-ordination of activities among the members of a group . . . Strictly speaking, the rules which we shall lay down [as the *semantical rules* of a natural language, on the basis of observed facts of how expressions are used by the speakers of the language] are not rules of the factually given language *B* [such as English]; they rather constitute a language system corresponding to *B* which we call the *semantical system B-S*. (1955, pp. 145, 149)

As long as we recognize that something as loose and fluid as a system of activities or habits cannot reasonably be expected to submit straightforwardly to an entirely general and precise model, we may, with no fear of the Twilight Zone, continue to pursue the best semantic theories we can.[2]

---

[2] Cf. Putnam: 'I want to suggest that semantics is a typical social science. The sloppiness, the lack of precise theories and laws, the lack of mathematical rigor, are all characteristic of the social sciences today. A general and precise theory . . . is still a long way off. But the fact that Utopia is a long way off does not mean that daily life should come to a screeching halt. There is plenty for us to investigate, in our sloppy and impressionistic fashion, and there are plenty of real results to be obtained' (1970, p. 142).

Pushing back the Twilight Zone: pragmatics

The goal of maximizing the fragments of language to which our semantic theories apply amounts to minimizing the fragments of language to which they do not apply – and for theories adequately covering the normal cases, this amounts to pushing back the borders of the Twilight Zone. How might this be accomplished? That is, when confronted with Twilight Zone cases, in which our normal practices with regard to the use of an expression do not apply in any consistent straightforward way, how might we nevertheless manage to extrapolate from normal practice?[3]

One strategy for pushing back the Twilight Zone is to make use of the distinction between semantics and pragmatics. This is the strategy pioneered by Grice. Consider, for instance, the case of my uttering the sentence 'It looks red to me' when I see a plainly red object in ordinary daylight. One principle governing normal uses of such a sentence is this:

> Say a sentence of the form 'It looks φ to me' whenever you want to indicate that the demonstrated thing gives you the kind of visual sensations that you normally get from things that are φ.

But another principle applying to normal uses of such a sentence is this:

> Say a sentence of the form 'It looks φ to me' only when you think there is some significant doubt about whether the demonstrated thing is indeed φ.[4]

Thus, in the given case these principles yield conflicting results – that is, our normal practices of reporting sensations based on these principles break down. Grice's strategy here is to distinguish between the

---

[3] I have been equivocating in my use of the expression 'the Twilight Zone' between what might be thought of as the *real* Twilight Zone and a merely *apparent* Twilight Zone. In the stronger sense the Twilight Zone has fixed (though blurry) borders, encompassing only genuine semantic indeterminacy; but in the weaker sense the borders of the Twilight Zone may shift as we discover coherent ways of extrapolating from our past linguistic experience that were not apparent at first glance.

[4] These principles could also be expressed indicatively, but I have chosen to formulate them as imperatives in order to avoid resolving any ambiguity between truth and felicity.

conditions on the normal usage of a sentence which are part of *what is said* in uttering the sentence, from those which are not. If we take the first principle but not the second as expressing a condition on what is said in an utterance of the sentence, then the semantic quandary is resolved – the Twilight Zone recedes, in that the semantic content of the utterance is unequivocally determined by normal practice (the second principle not being directly semantically relevant).[5]

Kripke himself makes use of this strategy, not on the puzzle about belief, but with regard to the referential use of definite descriptions. Suppose someone says 'the murderer of Smith is insane' when, contrary to the speaker's beliefs, the person the speaker means to speak of did not in fact murder Smith. One principle for the use of definite descriptions is this:

> An utterance of a sentence of the form 'the F is G' is true iff there is a unique thing which is F and it is also G.

But another principle is this:

> An utterance of a sentence of the form 'the F is G' is true iff the thing the speaker referred to (meant to refer to) as 'the F' is G.

If we suppose in the case at hand that the person the speaker has in mind is indeed insane, but that Smith was murdered by exactly one person, who is not insane, then we seem to be once again in the Twilight Zone, with normal practice breaking down in contradiction. One way to remove this case from the Twilight Zone would be to say that sentences of the form 'the F is G' have two separate meanings, in accordance with these two principles. Thus, there would be no contradiction, just as there is no contradiction in saying 'Betty likes bats' and 'Betty doesn't like bats' if one is referring in one case to a kind of sports equipment and in the other to a kind of flying mammal.[6] However, the method that Kripke prefers for pushing back the Twilight Zone here is

---

[5] Since the Twilight Zone is delineated only by *semantic* breakdown, it does not necessarily obtain wherever normal usage warrants incompatible ways of using an expression. Rather, the Twilight Zone obtains only where normal practice fails to determine *semantic* content.

[6] Aside from positing ambiguity, there are still more ways to deal with Twilight Zone phenomena, such as by appeal to indexicality; but I shall discuss here only the two methods to which this and the next section are devoted.

to use Grice's strategy. Kripke rejects the second principle, accounting for whatever plausibility it might have by distinguishing between the *semantic* referent of an expression of the form 'the F' and the *speaker's* referent – the thing the speaker means to refer to (what he or she wishes to talk about and thinks is the semantic referent).[7] Without the second principle to contradict the first, the Twilight Zone recedes.[8]

Pushing back the Twilight Zone: conceptual analysis

A different way to push back the Twilight Zone is by conceptual analysis. When normally compatible practices with regard to the use of an expression become incompatible, we might forestall semantic confusion by selecting some of those practices over others as more closely tied to the concept associated with the expression. Then, on the basis of those preferred practices – leaving aside the less preferred, incompatible practices – we would be able to extrapolate further before winding up in the Twilight Zone.

For example, our normal practices of attributing chairhood accord not only with SHAPE but also with the following:

> **Principle of Function (FUNC):**
> If something is suitable for exactly one person to sit on with back support, it is a chair.

As compatible as SHAPE and FUNC may be in the most normal cases, they collide when we get to chair-shaped objects that are not suitable for a person to sit on, or *non*-chair-shaped objects that *are* suitable for a person to sit on.[9] But when SHAPE and FUNC become incompatible, we need not surrender to the Twilight Zone. Rather, we might choose one – FUNC, say – as more semantically significant, as expressing something more essential to chairhood.[10] If so, then where SHAPE and FUNC conflict, our normal

---

[7] This is Grice's strategy, because what is said is determined by the semantic referent, not necessarily the speaker's referent.

[8] Kripke, of course, does not put it in quite these terms. On the face of it this case differs from the last, where the second principle was retained, though as pragmatic rather than semantic. The cases would look more alike if the principles in both were formulated all in terms of truth or none in terms of truth.

[9] The obvious shortcomings of my extremely oversimplified formulation of SHAPE may be overcome by a more sophisticated formulation – which I have omitted for ease of exposition.

[10] I use 'essential' here non-technically, remaining neutral with regard to essentialism.

practices of attributing chairhood might be strained, but they would not break down.

Another example of pushing back the Twilight Zone by conceptual analysis is provided by John Searle (with acknowledgments to H. Dreyfus):

> Suppose I go into a restaurant ... saying 'Give me a hamburger' ... Suppose ... that the hamburger is brought to me encased in a cubic yard of solid lucite plastic ... Has my order 'Give me a hamburger' been fulfilled or obeyed ...? My inclination is to say no, it has not been fulfilled. (1978, p. 216)

In the situation described there is a conflict between the following two principles, with which our use of the sentence 'Give me a hamburger' normally accords:

> **Principle of Edibility:**
> If somebody has given you a hamburger, you can eat it.
>
> **Principle of Ingredients:**
> If somebody brings you something containing a cooked beef patty between pieces of a round bun sliced in two, the person has given you a hamburger.

When these normally compatible principles become incompatible, one might conclude that normal practice has broken down. Instead, when push comes to shove, Searle takes the Principle of Edibility, but not the Principle of Ingredients, as semantically decisive.[11] If we so construe edibility, rather than ingredients, as more central to the concept of hamburger-giving, we may thereby put off the breakdown of our normal linguistic practice with regard to that concept.

A final example is provided by Peter Hacker:

> The expressions we employ in characterizing other people's thoughts, feelings, and experiences and in explaining what they do and say in terms of their experiences, beliefs, desires, and purposes have a use only in the stream of life . . . What prevents the literal applicability

---

[11] Searle does not make the point in these words, of course. Among other things, he discusses the case in terms of obedience-conditions of the imperative 'Give me a hamburger' – which may be construed quite differently from the truth-conditions of the indicative 'Somebody has given me a hamburger.'

> of concepts of thought, reason, and inference to our calculating devices are not deficiencies in computational power, which may be overcome by fifth generation computers. Rather, it is the fact that machines are not alive . . . Thought, inference, and reason are capacities of the animate. (1990, pp. 156, 168)

In the most normal, uncontroversial cases our use of the word 'thinks' and its synonyms and cognates respects these principles:

> **Principle of Animacy:**
> If something thinks, it is animate.
>
> **Principle of Calculation:**
> If something performs complex calculations, it thinks.

But our normal practices of attributing thought on the basis of these principles become questionable when we are confronted with something inanimate that performs complex calculations. In virtue of his views of the concepts of thought, reason, and inference, Hacker chooses the Principle of Animacy, rather than the Principle of Calculation, as capturing what is essential to thinking. Once again the Twilight Zone presumably recedes.

Whether or not any of these various attempts actually succeed, they illustrate a useful technique for carrying on with semantics in the Twilight Zone. The key to this technique is the underlying assumption that of the many principles with which our normal use of an expression might accord, some rather than others might be more closely connected to the concept associated with the expression and, hence, might be preferable as guides to extrapolation from normal cases to cases that are not so normal.

Back to belief

In light of these general remarks on semantics in the Twilight Zone, how might we address the puzzle cases of Jones and Pierre? One way would be by using Grice's strategy. Where our normal practices of attributing belief on the basis of principles such as DISQ, TRANS, SUB, and others seem to break down, we might avert the breakdown by interpreting one or another of these principles as pragmatic rather than simply semantic.[12]

---

[12] Other principles to consider include the converse of DISQ (in one version or another), as well as the principle (which Kripke uses without naming) that no logically competent person has directly contradictory beliefs.

Having discussed this approach at length elsewhere, I will not review the details here.[13]

Alternatively (or even simultaneously), we might try to rescue Jones and Pierre from the Twilight Zone by conceptual analysis. That is, we might avoid the conflict between the relevant principles by disregarding one or another of them, on the grounds that what they express is not really essential to the concept of believing. For example, recall DISQ:

> **Principle of Disquotation (DISQ):**
> If a normal English speaker, on reflection, sincerely assents to 'p', then he believes that p.

Doubts about DISQ might be aroused from the start by all the qualifications and explanations it requires:

> When we suppose that we are dealing with a normal speaker of English, we mean that he uses all words in the sentence in a standard way . . . The qualification 'on reflection' guards against the possibility that a speaker may, through careless inattention to the meaning of his words or other momentary conceptual or linguistic confusion, assert something he does not really mean, or assent to a sentence in linguistic error. 'Sincerely' is meant to exclude mendacity, acting, irony and the like. I fear that even with all this it is possible that some astute reader – such, after all, is the way of philosophy – may discover a qualification I have overlooked, without which the principle is subject to counterexample . . . Taken in it's obvious intent, after all, the principle appears to be a self-evident truth. (1979, pp. 137–8)

But even without doubting the general plausibility of DISQ, we may nevertheless ask about the nature of the connection between sincerely assenting to a sentence, on the one hand, and believing what it expresses, on the other. To what extent does this connection derive from the very concept of belief? The beginning of an answer to this question can be found in Nathan Salmon's gloss of Kripke's remark about the apparent self-evidence of DISQ: 'What makes the principle self-evident is that it is a corollary of the traditional conception of belief as inward assent to a proposition' (1986, p. 130). If Salmon is right in taking inward assent to a proposition as so central to the very concept

---

[13] See especially Berg (2012). Grice's strategy is also used in Salmon (1986).

of belief, then conceptual analysis can save Jones and Pierre from the Twilight Zone only if the principles incompatible with DISQ can be dismissed as unwarranted by the concept of belief. (Indeed Salmon argues this way, rejecting both the converse of DISQ, as well as the principle that no logically competent person has contradictory beliefs.) On the other hand, if belief is not conceptually bound to inward assent, then DISQ does not have the preferred status that Salmon would give it – and the question remains open.[14]

Conclusion

In 'A Puzzle about Belief' Kripke suggests that the puzzle cases about belief (both new and old) lie 'in an area where our normal apparatus for the ascription of belief is placed under the greatest strain and may even break down'. I have argued that from the view of extrapolation-based semantics – according to which, how we use words and what they mean depend on how they are normally used – such a Twilight Zone is not unique to belief ascriptions, but is to be expected wherever any word is used in unusual enough circumstances. Against those who view such phenomena as imposing fixed bounds on the semantics of natural language, I have shown two ways in which we might push back the bounds of the Twilight Zone – by appeal to the semantics/pragmatics distinction, and by means of conceptual analysis – and I have indicated very briefly how these techniques might be applied to the semantics of belief. Although the Twilight Zone inevitably confronts us, the truth is out there.

References

Berg, Jonathan (2012) *Direct Belief: An Essay on the Semantics, Pragmatics, and Metaphysics of Belief.* Berlin and Boston: De Gruyter Mouton.

Carnap, Rudolf (1955) *Foundations of Logic and Mathematics.* Chicago and London: University of Chicago Press; *International Encyclopedia of Unified Science* 1, 3, 1939.

Grice, Paul (1989) *Studies in the Way of Words.* Cambridge: Harvard University Press.

Hacker, P.M.S. (1990) *Wittgenstein: Meaning and Mind.* Oxford and Cambridge: Blackwell.

Kripke, Saul (1977) Speaker's Reference and Semantic Reference. *Midwest Studies in Philosophy,* 2; reprinted in Peter A. French, Theodore Edward Uehling, Jr.,

---

[14] Although I agree with Salmon about the principles he rejects, I reject DISQ as well; see Berg (2012).

and Howard K. Wettstein (eds), *Contemporary Perspectives in the Philosophy of Language*. Minneapolis: University of Minnesota Press, 1979, 6–27.

Kripke, Saul (1979) A Puzzle about Belief. In A. Margalit (ed.) *Meaning and Use*. Dordrecht: Reidel, pp. 239–83; reprinted in his (2011) *Philosophical Troubles: Collected Papers, Vol. 1*. New York: Oxford University Press, 125–61.

Putnam, Hilary (1970) Is Semantics Possible? In H. Kiefer and M. Munitz (eds), *Languages, Belief and Metaphysics*. Albany: SUNY Press; reprinted in his *Mind, Language and Reality: Philosophical Papers, Volume 2*. Cambridge: Cambridge University Press, 1975, 139–52.

Quine, W.V.O. (1955) The Scope and Language of Science. In L. Leary (ed.) *The Unity of Knowledge*. New York: Doubleday; reprinted in his *Ways of Paradox*, rev. edn. Cambridge: Harvard University Press, 1976, 228–45.

Quine, W.V.O. (1977) Intensions Revisited. *Midwest Studies in Philosophy*, 2; reprinted in Peter A. French, Theodore Edward Uehling, Jr., and Howard K. Wettstein (eds), *Contemporary Perspectives in the Philosophy of Language*. Minneapolis: University of Minnesota Press, 1979, 268–74.

Quine, W.V.O. (1987) *Quiddities*. Cambridge: Harvard University Press.

Salmon, Nathan (1986) *Frege's Puzzle*. Cambridge: MIT Press.

Schiffer, Stephen (1992) Belief Ascription. *Journal of Philosophy* 89: 499–521.

Searle, John (1978) Literal Meaning. *Erkenntnis* 13: 207–24.

Wittgenstein, Ludwig (1958) *Philosophical Investigations*, 3rd edn, trans. G.E.M. Anscombe. New York: Macmillan.

Part IV
Skepticism

8
Kripke's Infinity Argument

Oron Shagrir

In *Wittgenstein on Rules and Private Language* (*WR*), Saul Kripke (1982) advances two arguments against dispositional accounts of meaning.[1] One of them – the normativity argument – has been widely discussed. The other one – the infinity argument – has been less influential. My aim here is to investigate the scope of the infinity argument. After highlighting some differences between infinity and normativity, I will claim that the infinity argument falls short of defeating dispositional accounts of meaning. I will first claim that the argument fails to challenge even simple dispositional accounts of the meaning of perceptual terms, such as 'horse'. I will then contend that it is not conclusive against dispositional accounts of arithmetical terms, such as '+'. Finally, I will suggest that the significance of the argument should be located in the context of symbol machines. In this context, the argument points to difficulties with the idea that symbol machines are disposed to compute infinite arithmetical functions, such as *addition*. The moral is that the dispositionalist should be more careful when relying on symbol machines to account for the meaning of arithmetical terms.

In what follows, I assume the standard reading of Kripke, which has been advanced, for example, by Crispin Wright (1984; 1989), Warren Goldfarb (1985), Simon Blackburn (1984), and Paul Boghossian (1989). On this reading, the target of Kripke's arguments is *reductive* theories of meaning: dispositional theories that attempt to account for meaning in non-semantic and non-intentional terms. Among them are versions of

[1] I am grateful to Yemima Ben-Menahem, Itamar Pitowsky and Steve Yalowitz for reading and commenting on early drafts. Thanks to Saul Kripke and Mark Steiner for their insightful comments on the final version. This research was supported by The Israel Science Foundation, grant 857/03–07. "An earlier version of this paper was published in *Iyyun: The Jerusalem Philosophical Quarterly* 57 (2008): 3–24.

behaviorism, functionalism, and teleological and causal-informational theories. The crux of Kripke's arguments is ontological, not epistemological. The claim in these arguments is that there are no facts, to which the reductive theories can appeal, that constitute the correct ascription of meaning to people. Lastly, while Kripke discusses the arithmetical term '+', his arguments apply to all terms and expressions, including perceptual terms. Whether this reading is faithful to Kripke, and to what extent his arguments reflect Wittgenstein's, is beyond the scope of this chapter.

Infinity and normativity

Kripke's skeptic wonders what fact could constitute my meaning *addition* by '+' and not *quaddition* (quaddition is the two-place function whose values agree with addition when both arguments are smaller than 57, and 5 otherwise (*WR*, p. 9)). One possible answer is that meaning is dispositional:

> To mean addition by '+' is to be disposed, when asked for any sum '$x + y$', to give the sum of x and y as the answer (in particular, to say '125' when queried about '68 + 57'); to mean quus is to be disposed when queried about any arguments, to respond with their quum (in particular to answer '5' when queried about '68 + 57'). True, my actual thoughts and responses in the past do not differentiate between the plus and the quus hypotheses; but, even in the past, there were dispositional facts about me that did make such a differentiation. To say that in fact I meant plus in the past is to say – as surely was the case! – that had I been queried about '68 + 57', I *would* have answered '125'. By hypothesis I was not in fact asked, but the disposition was present none the less. (*WR*, pp. 22–3)

Kripke, however, resists this account. He says (*WR*, p. 24) that the relation between meaning *addition* and the use of '+' is a normative relation; that is, if I mean *addition* by '+', then there is a unique thing that I *ought* to do when I use '+'. The dispositionalist, however, provides only a descriptive account of this relation; he or she does not point to how I should use '+', but to how I in fact do and will use it. A dispositional analysis would work, therefore, only if there is no gap between my dispositions to perform and the correct applications of predicates. Kripke, however, provides two arguments to the effect that there is such a gap. His first argument – known as the infinity argument – contrasts my finite nature with the requirement for infinite application of predicates. On the one hand, as a finite being existing for a finite time, 'not only my actual performance, but also the totality of my dispositions, is finite' (*WR*, p. 26). My dispositions, that is, 'extend to only finitely many cases' (*WR*, p. 28). In particular:

> It is not true, for example, that if queried about the sum of any two numbers, no matter how large, I will reply with their actual sum, for some pairs of numbers are simply too large for my mind – or my brain – to grasp. When given such sums, I may shrug my shoulders for lack of comprehension; I may even, if the numbers involved are large enough, die of old age before the questioner completes his question. (*WR*, pp. 26–7)

On the other hand, if I mean *addition* by '+', I should be disposed to apply the term to any *m* and *n*, even if they are very large. It thus follows that there is a gap between the way I ought to use '+', which extends to infinitely many numbers, and the way I do and will use '+', which extends to finitely many numbers.

We can summarize the general argument as follows:

1. If my meaning *P* by a predicate *S* is dispositional, then I should be disposed to apply *S* in infinitely many cases.
2. 'The totality of my dispositions is finite' (*WR*, p. 26). My dispositions 'extend to only finitely many cases' (*WR*, p. 28).

Conclusion (by modus tollens): My meaning *P* by *S* is not dispositional.

The normativity argument is quite different. It points out the gap between my meaning *addition* by '+' and the misapplications of '+'. There is no dispute that I sometimes make mistakes in the sense that my actual use of '+' differs from the usual addition table: I sometimes forget to carry, lose attention, and so forth. But if meaning is equated with actual use, the dispositionalist cannot say that I mean *addition* by '+'. Since I am also disposed to make mistakes, the meaning of '+' could be also equated with the erroneous use. Thus the dispositionalist has to say why the meaning is equated with one disposition and not another, something he cannot do. 'According to him, the function someone means is to be *read off* from his dispositions; it cannot be presupposed in advance which function is meant' (*WR*, pp. 29–30). Yet, there is no fact, other than my intentions, that favors one disposition over another.

An important difference between normativity and infinity is this. The normativity argument does not challenge my disposition to provide the correct answer for all *types* of input pairs (m,n). The argument is that since I am *also* disposed to make mistakes, there is nothing to appeal to, other than my intentions, that can tell that '+' means *addition* and not *quaddition*. Kripke does not deny, for example, that I will usually reply '125' when queried about '67 + 58'. The argument is that given that I will sometimes reply '5', when I'm very tired, distracted, and so forth, there is nothing the dispositionalist can appeal to, other than my intentions, that could explain my meaning *addition* by '+' and not *quaddition*. In contrast, the infinity argument does challenge my disposition to provide the right answer to all types of pairs (m,n). It challenges the very possibility of a disposition that applies to infinitely many numbers. Of course, Kripke grants that we are disposed to reply '125' to '67 + 58'. But he denies that we are disposed to give the sum of m and n when m and n are large enough.

To summarize the difference, the normativity argument questions how it is possible to distinguish, in dispositional terms, between correct and incorrect usage. How can the meaning of '+' be constituted in one disposition, given that I also have the other disposition? The infinity argument questions how it is possible to apply '+' to infinitely many numbers. How can the meaning of '+' be constituted in a disposition, given that my disposition to produce the value of $m + n$ extends to only finitely many numbers?

The 'horse' case

On the standard reading, Kripke's arguments are meant to defeat dispositional analyses of all terms, even the analyses of 'simple' perceptual terms, such as 'horse' or 'green'. The infinity argument is meant to support the claim that there is an unbridgeable gap between my finite dispositions and the required, infinite application of 'horse'. On the one hand, 'my dispositions extend to only finitely many cases' (*WR*, p. 28). On the other hand, there are infinitely many actual and possible horses, including horses in the distant past and on Alpha Centauri. Thus we must conclude that I cannot be disposed to apply 'horse' to *all* horses, and, hence, my meaning *horse* by 'horse' cannot be dispositional.

Many contend that the argument is not convincing (see, e.g., Blackburn 1984, pp. 289–90; Boghossian 1989, pp. 528–30). This is not merely because the number of relevant horses might be finite, as one could argue (see, e.g., Goldfarb 1985, pp. 478–9). Even if the number is finite, it is very large, and perhaps unbounded, so the argument could still be made. The contention rather is that the infinity argument fails even if there were infinitely many horses. The true claim that I can apply 'horse' only finitely many times is consistent with being disposed to apply 'horse' to any horse, no matter how many horses there are. In what follows, I explicate this contention, and defend it against possible objections.

Consider a simple causal-informational dispositional analysis. According to this account, a speaker means by the term 'horse' a property *horse* just in case this speaker is disposed to apply the term 'horse' to objects with that property, namely, to horses. The disposition of the speaker to apply 'horse' to horses is grounded, in turn, in a causal nomological relation between the term 'horse' and the property *horse*. In particular, it is a counterfactual supportive truth that:

(1) If I were to encounter (get into a causal contact with) *any* particular horse, and asked what animal it is, I would call it 'horse'.

On influential versions of this account, advanced, for example, by Dretske (1981; 1988) and Fodor (1990), my meaning *horse* by 'horse' is associated with the content of a mental symbol **horse**. Whereas, the content of the mental symbol **horse** expresses the property *horse* by virtue of causal-nomological relations between **horse** and horses (objects that exemplify the property *horse*).

We should note that (1) does not require that I *actually* apply 'horse' to *all* horses. The requirement is just that I would apply 'horse' to *any* horse that I encounter in my lifetime. It is therefore consistent with Kripke's contention that I can apply 'horse' in finitely many cases. In fact, (1) is consistent with the stronger claim that I can *possibly* apply 'horse' in finitely many cases. To see why, assume that there are infinitely many horses, and that it is not possible for me to apply 'horse' more than ten times in my lifetime. This assumption is consistent with (1) because it is open for *any* horse to be in the class of ten applications of 'horse'.

It is now clear how the dispositionalist could reply to the infinity argument, at least with respect to perceptual terms. If the second premise – that my dispositions extend to finitely many cases – means that I can apply 'horse' in finitely many cases in my lifetime, then this premise is true. But it is also consistent with being disposed to apply 'horse' to all horses. Even if there are infinitely many horses, I can be disposed to apply 'horse' to any one of them. In that case, the first premise will be false. The meaning of 'horse' can be dispositional, without me being disposed to apply 'horse' infinitely many times. And if the second premise means that I am disposed to apply 'horse' to finitely many horses, then this premise is false. I am disposed to apply 'horse' to *any* horse, even if there are infinitely many horses, and even though I can apply 'horse' finitely many times.

Let us consider possible objections to this response. One may object that (1) does not fully capture the notion of disposition. The truth of (1) does not ensure that I am disposed to apply 'horse' to all horses. To be disposed to apply 'horse' to all horses is actually to apply 'horse' to any horse at some point in my lifetime. To explicate the objection, let us formulate (1) in an abbreviated form:

> (1) $\forall x((Hx \,\&\, Ex) \rightarrow Cx)$, where Hx = 'x is a horse', Ex = 'I encounter x', and Cx = 'I call x 'horse' (asked what animal x is)'; $\rightarrow$ should be read as a counterfactual conditional.

The objection, then, is that my disposition to apply 'horse' to all horses requires the truth of the stronger following counterfactual:

> (2) $\forall x(Hx \rightarrow (Ex \,\&\, Cx))$

Unlike (1), (2) does require that I call any of the infinitely many actual and possible horses by the word 'horse'. But since I cannot possibly accomplish this task, (2) is clearly false. Thus, my meaning *horse* by 'horse' cannot be dispositional.

My reply is that a dispositional analysis need not satisfy a strong condition of the magnitude of (2). Consider the disposition of a sample of salt to dissolve in water. We associate water-solubility with the claim: 'If this sample of salt were put in water, then it would dissolve.' But surely we understand this counterfactual in the weaker sense, analogous to (1), and not in the stronger sense, analogous to (2). Surely we do not expect a particular sample of salt to satisfy the counterfactual: 'If this sample of salt were put in *all* samples of water, it would dissolve in each of them.' In most cases, there will be nothing to put in water after our sample of salt has dissolved. Similarly, we associate the fragility of a particular piece of glass with the counterfactual: 'If (once!) dropped, the glass would break.' I thus see no reason why my disposition to apply 'horse' to horses is different from water-solubility and fragility, and requires the further constraint that I *actually* have to apply 'horse' to all horses. I may be disposed to apply 'horse' to horses without actually applying 'horse' to horses even once (see also Blackburn 1984, pp. 289–90).

There is yet another worry about (1) not capturing the notion of disposition. One may say that even if I am disposed to apply 'horse' to infinitely many horses, as (1) permits, I am still not disposed to apply 'horse' to *all* horses. I am not disposed to apply 'horse', for example, to the horses living far away on Alpha Centauri, since I cannot even survive the trip there to get into causal contact with the horses there. The objection, in other words, is that the notion of my horsy disposition requires the truth of the following counterfactual:

(3) $\forall x(Hx \rightarrow \Diamond(Ex \,\&\, Cx))$

This counterfactual is, however, false.

My reply is similar to the one before. A dispositional analysis need not satisfy a condition like (3). I am disposed to apply 'horse' to the horses on Alpha Centauri, even though I cannot get there. This sample of salt is water-soluble, even if it is not possible for it to survive the trip to Alpha Centauri, to dissolve in water there. We just require the truth of the counterfactual: 'If this sample of salt were put in the water on Alpha Centauri, it would dissolve.' Likewise, we need not require that I survive the trip to Alpha Centauri. We just need to require the truth of the counterfactual: 'If I were to get to Alpha Centauri, I would call any horse I encounter there "horse"' (see also Boghossian 1989, p. 529).

One may point out, correctly, that (1) is true only if read under a *ceteris paribus* clause. The truth of (1), that is, depends on certain ideal background conditions: that I am alive and awake, that the lighting is good, etc. If it is too dark outside, I may not call the horse in front of me 'horse', but 'cow'. On a first glance, there is nothing wrong about a *ceteris paribus* reading. Even Kripke agrees that '*ceteris paribus* notions of dispositions, not crude and literal notions, are the ones standardly used in philosophy and in science' (*WR*, p. 27). He, however, also thinks that the appeal to *ceteris paribus* clauses is illegitimate in the analysis of meaning. Whether I would have called the horses on Alpha Centauri 'horses' is something I don't know: 'How in the world can I tell what would happen if my brain were stuffed with extra brain matter, or if my life were prolonged by some magic elixir? Surely such speculation should be left to science fiction writers or futurologists' (*WR*, p. 27). Since we do not know how I am to act on Alpha Centauri, we specify ideal conditions that are in accord with what is meant. Under these conditions, (1) becomes true, but the specification is obviously circular.

The meaning of 'horse' resides in a *ceteris paribus* clause that gives rise to ideal conditions whose specifications rest on the prior assumption that 'horse' means *horse* (*WR*, p. 28).

I think that Kripke's worries about the *ceteris paribus* notions of dispositions are correct, and that they challenge a possible reply to the normativity argument. But they do not really challenge my reply to the infinity argument. Let me explain. The aim of the normativity argument is not to deny that I am disposed to apply 'horse' to horses. It is agreed that there are conditions under which I will call a horse I never encountered before, and perhaps never will, 'horse'. The concern is that since I am also disposed to apply 'horse' to cows – when the lighting conditions are bad and so forth – we cannot favor, without circularity, the *ceteris paribus* reading that picks out the application of 'horse' to horses over the application of 'horse' to horses-or-cows. Since I am *also* disposed to call cows 'horse', the *ceteris paribus* clause cannot tell which disposition is in accordance with the meaning of 'horse'. We simply favor the conditions that are in accordance with what we take to be the meaning of 'horse'.

The claim in the infinity argument is quite different. Granted that I have finite dispositions, and assuming that there are infinitely many horses, there must be horses to which I am not disposed to apply 'horse'. This would mean that there is a horse, perhaps one that lives on Alpha Centauri, to which, *under no conditions*, I will call 'horse'. If this were the case, then Kripke's complaint would have been just: we are taking the conditional 'If I were to get to Alpha Centauri, I would call any horse I encounter there "horse"' to be true, under a *ceteris paribus* reading, even though the ideal conditions implicit in the *ceteris paribus* clause do not and could not exist. Kripke, however, is in no position to claim that under all conditions the conditional is false. If the antecedent of the conditional is always false – there are no conditions under which I can encounter the horse on Alpha Centauri – then the conditional itself is always true. And if the antecedent is sometimes true – there are conditions under which I encounter the pertinent horse – it is certainly conceivable that under some of these conditions I will call this horse 'horse'. If Kripke thinks it is inconceivable, it is he who has to prove why, under all circumstances, I cannot call a horse I encounter on Alpha Centauri 'horse'. Short of an argument showing why such a case is inconceivable, which Kripke does not provide, there is no reason to suspect that the *ceteris paribus* reading of (1) is somehow illegitimate.

Lastly, one may object that (1) cannot be true because the infinitely many actual and potential horses differ from each other in many, perhaps infinitely many, respects. The worry is that a finite creature like me cannot have the appropriate powers to apply 'horse' to any of these very different horses. But, actually, I could have these powers. In fact, there are already many simple information-processing systems with such powers. Consider a flip-detector that flips '+' whenever the input voltage is higher than 2.5 volts, and '–' otherwise. There are infinitely many types of currents that can be detected. Hence, the '–' state of the detector has the powers to detect different voltages on the scale of [0,2.5], though there are infinitely many potential inputs with different currents. Similarly, there is no special reason why my mental symbol **horse** cannot detect any of the actual and potential horses, even if all these horses differ from each other.

The '+' case

We saw that the infinity argument is ineffective when applied to simple perceptual terms. But does the argument work against a dispositional analysis of other terms? It would be interesting to answer this with respect to arithmetical terms, such as '+', since these are the terms that Kripke invokes in his argument. The arithmetical case is interesting for another reason. One might argue that the analysis of '+' requires a far more powerful disposition than the analysis of 'horse'. If that is correct, then my criticism with respect to the 'horse' case is not immediately applicable to the '+' case. If the infinity argument works with respect to '+', it would still show that the meaning of *some* terms cannot be dispositional. It would still show that we cannot provide an all-inclusive account of meaning, solely in dispositional terms.

Here is why one might think that the analysis of '+' calls for a more complex disposition. In the 'horse' case, I should be able to discriminate between horses and non-horses. I should apply 'horse' to any horse I encounter, and just to horses. But I need not discriminate between types of horses. Nor is there a need to distinguish between previous horses I encountered and the one I encounter now. I apply 'horse' to only one type of objects, namely, to horses. Even if each horse constitutes a different type, I need not recognize the types of horses, but only that it is a horse. In the '+' case, besides the ability to discriminate between numbers and non-numbers, I should also be able to discriminate between different types of numbers (or, *representations of numbers*, for example, decimals). I should be able to answer '7' when asked for the value of '3 + 4', but '17' when asked for the value of '11 + 6'. The problem, however, is that there are infinitely many *types* of numbers. So

I must be able to discriminate between infinitely many types (m,n), and to produce for them infinitely many types $m+n$.

Put differently, the infinity problem in the 'horse' case is about tokens. The problem is that there are infinitely many tokens, namely horses, to which I have to be able to apply 'horse'. The infinity problem in the '+' case is *also* about types. In order to compute addition, it is not enough to tell tokens of '7' from other tokens. In addition, I should be able to discriminate between the other types of numbers. I should be able to tell tokens of '3' from tokens of '4'. But since there are infinitely many numbers, I must have the ability to discriminate between and to produce tokens of infinitely many types. But how can a finite object have this ability? How can a finite object have the required disposition given that, on the one hand, its dispositions extend to finitely many numbers, and on the other, that it should give as a reply the sum of m and n, when asked for the value of $m+n$, for any m and n?[2]

In response, one might say that we do think of infinitely many cases of the addition table; Kripke responds that anyone who says so is a liar (*WR*, p. 52, n. 34). The dispositionalist, however, might point to

---

[2] The ability to entertain or produce an unbounded number of types of expressions with finite means is known as productive or generative capacity. The ability to compute arithmetical functions is one example of productivity. Another celebrated example is the ability to recognize and generate an unbounded number of grammatical sentences (e.g. Chomsky 1965). Kripke's argument, then, seems to have a wider scope, challenging the idea that the mind/brain, as a finite object, has productive capacities, arguing that the dispositions of an object with finite means 'extend to finitely many cases'. But this challenge should be qualified. Productivity is sometimes viewed not just in terms of dispositions, but also as a *theoretical* maxim. For example, Fodor and Pylyshyn (1988, p. 33, n. 22) suggest that there is no need to assume that we possess infinite generative capacities: 'infinite generative capacity can be viewed, instead, as a consequence or a corollary of theories formulated so as to capture the greatest number of generalizations with the fewest independent principles' (see also Chomsky 1986). Theories of cognition generalize over individuals whose actual performance to produce $m+n$ varies quite dramatically. In addition, it is known that individuals can improve their performance by 'relaxing time constraints, increasing motivation, or supplying pencil and paper' (Fodor and Pylyshyn 1988, p. 34). Thus healthy theoretical principles such as generality, simplicity, and economy motivate us to attribute to individuals the capacity to produce $m+n$ for any m and n (see also Fodor 1990, pp. 94–5). Kripke, indeed, emphasizes that his argument is not meant to target this theoretical understanding of productivity (see *WR*, pp. 38–9 and n. 25; and also Wright 1989). His argument, rather, is that this theoretical claim is not grounded in *disposition*. If our alleged infinite powers are grounded in principles such as generality, simplicity, and economy, then, dispositionally speaking, we are not really adders but quadders.

a finite-size analog device that computes the function, when numbers m and n are represented by the rational magnitudes $1/m$ and $1/n$.[3] The device is finite in that it occupies a bounded region in the physical space, and completes the computation in a finite time. It requires an unbounded number of *types* of atomic components, for it should discriminate between an unbounded number of types of rational values. If, for example, we encode each natural number n by an activation value $1/n$, the device must be able to produce precise values for any n, as well as to distinguish between $1/n$ and $1/(n+1)$. Thus if the numbers encoded are very large, the distance between the rational coefficients that represent these numbers is very small. In that case, the device must support and discriminate between any two rational activation values.

Is it possible to have a device with these discriminative powers? Those who say 'No' remind us that a reductive account must anchor these powers in some *physical* object. As Kripke points out, an 'abstract mathematical object, gets us no further' (*WR*, p. 33); to answer the skeptic, we would need to show that the device is consistent with the *physical* space of possibilities (*WR*, p. 34). But, the deniers would claim, there is a lower bound on the size of the physical components, at least in practice. There is surely no reliable enough machine with these discriminative powers. If n and m are large enough, the device, which is always sensitive to some noise, cannot reliably distinguish between the magnitudes of $1/n$, $1/m$ and other close enough values.[4] And even if there were such a possible physical device, this would not show that *we* have these discriminative powers. There is no empirical evidence whatsoever that our brains have these capacities.

But there are those who are not so skeptical. They might point out that even if there is a lower bound on the size of components, the discriminative powers could be realized in other features, e.g. directionality of

---

[3] To take just one example, consider the following neural network. The net consists of two input units, i_1 and i_2, one output unit, o, and perhaps a number of hidden units. Assuming that the activation values of the input units range from 0 to 1, we will uniquely encode the numbers by the rational values Q_i in [0,1], for example, $Q_i = 1/i$ (where i is a natural number different from 0; if $i = 0$ then $Q_0 = 0$). The net can be seen as performing addition if and only if it computes the function $f('x','y') = ('x' \times 'y')/('x' + 'y')$ with the interpretation $I('x') = 1/x$. It is not necessary to specify here the inner structure of the net. A result by Siegelmann and Sontag (1995) indicates that for every function that is Turing-machine computable, there is such a corresponding network with rational coefficients that computes the values of the function.

[4] For discussion of the condition of a lower bound on the size of the components, see e.g. Gandy (1980).

particles. And even if the laws of physics, as we know them, do not allow reliable devices with these powers, we should always stand prepared to revise our physical theories if we have good arguments in favor of infinite dispositional capacities.[5] There are also those who suggest that the brain has far more computational power than we often attribute to it, and that this power is exhibited by an analog neural network.[6] Lastly, even if the device described here cannot be realized, it is just a simplistic example that reminds us that we cannot rule out a priori the existence of very powerful devices. There might well be another, far more sophisticated, idealized disposition that has these or other powers, and that anchors my meaning *addition* by '+'. We do not have a systematic account of permissible idealizations that rules out this possibility (see Boghossian 1989, p. 530).

We cannot conclude the ongoing debate here. But the debate does indicate that the infinity argument does not accomplish its task. Perhaps there is no disposition with the required discriminative powers. Perhaps I cannot be disposed to discriminate between infinitely many types of numbers. And perhaps I cannot be disposed to produce the value of $m+n$, for any m and n. But it is surely up to Kripke to provide a conclusive argument for these claims. If Kripke thinks that we don't have these dispositional powers, then the burden of proof is on him to demonstrate that we cannot. But the infinity argument falls short of doing that.

Symbol machines

The infinity argument does not present a serious threat to the dispositional approach to meaning. But does the argument have any value at all? I suggest that the significance of the argument lies in the context of symbol machines. More specifically, I contend that the argument challenges the idea that symbol machines are *disposed* to compute functions that are defined over infinitely many types, for example to produce as outputs $m+n$ for any m and n.

The case of symbol machines is of interest for various reasons. First, Kripke dedicates a lengthy discussion to machines as a variant of the

---

[5] A well-known example of someone who advertises for a revision in physics is Roger Penrose (1989). Penrose advances an argument for the claim that some conscious states must be a result of non-recursive processes. Since this result is at odds with most of what we know about physics, Penrose delves into the details of quantum physics, pointing out where the revision might take place.

[6] Kripke himself (2013, p. 91) says that nothing in principle rules out the existence of an empirically possible machine that calculates a decimal not computable in Turing's sense; see also Siegelmann (1998) who raises the possibility that the brain is an analog neural network, and that it computes non-recursive functions.

dispositional account (*WR*, pp. 32–7), apparently as a response to Dummett. Kripke's obvious concern is that his objector will wonder why I cannot be disposed to compute addition, given that familiar finite machines, which embody programs for addition, have this ability:

> We can interpret the objector as arguing that the rule can be *embodied* in a machine that computes the relevant function. If I build such a machine, it will simply grind out the right answer, in any particular case, to any particular addition problem. The answer that the machine gives is, then, the answer that I intended. (*WR*, p. 33)

In these passages, Kripke advances two criticisms of the use of machines as a way out of skepticism – its finitude and the possibility of malfunction – that are versions of the infinity and normativity arguments. There is also an interesting exegetical point here. Wittgenstein apparently has the same concerns, and he discusses machines explicitly in the *Investigations* (§193–5) and in the *Remarks on the Foundations of Mathematics* (I, §118–30; II, §87; III, §48–9).[7] Kripke not only refers to

---

[7] Here are some pertinent passages in Wittgenstein:

> But might it not be said that the *rules* lead this way, even if no-one went it? For that is what one would like to say – and here we see the mathematical machine, which, driven by the rules themselves, obeys only mathematical laws and not physical ones. (*Remarks on the Foundations of Mathematics*, III, §48)
>
> The machine as symbolizing its actions: the action of a machine – I say at first – seems to be there in it from the start. What does it mean? If I know the machine, everything else, that is its movements, seems to be already completely determined.
>
> We talk as if these parts could only move in this way, as if they could not do anything else. How is this – do we forget the possibility of their bending, breaking off, melting, and so on?
>
> But when we reflect that the machine could also have moved differently it may look as if the way it moves must be contained in the machine-as-symbol far more determinately than in the actual machine ... And it is quite true: the movement of the machine-as-symbol is predetermined in a different sense from that in which the movement of any given actual machine is predetermined. (*Philosophical Investigations*, §193)
>
> We say, for example, that a machine *has* (possesses) such-and-such possibilities of movement; we speak of the ideally rigid machine which *can* only move in such-and-such a way ... We say: 'It's not moving yet, but it already has the possibility of moving' – 'so possibility is something very near reality'. Though we may doubt whether such-and-such physical conditions make *this* movement possible, we never discuss whether this is the possibility of this or of that movement ... 'so it is not an empirical fact that this possibility is the possibility of precisely this movement'. (*Philosophical Investigations*, §194)

these paragraphs in Wittgenstein, but declares that, in fact, his 'criticisms in the text of the dispositional analysis and of the use of machines to solve the problem are inspired by these sections' (*WR*, p. 35, n. 24). It would be therefore even more interesting to review the arguments about machines that Kripke finds in Wittgenstein.

The case of symbol machines is of interest for another reason. The view that some symbol machines are disposed to compute addition is widespread, and explicitly advocated, for example, by Fodor and Pylyshyn (1988), Schwarz (1992) and Van der Velde (1995). The view is also used by Chomsky (1986) and Fodor (1990) to reply to Kripke's argument. Moreover, the view is often associated with another thesis, nowadays paradigmatic in cognitive science, that our mind/brain is a symbol machine, and that this fact can account for mental capacities that are involved with entertaining and producing infinitely many types. If my mind/brain is a sort of physical symbol system, then it can account for my alleged ability to produce the value of $m+n$, for any m and n, and perhaps even for my meaning *addition* by '+'. It would be interesting to see to what extent Kripke's argument contests this picture.[8]

Lastly, there is a highly interesting reconstruction of Turing's analysis of effective computability that links between an ideal human calculator and the paradigm example of a symbol system, i.e. a Turing machine (see Sieg 1994; 2002). On this reconstruction, Turing demonstrates that the concept of computation by a Turing machine is included in the concept of computation by an ideal human in the following sense. A Turing machine is a letter machine. It operates on one letter (symbol) at a time. A human calculator can operate on more than one letter at a time. He or she can operate over a bounded region of symbols. Thus

[8] The hypothesis that our minds/brains are 'physical symbol systems' appears in its most explicit form in Newell and Simon (1976). Fodor and Pylyshyn (1988) further argue that symbol machines are the *only* ones – as far as we know – that have the ability to entertain and produce an unbounded number of types of numbers. The argument of Fodor and Pylyshyn to which I refer here is about the productivity of thought (1988, pp. 33–6). Assuming that the human mind/brain has productive or generative capacities, Fodor and Pylyshyn thus infer that the human mind/brain must be a symbol machine. Fodor (1990, pp. 94–5) also invokes the idea of symbol machines to demonstrate that my meaning of '+' can be dispositional. Here I claim that Kripke's argument threatens the premise that our symbol systems have the required productive powers (unless 'productivity' is understood as a theoretical maxim, see note 2 above). Elsewhere, I argue that Fodor and Pylyshyn's other premise – that symbol machines are the only ones that can account for productivity – is fallacious, even when productivity is understood as a theoretical maxim (Shagrir 2000).

what can be done by a Turing machine can also be done by an ideal human calculator. On the other hand, the central thesis of the analysis is that the computational powers of human calculators do not exceed those of Turing machines. Turing demonstrated that what can be done by a human calculator in a single step, can be done, perhaps by a finite number of successive steps, by a Turing machine. It would thus be interesting to see to what extent Kripke's argument is relevant to this result.[9]

The idea of a symbol machine is attractive to the dispositionalist since, arguably, the machine produces the value of $m + n$ for arbitrary m and n, using only finite means. The machine is finite in several aspects. First, it operates on strings of symbols that can be as long as we wish, yet are defined over a bounded number of atomic types, via a fixed number of rules.[10] Second, the computation process is 'governed' by a rule, or a program, for *addition*, that consists of finitely many conditions (states). Third, each computation step involves a change in a bounded number of resources. In a Turing machine, for example, each single step is mostly involved with a change in one digit on the tape, in one state of the program, and in one-cell location of the read/write mechanism. It thus follows from these features that there are only finitely many *types* of operations, or single steps, the Turing machine can perform. Lastly, the computation process consists of finitely many steps.[11]

---

[9] This would be even more interesting in light of Sieg's claim that 'the essence of Turing's formulation is brought out by an aphoristic remark of Wittgenstein's on Turing's *Machines*. "These machines," Wittgenstein said, "are humans who calculate"' (2002, p. 395).

[10] A paradigm example is the decimal system whose members (decimals) represent numbers. The decimal system includes infinitely many types of symbols, each of which is a finite string of primitive or atomic symbols (digits). There is, overall, a bounded number of types of atomic symbols, i.e. ten, and all the other types of decimals are strings of digits, composed according to a finite number of construction and interpretation rules. The rules of syntax and semantics may be defined as follows:

Rules of syntax:
(1) '0', '1', ... '9' are primitive decimals (digits).
(2) If T is a string, and x is a digit, then Tx is a string.
Rules of semantics:
(1) $I('0') = 0$; $I('1') = 1$; ... $I('9') = 9$.
(2) $I(Tx) = 10 \times T + I(x)$.

[11] Assuming that the function is total, as is the case with *addition*. If the output is undefined, the machine never halts. For a detailed analysis of the finiteness constraints on (finite) machines, see Sieg (2002).

All this shows that producing the value of $m+n$ for any m and n is a finite process, yet it does not follow that it is bounded. If the strings are long enough, the machine must go through more computation steps. Since there are infinitely many decimals – some of which are very long strings – no bound can be put on these resources. There will always be sums $m+n$ whose production requires more of these resources. This may not raise a difficulty for the *abstract* Turing machine whose resources can be extended indefinitely. But it does raise a difficulty if the machines we deal with are *physical* objects, whose resources are arguably bounded. If the input strings are long enough, then the *physical* symbol machine will run out of memory space or break down before it produces the sum of these inputs. Thus the concrete physical symbol machine, one may argue, is not disposed to produce the value of $m+n$ for arbitrary m and n.

There is a standard strategy to take care of this difficulty. A symbol system maintains a functional distinction between program and memory. The program is fixed in advance, but memory can be extended indefinitely. We can therefore add more memory to the machine without altering its computational structure, that is without altering the program executed by the machine: 'in a system such as a Turing machine, where the length of the tape is not fixed in advance, changes in the amount of available memory *can be affected without changing the computational structure of the machine*; viz. by making more tape available' (Fodor and Pylyshyn 1988, pp. 34–5). 'Memory is external to the program, so that the memory capacity can be increased without changing the program, that is without changing the computed function itself' (Van der Velde 1995, p. 250). Thus if the physical machine is identified with the program it executes, it is disposed to entertain any input pair (m,n) and produce the value of $m+n$: under ideal conditions, when the working memory is unbounded, the machine will produce $m+n$ for any m and n. Consequently, if *we* (or our brains) are physical symbol machines, we are also disposed to entertain any input pair (m,n) and produce for it the sum $m+n$: 'if we did have unbounded memory, then, ceteris paribus, we would be able to compute the value of $m+n$ for arbitrary m and n' (Fodor 1990, p. 95).

This strategy is often rephrased in terms of a distinction between competence and performance. The distinction has been forcefully employed by Chomsky (1965, pp. 3–5) to emphasize that hearers/speakers have the *competence* to hear/understand arbitrarily long expressions even if they do not actually *perform* well when the expressions are too long. In his discussion of Kripke's arguments, Chomsky puts the distinction as follows:

> But the account of 'competence' ... deals with the configuration and structure of the mind/brain and takes one element of it, the component of L, to be an instantiation of a certain general system that is one part of the human biological endowment. We could regard this instantiation as a particular program (machine), although guarding against the implications that it determines behavior. (1986, p. 238)

The performance of the physical symbol machine is identified with its actual and potential behavior that depends, among other things, on the size of a memory, which is bounded. As a result, its performance is 'correct' with respect to a bounded number of input and output types. The competence of the machine, however, is associated with its program for *addition*. As such, the competence of the machines is revealed only when the program operates under ideal conditions, i.e. with unbounded memory: 'competence simply is performance under ideal processing conditions; i.e. without memory constraints. Competence will differ from performance when the system does not realize the required amount of memory' (Schwarz 1992, p. 215). And, under these ideal conditions, the machine entertains any type of input pair (m,n) and produces for it the value of $m + n$.

Kripke, however, criticizes this strategy. He does not deny the theoretical and practical virtues of the distinctions between program and memory and competence and performance, but he denies that the distinctions can help the dispositionalist.[12] Why? Simply because the disposition to entertain any pair (m,n) and produce for it the sum $m + n$, for arbitrary m and n, requires not only unbounded memory, but also unbounded iterative powers. To see this, assume that the state q_2 in my program is tokened whenever '1' occurs in the string. This requires the tokening of q_2 not only in the cases where the machine encounters the single string '1', but also in the cases where the machine encounters any string that consists of '1' (e.g. '101'). But this requires the tokening of q_2

[12] In fact, Kripke emphasizes that he does not reject Chomsky's competence-performance distinction: 'on the contrary, I personally find that the familiar arguments for the distinction ... have great persuasive force' (WR, p. 30, n. 22). Kripke also does not think that 'Wittgenstein himself would reject the distinction' (WR, p. 31, n. 22), provided that we take, as we should do, the notion of competence as *normative*, not descriptive.

over and over again in the cases where the machine encounters strings that consist of many '1's. It requires the tokening of q_2 an unbounded number of times. It requires, in other words, a *perpetuum mobile* working program.

This is often ignored since we think about the program as an *abstract* entity. And, indeed, there is no dispute that an abstract Turing machine can entertain arbitrarily long strings of decimals. But the situation is quite different with 'the actual physical machine, which is subject to breakdown' (*WR*, p. 35, n. 24). A concrete physical machine made of metal and gears, transistors and wires or neural tissues, 'is a finite object, accepting only finitely many numbers as inputs and yielding only finitely many as output – others are simply too big' (*WR*, p. 34). A physical machine, unlike an abstract machine, is constrained by physical laws, and, according to these laws, the machine is bound to break down, before it completes the addition of very long strings. A physical symbol machine cannot produce the sum $m+n$ for arbitrary m and n, even if its memory were unbounded. If the two input strings are too long, the working program will disintegrate before completing the mission. The physical symbol machine is, therefore, not disposed to produce $m+n$ for any m and n, even under ideal memory conditions.

I think that Kripke's comments on symbol machines are telling. The appeal to ideal memory conditions is both unnecessary and unhelpful in solving the infinity problem. It is unnecessary for two reasons. First, computing *addition* does not require an internal memory tape at all. As Kripke notes, *addition* can be computed by a finite state automaton (*WR*, pp. 35–7, n. 24). Unbounded memory is required for other arithmetical functions such as *multiplication*, but not for *addition*. It is thus surprising that the critics think that the appeal to unbounded memory can meet Kripke's argument, though the argument is not about memory constraints. Second, the assumption that there are ideal memory conditions is not only dubious, but also not necessary, even for computing multiplication. It is dubious because the number of particles in each possible physical world may be bounded. And it is unnecessary because we can appeal, instead, to the weaker and more plausible assumption that for every input pair (m,n), there is a possible physical world with enough, but finite, memory, such that this machine (program) can produce the value of $m \times n$.[13]

The appeal to ideal memory conditions is unhelpful because the main problems are with the *program*, not memory. One problem has to do with normativity. Granted that 'actual machines can *malfunction*: through

---

[13] I discuss these points in detail elsewhere (Shagrir and Pitowsky 2003).

melting wires or slipping gears they may give the wrong answer' (*WR*, p. 34), the dispositionalist should be able to tell why the competence of the machine is computing *addition* and not *quaddition*. Associating the competence with a program, even if it were justified, is of no help. If 'program' refers to the abstract rule we take the machine to implement, and not to the physical part that implements this rule, then 'the physical object is superfluous for the purpose of determining what function is meant' (*WR*, p. 35). The competence of the machine is really determined by the intentions of the designer. And if 'program' refers to the implementing physical object, then we are back to square one, as the physical part can malfunction too.

The other problem has to do with infinity. Even if we had the means to sort out proper functioning from malfunctioning, the dispositionalist cannot identify proper functioning (competence) with a function that the system is not disposed to compute. And since the working program cannot produce $m+n$ for any m and n – even if memory is unbounded – the competence of the machine is not computing addition. 'Usually this is ignored because the designer of the machine intended it to fulfill one program.' But, as Kripke emphasizes, 'the appeal to the designer's program makes the physical machine superfluous; only the program is really relevant. The machine as a physical object is of value only if the intended function can somehow be read off from the physical object alone' (*WR*, p. 34). Yet the problem is that we cannot read off the addition function from the physical object alone, since there are no conditions under which the physical object can compute the value of $m+n$ for arbitrary m and n.

How convincing is the argument? I suggest that we assess it at two different levels. At one level, the argument highlights two difficulties with the attempt to anchor arithmetical dispositions in symbol machines. One difficulty is that we cannot tie the unbounded powers to memory alone. There is also the issue of the program. Although a program is finite and fixed in advance in the sense that it consists of a fixed number of states, its execution sometimes requires an unbounded number of iterations. The other difficulty is that we cannot refer to programs as abstract objects. The dispositional approach, as a reductive approach, must refer to programs (or their manifestations) as concrete physical objects, i.e. as objects that obey empirical principles. When taking the two difficulties into account, the argument indicates that the dispositional analysis depends on the claim that there are concrete physical objects (programs) that support unbounded iterative powers, e.g. that can return the value of $m+n$ for any m and n.

I think that the significance of Kripke's argument lies at this level. As we saw above, dispositional accounts of meaning (and content) appeal to symbol machines for a reason. They aim to demonstrate that we can anchor arithmetical dispositions in a physical object, i.e. a symbol machine. Viewing things this way, the burden of proving this anchoring is on these accounts. We cannot accept the dispositionalist's claim as long as we doubt that there is such a physical object. But Kripke's argument raises precisely such a doubt. It points out that by focusing on the (non-) issue of memory, the dispositional accounts underestimate the issue of the program. In this respect, Kripke's argument is illuminating.

At another level, the argument aims to show that there cannot possibly be a physical object with the required disposition, i.e. unbounded iterative powers. At this level, the argument is less convincing. Of course, the argument does indicate that it is unlikely that we find in our environment, not to mention the brain, a physical symbol system with the required unbounded capacities. Still, there are various suggestions for physical systems that, under extreme idealization, have very powerful capacities.[14] And there might be other, very sophisticated, symbol systems that we haven't thought about. At this level, the burden of proof is on Kripke to show that there cannot possibly be objects like these. Yet this has not been done.

Summary

The infinity argument fails to challenge even the simplest dispositional analysis of perceptual terms. It points to a difficulty with an analysis of arithmetical terms, but falls short of showing that my meaning '+' cannot possibly be dispositional. Still, Kripke also discusses a specific family of analyses of the meaning of '+'. The analyses that Kripke considers are rooted in the idea that we follow a rule much like a symbol machine executes programs. Following Wittgenstein, Kripke forcefully demonstrates that this rule-following idea conflates abstract programs and concrete physical objects. Unlike an abstract program, a concrete physical object obeys empirical principles. Thus the dispositionalist is required to show us how a physical program can return the value of $m+n$ for any m and n, and, specifically, that is has unbounded iterative powers.

---

[14] Kripke (2013, p. 91; see also p. 100, n. 56) now takes the view that there is no reason to suppose that the decimal description of physical magnitudes (for example, electron–proton mass ratio) is Turing computable. See also Copeland's (2002) suggestion for an accelerating Turing machine, i.e. a symbol system that completes infinitely many steps in a finite span of time. It is also known that General Relativity is consistent with the existence of machines that complete infinitely many steps in a bounded span of time (Hogarth 1992; 1994); but see also Earman and Norton (1993). For discussion see Shagrir and Pitowsky (2003).

References

Blackburn, S. (1984) The Individual Strikes Back. *Synthese* 58: 281–301.

Boghossian, P.A. (1989) The Rule-Following Considerations. *Mind* 98: 507–49.

Chomsky, N. (1965) *Aspects of the Theory of Syntax*. Cambridge, MA: MIT.

Chomsky, N. (1986) *Knowledge of Language*. New York: Praeger.

Copeland, B.J. (2002) Accelerating Turing Machines. *Minds and Machines* 12: 281–301.

Dretske, F.I. (1981) *Knowledge and the Flow of Information*. Cambridge, MA: MIT.

Dretske, F.I. (1988) *Explaining Behavior*. Cambridge, MA: MIT.

Earman, J. and Norton, J.D. (1993) Forever is a Day: Supertasks in Pitowsky and Malament–Hogarth Spacetimes. *Philosophy of Science* 60: 22–42.

Fodor, J.A. (1990) A Theory of Content II: The Theory. In his *A Theory of Content and Other Essays*. Cambridge MA: MIT, pp. 89–136.

Fodor, J.A. and Pylyshyn Z.W. (1988) Connectionism and Cognitive Architecture: A Critical Analysis. *Cognition* 28: 3–71.

Gandy, R. (1980) Church's Thesis and Principles of Mechanisms. In J. Barwise, H.J. Keisler, and K. Kunen (eds) *The Kleene Symposium*. Amsterdam: North-Holland, 123–48.

Goldfarb, W. (1985) Kripke on Wittgenstein on Rules. *Journal of Philosophy* 82: 471–88.

Hogarth, M.L. (1992) Does General Relativity Allow an Observer to View an Eternity in a Finite Time? *Foundations of Physics Letters* 5: 173–81.

Hogarth, M.L. (1994) Non-Turing Computers and Non-Turing Computability. *Proceedings of the Philosophy of Science Association* 1: 126–38.

Kripke, S.A. (1982) *Wittgenstein on Rules and Private Language*. Oxford: Blackwell.

Kripke, S.A. (2013) The Church–Turing 'Thesis' as a Special Corollary of Gödel's Completeness Theorem. In B.J. Copeland, C.J. Posy, and O. Shagrir (eds) *Computability: Turing, Gödel, Church, and Beyond*. Cambridge MA: MIT, 77–104.

Newell, A. and Simon, H.A. (1976) Computer Science as Empirical Inquiry: Symbols and Search. *Communications of the Association for Computing Machinery* 19: 113–26.

Penrose, R. (1989) *The Emperor's New Mind*. New York: Penguin.

Pitowsky, I. (1990) The Physical Church Thesis and Physical Computational Complexity. *Iyuun* 39: 81–99.

Schwarz, G. (1992) Connectionism, Processing, Memory. *Connection Science* 4: 207–26.

Shagrir, O. (2000) Productivity and the Classical–Connectionist Debate. In M. Scheutz (ed.) *New Computationalism, Conceptus-Studien* 14: 37–50.

Shagrir O. and Pitowsky I. (2003) Physical Hypercomputation and the Church–Turing Thesis. *Minds and Machines* 13: 87–101.

Sieg, W. (1994) Mechanical Procedures and Mathematical Experience. In A. George (ed.) *Mathematics and Mind*. Oxford: Oxford University Press, 71–117.

Sieg, W. (2002) Calculations by Man and Machine: Conceptual Analysis. In W. Sieg, R. Sommer, and C. Talcott (eds) *Reflections on the Foundations of Mathematics*. Natick, MA: Association for Symbolic Logic, 390–409.

Siegelmann, H.T. (1998) *Neural Networks and Analog Computation: Beyond the Turing Limit*. Boston: Birkhäuser.

Siegelmann, H.T. and Sontag E.D. (1995) On the Computational Powers of Neural Nets. *Journal of Computer System Sciences* 50: 132–50.
Van der Velde, F. (1995) Symbol Manipulation with Neural Networks: Production of a Context-Free Language Using a Modifiable Working Memory. *Connection Science* 7: 247–80.
Wittgenstein, L. (1953) *Philosophical Investigations*. Oxford: Blackwell.
Wittgenstein, L. (1956) *Remarks on the Foundations of Mathematics*. Oxford: Blackwell.
Wright, C. (1984) Kripke's Account of the Argument against Private Language. *Journal of Philosophy* 81: 759–78.
Wright, C. (1989) Wittgenstein's Rule-Following Considerations and the Central Project of Theoretical Linguistics. In A. George (ed.) *Reflections on Chomsky*. Oxford: Blackwell, 233–65.

9

Kripke's Paradox of Meaning

Paul Horwich

The central issue

Given the common-sense assumption that words possess distinctive meanings – e.g. that Jan's word, 'pièś', has the property of *meaning DOG* – we can reasonably address ourselves to the question of where such phenomena come from, how facts of this sort are to be explained.[1] More specifically:

- To what, if anything, are meaning-properties, such as '*w* means DOG', conceptually (a priori) analyzable?
- To what, if anything, are they empirically (a posteriori) reducible?
- Which causal processes, if any, are responsible for their exemplification?

One may raise such questions about any property whatsoever – being red, being magnetic, being a dog, etc. – and there are established methodologies for trying to answer them. But it is widely thought that peculiar difficulties exist in the case of *meanings* – special and stringent requirements on adequate accounts of how these properties are engendered.

The central problem is felt to be that of doing justice to their *truth*-theoretic (i.e. *referential*) import. For example, because of what it *means*,

[1] The main ideas in what follows were aired at the Haifa Kripke Conference in the spring of 1999. Those ideas formed the basis of the paper that I gave in Warsaw, ten years later, at the Polish Philosophical Congress, and which was then published in the *Polish Journal of Philosophy* (III/1, 2009, pp. 23–32). A revision of that publication became Chapter 6 of Horwich (2010) and the present chapter is reprinted from that book. The only changes are a handful of minor stylistic improvements and some new notes.

the English word 'planet' is true of Mars and is true of Jupiter, but is *not* true of Aristotle or of the number three. Thus, in virtue of a word's being given a certain meaning, it 'reaches out' into the world and 'grabs on to' a certain specific collection of things – perhaps infinitely many of them and often including objects that are inaccessible to us. But how could this so-called *intentionality* or *aboutness* be made sense of? What sort of activity on our part – mental or behavioral or social – could result in our investing a certain word, *w*, with a certain meaning, *given that this would have to entail a staggering, infinite profusion of facts of the forms, 'w is true of x' and/or 'w is not true of y'*?

The issue to be addressed in this chapter is whether that datum – the referential import of meaning – presents a substantial difficulty or not. Does it provide a legitimate and hard-to-satisfy adequacy condition on good answers to our initial questions about how meaning-facts are engendered? Is that adequacy condition not merely stringent, but *impossible* to satisfy (as Saul Kripke argues in his *Wittgenstein on Rules and Private Language*)?[2] And must we conclude with him that there cannot be any genuine facts of meaning? If so then we have a paradox; for it seems obvious that words *do* have distinctive meanings.

Elaboration of the apparent difficulty

The explanatory route *from* our meaning-giving activity with, for example, the English word 'dog' – call it Act57('dog') – *to* that word's being true of all and only the dogs, would presumably have to take the following form:

1. Act57('dog')
2. Act57('dog') $\rightarrow$ 'dog' bears relation *R* to every dog and only to dogs

∴ 3. 'dog' bears R to every dog and only to dogs

4. Word *w* is true of *x* $\Leftrightarrow$ *w* bears *R* to *x*

∴ 5. 'dog' is true of every dog and only of dogs

Such an explanatory deduction would show how certain underlying facts about a term will result in its being true of dogs and only of dogs – and

---

[2] Oxford: Blackwell, 1982. The following account of what I'm calling 'Kripke's paradox' diverges somewhat from his own presentation of it (see especially pp. 22–32). However, my aim here is not to rehearse his discussion, but to articulate and assess what I take to be the sharpest formulation of the problem with which he is concerned. In particular, I will not dwell, as he does, on issues deriving from the *normative* import of meaning, though I will indicate, in note 7, how I think they can be dealt with.

show thereby how those facts might be responsible for its meaning what it does. However, it is no easy matter to find a relation, *R*, able to play the role prescribed. For remember that our basic concern is with what we *do* – computationally, or neurologically, or behaviorally, or communally, etc. – in order to put words into their referential relations with objects. Thus the sort of verbal 'activity' that we are assuming must entail the instances of *R* (see line 2) is *non-semantic* activity. It doesn't include, for example, *the activity of using 'dog' to refer to dogs*. And so *R* itself will have to be something that can be articulated in non-semantic terms. Otherwise its instances could not be entailed by Act57('dog'). But what relation could that be? What non-semantic relation links 'dog' to dogs, 'neutrino' to neutrinos, 'plus' to the triples <*x*,*y*,*z*> satisfying *x* plus *y* equals *z*,..., and so on, for all the predicates in our language?

A natural candidate for *wRx* is something along the following lines:

> We are disposed to apply *w* to *x*.

However, this particular suggestion overlooks the fact that we sometimes make *mistakes*. Sometimes we are disposed to call a given thing 'a dog' even when that term is *not* in fact true of the thing. On a moonless night we might wrongly apply it to a large and distant cat.

It is tempting to imagine that this difficulty can be finessed by modifying the initial proposal, as follows:

> We are disposed *in ideal circumstances* to apply *w* to *x*.

But a powerful objection to this new idea about the identity of relation *R* is that we have absolutely no reason to believe that any such 'ideal circumstances' exist. Why should there be general conditions of inquiry in which, whenever the question arises as to whether a given predicate is true of a given object, we would inevitably reach the correct answer? Certainly, no philosopher has ever come close to specifying what those conditions are.[3]

This sort of reasoning is the core of Kripke's skeptical argument. For if there is indeed nothing about our relationship to a word that could

---

[3] Even if we were to relax the assumption that a *single* relation, *R*, accounts for *every* instance of 'being true of' no matter which predicate is at issue – that is, even if we were to allow that a *variety* of relations, *R*1, *R*2, . . . , *Rk*, might engender different instances of it (perhaps one relation for color terms, one for substance terms, one for size terms, etc.) – the difficulty of specifying, for each such category, its 'ideal conditions of inquiry', would remain insuperable.

provide it with its distinctive referential import, and if (as seems obvious) any fact about its reference – hence, its meaning – would have to somehow result from some characteristic neural or computational or behavioral feature, then there can be no such thing as reference or meaning.[4]

Deflationism with respect to 'true of'

The thesis of the present chapterpaper is that this entire 'problem of aboutness' rests on a misconception about truth. More specifically, I will try to motivate two related claims: first, that no such problem can arise from a *deflationary* perspective on truth; and, second, that this provides us with an additional reason to adopt that perspective. So let me now summarize the salient features of deflationism, and then proceed to describe their bearing on Kripke's paradox.

[4] One might hope to escape Kripke's paradox simply by denying that our meaning-giving activity with a word must be specifiable in *non-semantic* terms – allowing, more liberally, that such activity may contain *intentions* and other propositional attitudes. It may be thought, for example, that 'There's a dog' means what it does in virtue of the speaker's intention to communicate his belief that a dog is present. But, on reflection, this move merely relocates the problem. Instead of the question of how *public linguistic expressions* acquire their semantic contents, we now face the parallel and equally hard question of how mental/neurological states manage to acquire *their* particular contents (and thereby come to qualify as the particular intentions, beliefs, etc., that they are). Moreover, the most promising approach to this parallel question is to suppose (with Jerry Fodor) that such states are just 'meaningful sentences in the head' – an assumption that would bring us right back to square one!

So we may well be led to suspect that semantic facts (concerning both sentences and mental states) are *explanatorily fundamental*. Some such *primitivist* move is recommended by Paul Boghossian (1989). But, as Kripke had observed, that approach would leave us with no prospect of any explanation of how a predicate's meaning yields its peculiar extension. In addition, we might reasonably object that the primitivist approach merely trades our initial paradox for another. For, on the one hand, the suggestion is that semantics facts are entirely ungrounded in, and uncaused by, physical phenomena. But, on the other hand, such facts are surely capable of *influencing* physical phenomena – in particular, a person's *utterance* of a given sentence on some occasion is surely explained, in part, by the meaning he or she attaches to that sentence; and this can be so (assuming 'the causal autonomy of the physical') only if the meanings of expressions *are* somehow engendered by physical phenomena.

Thus, insofar as our aim is to demystify semantic facts, it doesn't help matters to question whether they are the products of non-semantic activity.

According to deflationism, and contrary to traditional thinking, sentential truth is not a deep 'substantive' property – i.e. a property about which one might expect a theory of the form

s is true $\equiv s$ is Q

where 'Q' stands for some correspondence property, or some verifiability property, or some pragmatic property, or some consensus property, etc. Rather, the fundamental and defining principle is

s means that $p \rightarrow (s$ is true $\leftrightarrow p)$

For it is our acceptance of such conditionals – *not* of any traditional explicit definition – that explains why and how we deploy the notion of sentential truth. It is a useful device of generalization. For example, we can say 'Every instance of 'p v $-p$' is true' instead of being stuck with the intractably cumbersome infinite conjunction '(A v $-A$) & (B v $-B$) & (C v $-C$) & ...' (where 'A', 'B', etc. are specific sentences). And the general truth-claim can capture all those specific distinctions – i.e. entail each of them (but without going too far – if and only if we assume the above meaning-to-truth conditional).[5]

Similarly, 'w is true of x' doesn't stand for a substantive (i.e. potentially reducible) relation. Rather, we understand it – *relative to a prior understanding of meaning-attributions*, such as 'w means DOG' – through our acceptance of the conditionals:

w means DOG $\rightarrow$ w is true of all and only dogs
w means CAR $\rightarrow$ w is true of all and only cars
... and so on.[6]

---

5 Fuller grounds for the defining fundamentality of the above meaning-to-truth schema are offered in Horwich (1998a). It would be more accurate to say that the truly basic principles – from which that one is immediately derived – are the equivalence schema for *propositional* truth:

$<p>$ is true $\leftrightarrow p$

(where '$<p>$' is an abbreviation of 'the proposition that p') and the obvious definition of sentential truth (for *tokens*, of course) in terms of *propositional* truth:

s means $<p> \rightarrow (s$ is true $\leftrightarrow <p>$ is true$)$

But nothing in what follows would be affected by this correction.

6 'w means DOG' is an artificial notation introduced to express the distinctive meaning-property possessed by our word 'dog' and by synonymous terms such as the Polish 'piès', the Arabic 'caleb', and so on. Thus one might think of it as w's property of *meaning what is in fact meant by our word 'dog'*. There are interesting issues as to whether such meaning-properties are really as relational as they seem. Do they each involve the relation, *means*, together with one or another meaning-*entity* (e.g. DOG)? And, if so, what do those ingredients themselves consist in? But these issues have little bearing on our present concerns.

Deflationism implies that the problem of explaining meaning's referential import is a *pseudo*-problem

In general, if a predicate '*f*' (e.g. 'ice') is defined in terms of an expression '*g*' (e.g. 'frozen water'), and if something, *k*-ness (e.g. 'H_2O below 0°C') is proposed as the source (or cause, or origin) of *g*-ness:

$$\begin{array}{lr} x \text{ is ice} = \text{(by definition) } x \text{ is frozen water} & \\ \Uparrow & \text{(causal hypothesis)} \\ x \text{ is } H_2O \text{ below } 0°C & \end{array}$$

we do not think that the hypothesis stands in need of support by reference to some way of explaining, *independently of the definition*, why it is that if something is *k* (H_2O below 0°C) then it is *f* (ice). Rather, we *first* justify the hypothesis on the basis of considerations that involve no use of '*f*', and we are then entitled to cite it, together with the definition, to explain why that conditional holds.

In particular, *if* deflationism is correct – *if* 'true of' is indeed defined, as suggested above, in terms of 'means' – then the explanatory route leading *from* a word's meaning-*engendering* property (e.g. that 'dog' has non-semantic property Act57(*w*)) *to* its extension (e.g. that 'dog' is true of exactly the dogs) must proceed *via* the intermediate fact that the word means what it does (e.g. that 'dog' means DOG).

Therefore, unless deflationism has somehow been excluded from consideration, one has no right to insist that the phenomena responsible for a word's meaning DOG must provide a *direct* explanation of why it is true of dogs – that is, an explanation that does not rest on the pertinent meaning-to-truth conditional. In other words, one has no right to require (as was done à la Kripke on pp. 192–4) that the non-semantic source of '*w* means DOG' entails something of the form '$(x)(wRx \leftrightarrow x$ is a dog)' – where *R*-ness either *constitutes* 'being true of', or is, in some other way, necessary and sufficient for that semantic relation to hold. Therefore, absent some refutation of deflationism, the above-argued non-existence of any such relation, *R*, can cohere perfectly well with the reality of meanings, and with their being the product of our mental and/or behavioral activity.

Indeed, this coherence, together with the apparently insuperable difficulties that plague the initially presupposed (inflationary) approach, provide strong additional evidence in favor of our deflationary alternative.

To repeat: the deflationist position is not to deny that the meaning-giving property of the word 'dog' fixes its extension, but to suppose that it does so only because it *first* fixes the word's meaning. For we can then invoke the explanatorily fundamental account 'true of' in terms of 'meaning' – including, '*w* means DOG $\rightarrow (x)(w$ is true of $x \leftrightarrow x$ is a dog)' – to explain (by transitivity) why it is that the word is true of exactly dogs.[7]

This perspective presupposes that there is some way of discovering – independently of truth-theoretic considerations – which facts underlie the meanings of words. But no clue has been given as to how that might be done.

I would suggest that we address this issue by reference to the normal methodology, familiar from *outside* semantics, for settling matters of empirical reduction. In general, the question of how a property (e.g. being made of water) is constituted is typically approached by looking for an underlying property (e.g. being made of H_2O molecules) that explains the characteristic symptoms (e.g. boiling at 100 degrees centigrade) of the superficial property.

Now – turning to the question of how the constitutors of *meaning*-properties are to be identified – the main symptoms of a word's meaning are its various *uses* (e.g. facts of the form: 'such-and-such sentence containing it was accepted on such-and-such occasion'). So, we should

[7] Kripke's own skeptical argument trades not merely on the *referential* import of meaning, but also on its *normative* import. For example, it is presumably in virtue of what 'dog' means that one *should* apply it only to dogs. So one might expect to be able to test any candidate meaning-constituting property by whether it would have that normative consequence. But – so the argument goes – we can't easily find anything that would pass such a test. However, there is a solution to this problem that is somewhat analogous to what has just been said about the *truth*-theoretic properties of terms. We can and should explain why it is that

If Act57(*w*), then *w* should be applied only to dogs

by reference to the following pair of explanatorily more basic facts:

(i) If Act57(*w*), then *w* means DOG
(ii) If *w* means DOG, then *w* should be applied only to dogs

Facts of type (i) are discovered via the methodology sketched immediately below;. And facts of type (ii) are instances of 'the value of truth'. For discussion of whether and how the latter might be explained, see Horwich (2013).

be looking for whatever underlying property of the word will play a core role in explaining its overall deployment.

And, quite plausibly, there is such a property. As just noted, we *do* feel that our verbal output (internally in thought, as well as externally) is, in part, the result of what we mean by our words. And, if that is right, then there should be, at the non-semantic level, some property of each word that accounts for this causal capacity.

What sort of property might that be? Arguably, it's a *basic propensity of use* – a law-like tendency to accept certain specified sentences containing the word in certain specified conditions. For instance, 'dog''s being governed by some such 'law' may (in virtue of the core role of that fact in explanations of the word's overall deployment) constitute its meaning what it does – i.e. its meaning DOG.[8]

A telling analogy

Suppose we define the relational term 'schmoo' by the stipulation that if something is made of plastic then it is schmoo of each dog. Thus a credit card qualifies as schmoo of Pooch, but a nickel does not.

Would it then be reasonable to complain to a chemist who offers a reductive theory of plastic – 'plastic = XYZ' – that her theory can be accepted only if she provides a *direct* explanation (i.e. one that does not simply combine her theory with the schmoo-stipulation) of why things made of XYZ are schmoo of precisely the dogs – and not (say) all dogs except for Fido who lives on Alpha Centauri?

Of course not! No such direct explanation is conceivable. Given the definition of 'schmoo', the only possible route from 'XYZ' to 'schmoo of the dogs' goes via 'plastic'. So the legitimacy of the first of these two steps cannot rest on anything to do with 'schmoo'. The chemist is perfectly entitled to accept her theory on other grounds, and then to explain the relationship between 'XYZ' and 'being schmoo of dogs'

---

[8] For clarification of this proposal, for arguments in favor of it, and for responses to objections, see Horwich (1998b, ch. 3; 2005, ch. 2; and 2010, ch. 7). I see no prospect of any non-trivial *conceptual* analysis of '*w* means DOG'. One might try '*w* means what my word "dog" actually means', or '*w* has the same meaning as my word "dog"'. But these are trivial (given the convention that allows us to name the meanings of our expressions by writing them in capital letters). A *non*-trivial proposal would be '*w* has the same basic use property as my word "dog"'. But although this is, quite plausibly, a priori equivalent to '*w* means DOG (to me)', there is good reason to doubt that it provides an *analysis* of it, rather than an a priori specification of how to go about identifying the correct a posteriori reduction.

by deriving it from that theory in combination with the definition of 'schmoo'.

Three objections

Objection A

> There is a striking *dis*analogy between the hypothetical 'schmoo' example and the case of 'true of'. For 'schmoo' is introduced by means of a *stipulation* about how it is to be used in relation to the words 'plastic' and 'dog', *which are already understood*. However, it almost certainly was *not* the case that, only *after* we began to deploy ordinary terms such as 'dog', and predicates of meaning-attribution such as '*w* means DOG', did we introduce 'true of' via conditionals such as '*w* means DOG $\rightarrow (x)(w$ is true of $x \leftrightarrow x$ is a dog)'.

Granted. But this difference, although real enough, is irrelevant. To see why, remember that we are quite happy to say that 'bachelor' abbreviates 'unmarried man' – despite the historical absence of any *explicit stipulation* to that effect. This is because of how we use these expressions: more specifically, because we can see that the best way to explain our use of 'bachelor' is in terms of our treatment of it as intersubstitutable with 'unmarried man'. Still, it is clear that, if someone did happen to incorporate the word into his or her vocabulary via an explicit stipulation, it would acquire precisely the basic use that it actually has, and hence the same meaning. Similarly, in order for the meaning of 'true of' to depend – in the way that deflationists claim it does – on the meanings of such terms as 'DOG', '*w* means DOG', 'CAR', '*w* means CAR', etc., it suffices that the best explanation of our overall use of 'true of' be that anyone who understands a predicate, '*f*', and its corresponding meaning-attribution, '*w* means *F*', accepts the conditional, '*w* means $F \rightarrow (x)(w$ is true of $x \leftrightarrow x$ is an $f)$'. That this explanatory hypothesis is correct would perhaps be more obvious if 'true of' had been introduced, in a 'schmoo'-like way, via the stipulation that these conditionals hold. But it can be correct – and plausibly *is* correct – in the absence of any such mode of introduction.

Objection B

> In order to justify the hypothesis that 'being water' is constituted by 'being made of H_2O molecules', it was vital to show that certain known implications of something's having the superficial property

> (e.g. boiling at 100 degrees) would be explained by its having the proposed underlying property. So, why should we not think, similarly, that in order to justify the hypothesis that a word's meaning DOG is constituted by its having 'Act57(*w*)', it would be vital to show that a certain prominent implication of a word's meaning DOG – namely, its being true of dogs – would be explained by its having 'Act57(*w*)'?

The answer lies in a crucial difference between the two cases. On the one hand, 'boils at 100 degrees' is *not* defined in terms of 'water'. Rather, we have an independent understanding of it. And that is why we can take it to be an adequacy condition on the credibility of the theory, 'water = H_2O', that there be a *direct* account of how being made of H_2O gives rise to that particular boiling point. But, on the other hand – assuming deflationism is correct – 'true of' *is* defined in terms of 'means'. So it cannot be supposed that a theory of how '*w* means DOG' is constituted will be credible only relative to a prior account of how the alleged constituting property gives rise to *w*'s extension.[9]

Objection C

> Someone can perfectly well accept that '*w* means DOG→*w* is true of the dogs' is both true by definition and explanatorily fundamental, and yet suppose – in stark opposition to deflationism – that this conditional helps to define '*w* means DOG' in terms of a *prior* notion of '*w* is true of the dogs' (rather than the other way around). And from this point of view, we *can* reasonably impose as a constraint on any analysis of '*w* means DOG' that it squares with a plausible analysis of '*w* is true of dogs'.

No doubt this alternative approach – which is the traditional one – deserves the serious consideration that (in effect) Kripke gave it. But, as he showed – and as I indicated on pp. 192–4 – it just doesn't pan out. We are not able to come up with a decent *direct* explanation of how our activity with a word could bring about its being true of dogs.[10]

---

[9] This response can be articulated without bringing in considerations of *definition* or *understanding*. The basic point is that, on the one hand, the water-to-(boils-at-100 °C) fact is *not* fundamental; so there can be an explanation of it in terms of the fact that H_2O boils at 100 °C; and so this can be regarded as helping to justify the reductive hypothesis that water *is* H_2O. But, on the other hand (according to deflationism), the meaning-to-truth facts *are* fundamental. So we can't explain 'dogs''s extension-condition in terms of its use without going through the word's meaning.

[10] Nor can we say what is the further characteristic of a word that, when added to its being true of dogs, suffices for it to mean DOG.

There remains, however, a theoretical reaction to this negative result that is far more attractive than either meaning-skepticism or meaning-primitivism (see note 4). For the deflationist order of definition *can* be vindicated. We *are* able to see how our acceptance of instances of '*w* means $F \rightarrow w$ is true of the *f*s' would, relative to an understanding of '*F*' and of '*w* means *F*', explain our overall use of 'true of'. And we *are* able see how a word's non-semantic meaning-giving activity – the reductive ground of *w*'s meaning *F* – might and should be identified independently of any truth-theoretic considerations. So we *can* adequately defend the deflationist view that the explanatory route from the meaning-giving activity with a word to its extension goes via its meaning-property. This case in favor of our approach is then further bolstered by its simple way of avoiding both the implausibility of skepticism and the implausibility of primitivism. Thus there is good reason to conclude that deflationism about truth, when combined with a use-theory of meaning, provides the only viable perspective on these phenomena.[11]

References

Boghossian, P. (1989) The Rule Following Considerations, *Mind* 98: 507–49.
Horwich, P. (1998a) *Truth*, 2nd edn. Oxford: Oxford University Press.
Horwich, P. (1998b) *Meaning*. Oxford: Oxford University Press.
Horwich, P. (2005) *Reflections on Meaning*. Oxford: Oxford University Press.
Horwich, P. (2010) *Truth-Meaning-Reality* Oxford: Oxford University Press.
Horwich, P. (2012) *Wittgenstein's Metaphilosophy*. Oxford: Oxford University Press.
Horwich, P. (2013) Belief-Truth Norms. In T. Chan (ed.) *The Aim of Belief*. Oxford: Oxford University Press.
Kripke, S. (1982) *Wittgenstein on Rules and Private Language* Oxford: Blackwell.

[11] I would like to thank Paul Boghossian for the stimulus of our many lively conversations about this problem over the last twenty odd years. I have never been able to persuade him of my deflationary solution (or, for that matter, to persuade anyone else, as far as I know!); and so I have been led, in a succession of publications, to try to improve my formulation of it. This essay is my latest attempt to hit the nail on the head. See also Horwich (2012, ch. 5).

10

Skeptical Arguments in Hume and Wittgenstein

Mark Steiner

Hume and Wittgenstein

It's hard to think of two philosophers more distant than David Hume and Ludwig Wittgenstein. Wittgenstein himself is supposed to have said that he 'couldn't bear' to read Hume. It's easy to see why: in *Philosophical Investigations* (*PI*) (Wittgenstein 1968) Wittgenstein 'trashes' Hume's basic tenets.[1] Hume's thesis that every word expresses an 'idea' derived from an 'impression' is more noxious to Wittgenstein than Augustine's idea (quoted at the beginning of *PI*) that every word is a name. For Hume's doctrine makes every word a name of a private object, and every language a private language. Also, Wittgenstein has no truck with any absolute notion of a simple idea (a mistaken notion which he traces to Plato's *Theaetetus*), yet Hume made 'simple ideas' the basis of all knowledge.

Nevertheless, I maintain, Hume and Wittgenstein show remarkable similarities. Of course, it was Saul Kripke who drew attention to the parallels between the two, particularly the use by them of 'skeptical arguments'. In this chapter I will argue that this and many other analogies that Kripke does not mention all stem from a common conception of philosophic method.

Philosophy as struggle

Let's get right to the point: Hume and Wittgenstein see no role for philosophy (the kind they do) beyond the descriptive. In particular, philosophy can put forward no explanations. The construction of

[1] Not by name, of course.

philosophical theories in order to explain empirical regularity is the original sin of academic philosophy[2] (what they don't do).

Though both hate philosophical explanations, it is remarkable that they come to this aversion from opposite motivations. For Hume, the descriptive approach to philosophy stems from his wanting philosophy to imitate science – Newtonian science. Newton had argued that there is no need to explain every phenomenon by an underlying mechanism – mathematical laws, derived from 'the phenomena', do fine by themselves. 'Hypotheses' – explanatory stories which explain, without being derived from, the phenomena – are unnecessary and often misleading.

Hume sees himself as the Newton of the mind. The parallels to Newton's law of gravitation are the so-called 'laws of association' which describe (without explaining) how one idea leads to, 'attracts', another.[3] These laws replace the rationalist conception of 'innate ideas' used to explain, among other things, the prevalence of the same concepts in every language:

> These are therefore the principles of union or cohesion among our simple ideas ... Here is a kind of ATTRACTION, which in the mental world will be found to have as extraordinary effects as in the natural, and to shew itself in as many and as various forms. Its effects are every where conspicuous; but as to its causes, they are mostly unknown, and must be resolved into *original* qualities of human nature, which I pretend not to explain. Nothing is more requisite for a true philosopher, than to restrain the intemperate desire of searching into causes, and having establish'd any doctrine upon a sufficient number of experiments, rest contented with that, when he sees a farther examination would lead him into obscure and uncertain speculations. (*Treatise* (T), I, I, IV)

Hume criticizes Locke's attempts to explain the provenance of our ideas by a causal theory of perception. Hume replies that we have *no* causal explanation of the origin of our simple impressions. We couldn't

---

[2] I will use the term 'academic philosophy' as a general term of opprobrium for philosophers who hanker after philosophical theories and explanations, i.e. the philosophical targets of Hume, Wittgenstein, or both.

[3] I recently discovered the same idea, quoting the same passage, in Gjertsen (1988). Also, Hilary Putnam in a seminar I attended two years ago used the phrase 'Newton of the mind' in reference to Hume's pretensions. All three arrived at the phrase independently.

have one either: by the end of Book I he makes clear what he has hidden from the reader throughout, that the causal connection is only among 'impressions'. The causal theory of perception is thus incoherent, not only because it postulates an extra mental knowable, but because it postulates causality between a perception and something else.

Wittgenstein, notoriously, agrees that philosophy can be descriptive only. But a Newtonian 'empirical' science of the mind would repel him. He came to his descriptivism because he wanted philosophy to be *unlike* science – the science he was familiar with, contemporary science, which does invoke explanatory 'hypotheses'. Trying to copy science had led, in his view, to the corruption of (academic) philosophy.

So Hume and Wittgenstein concur that philosophy cannot explain the empirical, though they arrive at this conviction from opposite points of view. They also share a detestation of academic philosophy. They repeatedly side with the common man – or at least their perception of the common man – against professional philosophers. After all, they feel, the common man pretends not to explain by philosophy what philosophy cannot explain.

Hume points out, for example, that the common man believes in an external world – existing even when not perceived. Yet the common man refuses to explain his knowledge of the external world by a causal theory of perception, and identifies objects with perceptions, *à la* Berkeley. The common man thus ends up believing in unperceived perceptions, i.e. perceptions not in any mind. Now though the existence of 'unperceived perceptions' is doubtful, it is not logically impossible.[4] On the other hand, the causal theory of perception *is* a conceptual muddle. Hence, although the common man and the academic philosopher both err, the error of the academic philosopher is far more noxious.

Wittgenstein, for his part, attacks academic philosophy for perverting language on behalf of an illusory theory of language. Again and again he remarks that only when one is doing (academic) philosophy do we make queer and muddled statements never heard in ordinary conversation. His ambition is to 'bring back words to their ordinary use'.

---

4 This follows from Hume's view of the mind as a 'bundle of perceptions'. There is nothing there but the bundle, and perceptions do not 'inhere' in the mind; rather, they constitute the mind. An unperceived perception is then nothing but a perception not connected to the rest of the bundle. Hume held that there is excellent evidence that this never happens, but that it is logically possible. Naturally, Berkeley would have regarded the existence of unperceived perceptions as a logical contradiction. Cf. T (I, iv, ii) and Price (1940).

But then what do we need philosophy for? What special expertise is needed for simply describing the facts? The answer that both Hume and Wittgenstein give is that there is a systematic drive to construct philosophical explanations. This drive appears as a projective superstition: we project ourselves onto reality and then marvel when we find ourselves mirrored therein. Everyone is prone to this superstition; but Hume and Wittgenstein regard academic philosophers as much more susceptible. In fact, philosophical explanations are based on the very pseudo-properties that result from this projection.

On this view, then, academic philosophy is, or results from, what the Talmud calls an 'evil inclination' – it embodies a tendency for self-deception. And true philosophy is not a special doctrine, but a skill: the ability to describe the facts without being deceived.[5] One might also call it a struggle – a struggle against superstition.[6] Wittgenstein is, of course, well known for holding this view; but Hume held it too, most famously in the case of causality.

In observing a cause A and its effect B, we observe only A, B, and – previously – a constant conjunction of events like A and events like B.[7] This does not satisfy us. We find ourselves looking for something *about* A and B which *explains* why B, given A, *had* to happen, why the future tends to be like the past. What we are looking for, in short, is a 'necessary connection' between A and B.

But the idea of a necessary connection among events is a superstition. The constant conjunction of events like A with events like B conditions us to expect that this conjunction will continue. Confounding internal

---

[5] 'We may not advance any kind of theory. There must not be anything hypothetical in our considerations. We must do away with all explanation, and description alone must take its place. And this description gets its light, that is to say its purpose, from the philosophical problems. These are, of course, not empirical problems; they are solved, rather, by looking into the workings of our language, and that in such a way as to make us recognize those workings: in despite of an urge to misunderstand them. The problems are solved, not by giving new information, but by arranging what we have always known. Philosophy is a battle against the bewitchment of our intelligence by means of language.' (*PI*, 109)

[6] This struggle takes a physical toll on both philosophers: Hume regards philosophy as so daunting that he must seek relief in backgammon; Wittgenstein (according to the testimony of Norman Malcolm) races off to grade B movies after his lectures, sitting in the front row to flood his mind with inanities so as to forget for a minute the torments of philosophy.

[7] I will ignore the very difficult problem of specifying what the criterion for 'like' is here.

with external determination,[8] we project this expectation upon external reality, as an explanatory 'necessary connection'.

This is not the only projective superstition for Hume. The common man's belief[9] in external 'bodies' is also caused by an error: the relative stability ('constancy') though time of our perceptions leads us to ascribe more identity to them than they have. Also, the 'coherence' of our perceptions leads us to ascribe more causality to the world than there actually is – we postulate unconsciously that our impressions continue to exist unperceived (i.e. outside any mind) and thus allow unperceived (*though perceivable*) causes, a contradiction for Hume.[10]

The common man, then, is certainly misled. He misdescribes his own perceptions. Academic philosophy, however, by attempting to extricate itself from the fallacy of the common man, falls prey to the causal theory of perception and inventing mythical objects to explain why we have perceptions in the first place, and why they are as constant as they are. These mythical objects also 'explain' the coherence in our perceptions by filling in the causal gaps in the perceived world. It follows that academic philosophy (in the persona of Locke – and Descartes) is far more superstitious than the common man.

---

[8] This view of Hume's conflicts with what he says elsewhere in the *Treatise*, however. The distinction between internal and external causality collapses later in the book, both in that Hume sees no reason for failing to identify objects outright with sensory impressions, and also in that the causal relation holds only among 'perceptions'. This ambivalence brings the whole project of the *Treatise* to self-destruction. Another point is that Hume's view that we project internal determination onto nature does not mean that Hume holds, with Berkeley, that we can *directly* sense 'being compelled'. Hume explicitly denies that we can form the idea of necessary connection from our own case. Rather, it is the confounding of internal with external causality which produces the illusion of necessary connection in both cases.

[9] There is an inherent problem in Hume's explanation of the belief in an external world, and in other problematic beliefs. Strictly speaking, these do not count as *beliefs*, because they do not correspond to ideas. It might be better to say in those cases that one deludes oneself into thinking one has a belief.

[10] There is no doubt about it but that Hume is committed to the absurd view that causes are all perceived. This follows from his premise that the causal relation is a relation between 'perceptions' (T I, iv, ii; cf. the discussion of reasoning backwards from a noise to a man who made the noise) and the view that there are no unperceived perceptions. One way out would be to say that perceptions are all in the mind (they are all perceived), but there are possible perceptions in possible minds as well, and unperceived causes are to be identified with these 'perceivables'. This is precisely Kant's reply to Hume in the *Prolegomena*. Unfortunately, Hume rejects modalism as being incompatible with empiricism (and it is indeed true that empiricism has generally rejected the modalities to this very day). Recall, however, that it is *not* absurd to hold that *perceptions* are sometimes unperceived – only that *causes* are.

Let us compare Wittgenstein with Hume, now, on the matter of projective superstition. Discussing the proposal that *reading* is being 'guided' by the text, Wittgenstein uses strikingly 'Humean' formulations:

> It would never have occurred to us to think that we *felt the influence* of the letters on us when reading, if we had not compared the case of letters with that of arbitrary marks. And here we are indeed noticing a *difference*. And we interpret it as the difference between being influenced and not being influenced . . .
>
> I should like to say: 'I experience the because'. Not because I remember such an experience, but because when I reflect on what I experience in such a case I look at it through the medium of the concept 'because'. (*PI*, 170)

Wittgenstein gives a much more striking and systematic example of projective superstition in his discussion of rule following. My treatment of this subject is 'Kripkean', though I do not claim to follow Kripke in every detail.

Suppose we train a student in the command 'add 2' and note that he says 2, 4, 6,..., 1,000; then he begins to say 1,004, 1,008,.... We respond that he is no longer following the rule. If he had gone on to say 1,002, 1,004,..., we would have said that he was continuing to follow the rule. According to Wittgenstein, there is no fact that we are ascribing or denying in virtue of which our student is, or is not, following the rule. In both cases we are *evaluating* our student's performance as 'correct' or 'incorrect' – not describing it. The superstition begins when we project our own evaluation as an explanatory fact about the student, and then look for it, say, in his brain.[11]

Do we then ascribe rule following by fiat? Absolutely not. Our evaluation of the student, like all rational evaluations, is grounded in empirical regularities: most people when trained the same[12] way, behave the same

---

[11] Wittgenstein does not *deny* that there could be an empirical *correlation* between brain states and rule following; what he emphasizes is that the feeling that there *must* be such a correlation is a superstition. Furthermore, any such correlation plays no role in our everyday ascription of rule following, as speakers have no access to the correlation.

[12] Though Wittgenstein insists that there is no fact underlying our judgments of 'same' and 'different', just as there is no fact underlying our following rules (and for the same reasons), he also insists that the absence of such facts does not prevent us from making correct statements concerning identity and similarity, just as it does not prevent us from following rules. The same training produces both abilities (read carefully *PI*, 208ff.). Hence the statement that most people when trained the same way, behave the same way is entirely innocent, and, in Wittgenstein's eyes, true.

way. If this were not true, there could be no rules at all. Nevertheless, when we say our trainee is following the rule, we are not *saying* 'He is doing what most people, trained in this way, would do'. Rule following is evaluation, not description: when we evaluate someone's behavior we *take a position*, for example, with respect to rewarding or punishing that behavior, in furtherance of societal goals. One of those goals may be to increase the uniformity of human behavior. (This is not always a worthy goal, but it sometimes is: for example, in the practice of counting and measuring, or in logical reasoning.) Every empirical regularity may have exceptions. We 'harden' a regularity into a rule, regarding departures from the regularity as deviant 'mistakes'.

This is the correct description of what happens (as Wittgenstein sees it). However, there is a persistent tendency to misdescribe what happens, to conflate rules with regularities. Rules are norms or ideals; regularities are empirical facts[13] (according to Wittgenstein's common-sense realism). Hence, conflating them gives us a 'synthetic a priori'[14] – a fact which is, at the same time, an ideal.

Confusion of rule with regularity occurs rampantly in the philosophy of logic. For example, we tend to think of the laws of logic as coercive. The origin of this superstition is as follows. The laws of logic are nothing but rules for using expressions like 'for all', 'if–then', etc. There is general regularity in the use of such expressions, as a result of being trained in their use, but there are also deviations. We project outward our desire to increase the uniformity of the use of logical particles and profess to detect some impersonal, 'supercausal' force which could survive even the total breakdown of the regularity. We ourselves are determined by our training to use logical particles in a certain way. Our student doesn't follow suit; so we project our own causal determination onto his deviation, as though we share the determination with him in a supercausal sense.

The myth of 'supercausation' takes two forms in academic philosophy: Platonism and mentalism. Platonism postulates ideal relations between logical premise and conclusion, which hold even if actual reasoning falls short of the ideal. Note that Platonism here is the Platonism of rules. Wittgenstein regarded this as more pernicious, because more subtle, than the usual Platonism of objects.

---

[13] Though many writers seem to feel that Wittgenstein did not believe in 'facts', the truth seems to be that he held that this word, like many others used in philosophy, has a perfectly sound ordinary use – primarily in what are called empirical contexts.

[14] This is Wittgenstein's own term.

Mentalism postulates an objective relation between a state of mind of the student and hypothetical behavior. This relation can't be one of causation, since we see that the student did not reason correctly; so we think of it as a 'supercausal' relation between some fact about the intention and the student's behavior *in an ideal world.*[15] Mentalism turns out to be the flip side of Platonism.

I'd like to conclude this section by rewriting the history of philosophy in light of this analysis. I see Maimonides, Hume and Wittgenstein as representatives of a nameless philosophy unrecognized by historians: a school that holds that philosophy is a struggle against superstition. Maimonides fought against anthropomorphic descriptions of God, meaning any projection of man's characteristics onto the deity in an attempt to explain nature. Hume continued this tradition, attacking the concept of 'necessary connection' as a projection of ourselves onto the constant conjunctions of nature. Finally, Wittgenstein decried projecting our norms and conditioning on others' behavior as though they were factual.

The role of skeptical arguments in all this

I would now like to explain the relation of Hume and Wittgenstein to philosophical skepticism. Let us distinguish, with Berkeley's First Dialogue (1988, 121–3), between skepticism of doubt, and skepticism of denial. Skepticism of *doubt* questions propositions (or classes of propositions) ordinarily taken as certain, for example 'there are trees'. Skepticism of *denial* advocates flat repudiation of such propositions.

Not only do Hume and Wittgenstein not endorse *skepticism of doubt,* they condemn it in the same terms. Hume argues (T I, iv, i) that skepticism is psychologically impossible, which is for him the ultimate refutation of any doctrine. Wittgenstein not only agrees on this point, but adds that skepticism is a sure sign of linguistic confusion.

However, both Hume and Wittgenstein *use* skeptical *arguments* without *identifying with* or *endorsing* skepticism itself. Skeptical arguments serve as a weapon against, as a *reductio ad absurdum* of, academic philosophy and its search for philosophical knowledge as something which can play an explanatory role.

[15] Again, note the slipperiness of the word 'fact' – for Wittgenstein, the term in ordinary language is connected with empirical truth. It is harmless to stretch it further, as long as we don't try to explain things with the word 'fact'. I'll discuss Saul Kripke's use of the word later.

In fact, they hold, the search for philosophical knowledge is misguided: you can have certainty without knowledge.[16] Classical epistemology is useless. Worse, the very quest for philosophical knowledge leads ineluctably to the very doubt it wants to lay to rest.

To show this, both Hume and Wittgenstein employ skeptical arguments, whose conclusion *for them* is denial, not doubt. But they show that, *for academic philosophy*, denial of one proposition leads to doubting others: academic philosophy self-destructs. Here are some examples of this strategy.

Hume

Trying to explain causal reasoning by 'necessary connections', argues Hume, undermines it: there are no necessary connections. As he puts it, the expression 'necessary connection' fails to express an idea beyond 'regularity' or 'constant conjunction'.[17]

Hume's own position, on the other hand, turns philosophy on its head: it is the necessary connection which depends on our willingness to make causal inferences, rather than the other way around. 'This is what we do', he in effect says, anticipating Wittgenstein. Skepticism becomes irrelevant when knowledge is not the goal.

Another example is that Hume holds that the causal theory of perception, apart from its other bad features, subverts belief in the external world. With Berkeley[18] he argues that the causal theory of perception gives rise to Cartesian skepticism; but he has no solution to it. Also, Locke's distinction between primary and secondary qualities makes every physical object vanish.[19] If color is an artifact of perception, not a property of bodies, then so is extension – the impression, hence the idea, of extension, is inseparable from that of color.

Wittgenstein

First, let us discuss the 'rule following paradox'. Kripke attributes the following skeptical argument to Wittgenstein. There is no fact about a subject

---

[16] I shall not discuss the opposite: whether you can have knowledge without certainty, where I believe Hume and Wittgenstein differed.

[17] *Treatise*, Book I, Part III, Section IV.

[18] There is a scandalous number of arguments in Hume's *Treatise* 'borrowed' from Berkeley. Many more that are not actually plagiarized are at least based on Berkeley's foundations, to which Hume should have given credit.

[19] This argument also bears an uncomfortable resemblance to Berkeley's attacks on Locke.

in virtue of which the subject is or is not following a rule. Therefore, (a) there is no way of knowing whether anybody is following a rule; but this entails the even more radical-sounding position: (b) nobody ever follows a rule. Again we move from skepticism of denial to skepticism of doubt.

Kripke criticizes this on the grounds that it is wrong on principle to attribute skepticism to Wittgenstein. Kripke also ignores Wittgenstein's own interpretation of the rule following argument:

> This was our paradox: no course of action could be determined by a rule, because every course of action can be made out to accord with the rule. The answer was: if everything can be made out to accord with the rule, then it can also be made out to conflict with it. And so there would be neither accord nor conflict here.
>
> . . . There is a way of grasping a rule which is *not* an interpretation, but which is exhibited in what we call 'obeying the rule' and 'going against it' in actual cases. (*PI*, 201)

Wittgenstein here *states* the paradox, and replies with *two comments*. The paradox was that any behavior can be seen, under a suitable interpretation, as following any rule. So it is impossible to follow a rule. Wittgenstein's *first comment* is that the paradox is itself logically incoherent, since the notion of a rule or norm includes the possibility of its being broken. His *second comment* is: it is irrelevant that we can interpret any behavior as following any rule, since interpretation is not always necessary for attributing rule following.[20]

Properly understood, however, Kripke's proposal – that Wittgenstein offers a skeptical argument – stands. Wittgenstein's 'paradox' flows from the assumption, pinpointed by Kripke, and often presupposed in academic philosophy, that there is *always* a philosophical explanation of rule following.[21] The skeptical paradox is a *reductio ad absurdum* of that assumption. Wittgenstein himself does not feel a need to explain rule following at all costs: 'explanations come to an end somewhere' (*PI*, 1). As above, he uses, but does not identify with, his skeptical arguments.

---

[20] It is important to realize that Wittgenstein does not deny that we often *do* attribute rule following on the basis of an interpretation. All he means to say is that it is incoherent to suppose that we *always* do.

[21] It is important to note that Wittgenstein does not believe that there is *never* an explanation for rule following, only that there are *some* cases where the quest for explanation is inappropriate. The belief that there must always be an explanation leads academic philosophy to supply one where science cannot.

Wittgenstein's two comments, accordingly, do not *refute* the skeptical argument, but rather assail its presuppositions. The first comment – rules presuppose the possibility of breaking them – highlights the difference between natural laws and human norms. This is precisely the distinction trodden upon by the academic philosopher: if there is a fact in virtue of which a subject *s* follows rule *r*, why could that fact *not* hold all the time?[22] The second comment – against the view that attributing rule following is supplying an interpretation – can also be seen as denouncing the thesis that behavior is always to be explained by a fact about the subject, since an explanatory fact would determine an interpretation.

Wittgenstein's own 'descriptivist' views on rule following are therefore the following. First, we can, and do, attribute rule following to subjects solely on the basis of their previous training and behavior. It is true that this training and behavior are compatible with other rules than the ones we attribute, since any finite sample of behavior – by an appropriate interpretation – can be made to accord with any rule. But this is irrelevant, since we attribute rule following in those cases without constructing any interpretation. We simply find ourselves attributing the rule, for we ourselves have been trained in the same language and form of life as the student and there is empirical agreement among trainees who have been trained the same way. As above, however, this agreement is not what we attribute to the trainee; rather, the agreement is

---

[22] Wittgenstein errs if he thinks that only an academic philosopher identifies laws with norms. Religious thought often sees the heavenly bodies as obeying the will of God; a model to be emulated by wayward humans. Pious Jews recite every month to this day a prayer upon the sighting of the new Moon, which contains the following lines:

> Blessed art Thou, O Lord our God, King of the Universe,
> Who created by His word the Heavens
> And by the breath of His mouth all their hosts
> An allotted time He assigned to them
> That they not change their task
> They rejoice and are glad to do the Will of their Maker,
> They are true laborers, for their work is true.

(Modern versions of this prayer have been piously emended to 'He is a true laborer, for His work is true'.) In fact, medieval Jewish thinkers looked forward to the Messianic age, when the evil inclination would disappear and humanity would serve God without any deviation whatever.

presupposed by the attribution.[23] To attribute rule following is *evaluating* the behavior. To the question, how do we know that the student is following the rule we attribute, the answer is: we don't *know* – but, again, lack of knowledge does not entail uncertainty. Knowledge is simply inappropriate here.

It is, further, consistent with a rule attribution that the student may deviate from what we consider to be the rule. In that case, we say that the student is no longer following the rule; he or she made a mistake; etc. Each of these is an evaluation – though empirical regularities (logically) underlie our ability to evaluate.

Since every rule is based on a regularity, when we attribute rule following to a subject, we can predict what the subject is likely to do next. Most people, for example, if they count by 2 'correctly' to 1,000 will continue '1,000 . . . 1,002' and not '1,000 . . . 1,004'. This predictability is one of the sources of the superstition that there is an explanatory fact behind rule following.

Let us now look at Wittgenstein's 'private language argument'. Though Kripke does not mention this, the argument also takes the form of a skeptical argument:

> Let us imagine the following case. I want to keep a diary about the recurrence of a certain sensation. To this end I associate it with the sign 'S' and write this sign in a calendar for every day on which I have the sensation. – I will remark first of all that a definition of the sign cannot be formulated. – But still I can give myself a kind of ostensive definition. – How? Can I point to the sensation? Not in the ordinary sense. But I speak, or write the sign down, and as it were, point to it inwardly. – But what is this ceremony for? For that is all it seems to be! A definition surely serves to establish the meaning of a sign. – Well, that is done precisely by the concentrating of my attention; for in this way I impress on myself the connexion between the sign and the sensation. – But 'I impress it on myself' can only mean: this process brings it about that I remember the connexion *right* in the future. One would like to say: whatever is going to seem right

---

[23] For this reason, I do not agree with Kripke that the criterion for attribution of rule following must be the trainee's agreement with the linguistic community. That the trainee will agree with the community is predicted by the empirical regularity among trainees. In most cases, it is enough to observe the past behavior of a trainee – this is enough of a criterion, for Wittgenstein, in order to attribute rule following in general, and this or that rule in particular.

> to me is right. And that only means that here we can't talk about 'right'. (*PI*, 258)

Wittgenstein thus puts forward a skeptical argument about remembering the connection between sign and sensation. This he counters by a move that resembles the move against the rule following paradox: he denies, as a matter of grammar, that we can equate 'seeming right' to 'being right'. Against what is this skeptical argument aimed? I think that he is taking aim at the view that we can *refer* to our own sensations and other mental events. The skeptical argument known as the private language argument is thus a *reductio ad absurdum* of this view.

Some preliminary explanation is in order, because Wittgenstein, after all, states explicitly that we *do* refer to our sensations:

> How do words *refer* to sensations? – There doesn't seem to be any problem here; don't we talk about sensations every day, and give them names? But how is the connexion between the name and the thing named set up? This question is the same as: how does a human being learn the meaning of the names of sensations? – of the word 'pain' for example. Here is one possibility: words are connected with the primitive, the natural, expressions of the sensation and used in their place ... the verbal expression of pain replaces crying and does not describe it. (*PI*, 244)

However, it is crucial to understand that Wittgenstein holds that academic philosophy distorts the plain meaning of words like 'refer' in a vain attempt to fashion a technical philosophical vocabulary which can then be used in philosophical, explanatory theories.[24] In their ordinary sense, semantic terms like 'refer' do not refer to any one relation between words and 'things'. Rather, the criteria for 'reference' depend on the aspect of life involved. In arithmetic, for example, we say that the numeral '3' refers to the number three *rather than* to the number two, and similarly for more complicated arithmetic expressions. But it makes no sense to say that the numeral '3' refers to a number three *rather than* to a boat. Similarly, within the practice of expressing our sensations it makes sense to say that 'pain' refers to a sensation we would

---

[24] In reading Wittgenstein, one must also be careful to distinguish where he is using words in their ordinary sense from where he is using words in their academic or technical sense (which he, of course, opposes). What I have said concerning 'refer' holds for expressions like 'true', 'fact', and many others.

prefer to avoid, and that 'pleasure' refers to the opposite.[25] Academic philosophy, however, sees referring to persons and physical objects as the paradigmatic reference – and here it is possible to fix the reference of a name merely by pointing to the referent, setting up a relationship between word and object. It then generalizes this idea to cases like 'mathematical objects' or sensations, assuming that reference to these is also a kind of 'pointing', perhaps a mental 'turning of attention', and then superstitiously looking for the object of the pointing. Thus, when I say that Wittgenstein denies that we can 'refer' to our sensations I mean this in the academic sense of 'refer', i.e. refer 'ostensively', not the ordinary sense. I mean that we cannot name our sensations in the way we can name our children, ostensively.

Not that we understand clearly what ostensive definition and reference to objects and persons is. On the contrary, clarity about this matter might have blocked the misuse of the ostension paradigm in the philosophies of mathematics and of mind. This is one reason why Wittgenstein expends much effort in getting clear concerning the nature of ostensive definition and naming objects at the beginning of *PI*. He opens with a discussion of the 'Augustinian' view that every word is a name. This, of course, is an inadequate view of language, and he remarks:

> That philosophical concept of meaning has its place in a primitive idea of the way language functions. But one can also say that it is the idea of a language more primitive than ours. (*PI*, 2)

Wittgenstein goes on to describe a 'language game' in which every word ('slab', 'beam') could in fact be regarded as a name: this language game is a model for Augustine's 'primitive' philosophical theory.

What is wrong with Augustine's theory is that it captures only part of the language; this is a standard problem with academic philosophy, Wittgenstein believes – that it attempts, in a 'scientific' spirit, to blow up a particular phenomenon of language as though it were universal. Here, Augustine projects the function of referring to observed bodies as though it were the only thing language does. Nevertheless, Augustine's view is consistent, in that there *could be* a language containing only 'names'. We can see Wittgenstein's language game as a model for Augustine's theory.

Nobody in contemporary philosophy holds that every word in a language is a name: consider words like 'but'. Yet there are modern philosophies that hold that every word or phrase that functions grammatically

---

[25] Thus Wittgenstein's position prefigures Carnap (1956).

like a name refers, at least in a true sentence, to an object. Both Platonism and mentalism result from such views. Platonism is abetted by the existence in mathematics of numerals which purport to be the names of the numbers. (Nominalism is an overreaction which says that the numerals refer to themselves, or else are 'non-referring names'.) And mentalism hives off our tendency to talk as though we were referring to mental events.

In speaking of reference, Wittgenstein emphasizes its public, rule-guided nature. This is in opposition to the view he attributes to Russell, that the ultimate reference is a private act of ostension, a 'directing of attention' to the thing pointed to. To this Wittgenstein replies that there is no one characteristic process that is the essence of such directing of attention: attending to the shape of a picture does not evoke the same experiences as attending to its color (*PI*, 33). And even if there were, 'it would still depend on the circumstances – that is, on what happened before and after the pointing' (*PI*, 35).

Wittgenstein concludes that the entire picture of referring via a unique mental activity of 'attending' is a superstition:

> And we do here what we do in a host of similar cases: because we cannot specify any *one* bodily action which we call pointing to the shape (as opposed, for example, to the color), we say that a *spiritual* [mental, intellectual] activity corresponds to these words. (*PI*, 36)

Note that Wittgenstein here is discussing referring to 'public' things like shapes and colors – 'public' here meaning that many people can witness them at once. He is not arguing, of course, that we cannot refer to these things, only that reference is not a private matter. (And even as a public matter, there is not *one* thing we mean by 'reference'.)

Now consider private events like sensations, to which the subject alone has 'access'. The *only* way we could 'point' to private events would be precisely by such a private act of 'attending'. Wittgenstein's conclusion is, therefore, that we do not (and cannot) refer to sensations – where 'reference' is understood on the model of ostension, creating a relation between name and bearer. If there is reference to sensations, it involves (not 'is') a relation between a name and the 'natural expression' of these sensations, not the sensations themselves.[26]

---

[26] Wittgenstein never takes the extreme 'behaviorist' line that there *are* no sensations, only that they play no explanatory role.

Now, there are a number of philosophies which make ostensive reference to sensations as a central feature of their systems: empiricism (Locke, Berkeley, Hume, the early Russell) in particular has this tendency; but other philosophies (such as that of Descartes) do too. These philosophies (what Thomas Reid called the 'Ideal System') define the meaning of a word as the 'idea' the word refers to. Here 'reference' can mean only an 'internal pointing' to the 'target' of such pointing, the idea. (Compare what Wittgenstein says above about the 'reference' of words like 'sensation' or 'pain'.) Wittgenstein's judgment of all these philosophies is (or would be) very harsh – they are much worse than Augustine's 'primitive' view of language, for they are not even coherent. Augustine's view, Wittgenstein says, is not true, but it would be *true of* a language more primitive than our own, and therefore Augustine's view can be modeled by the 'slab' game. The philosophies involving 'reference' to sensations make every language into a private language and are therefore incoherent. These 'private language philosophies' cannot even be modeled by a language game, because in a private language reference is not a rule-guided activity.

Wittgenstein's own view, that we do not refer ostensively to sensations, is not 'behaviorism', understood as the radical view that there is no mental life, or that mental discourse is meaningless or false.[27] 'I am in pain' for Wittgenstein has a perfectly good meaning, as we have seen: it is the socialized version of infantile crying or grunting. Society teaches us to imitate the third person 'He is in pain' as this is more useful and informative for society. Wittgenstein tends to treat all first-person psychological 'reports' in this way. For example, 'Now I can go on' (said by somebody who has just understood what rule he is supposed to be following) *may* be nothing but a *signal*, he says, not a description of my 'mental state'. It's like the cry 'Eureka!':

> We can also imagine the case where nothing at all occurred in B's mind except that he suddenly said 'now I know how to go on' – perhaps

[27] Wittgenstein would have probably understood the term 'behaviorism' as referring to the 'eliminative' view of John Watson, namely that the language of 'folk psychology' embeds a faulty theory and ought to be replaced, at least for scientific purposes, by a behaviorist language. The reductive view of B. F. Skinner, that ordinary language psychological discourse is to be preserved, but reinterpreted, is probably more congenial to Wittgenstein. It was Norman Malcolm, Wittgenstein's disciple, who attempted to bring about a rapprochement between the Wittgensteinians and the Skinnerians in a lecture in which he argued that Wittgenstein and Skinner were not far apart.

> with a feeling of relief; and that he did in fact go on working out the series without using the formula. And in this case too we should say – in certain circumstances – that he did know how to go on.
>
> *This is how these words are used.* It would be quite misleading, in this last case, for instance, to call the words a 'description of a mental state'. – One might rather call them a 'signal'; and we judge whether it was rightly employed by what he goes on to do. (*PI*, 179, 180)

The asymmetry between first-person and third-person 'reports' is another example of a plain fact which is concealed by the academic philosopher's lust for theoretical symmetry in defiance of the facts.

We can now approach the private language argument itself, thought of as a skeptical argument, designed to refute the thesis that we can make reference to our sensations and inner life in general by a mental act analogous to physical pointing. I see the argument as a constructive dilemma which goes as follows (not following Wittgenstein's order of presentation), where, as usual, the term 'refer' is used as a surrogate for pointing to an object:

- To refer to any object one must be able to refer to it again at another time.[28]
- This ability to reidentify an object is either based on evidence or is infallible.
- But there is no evidence that could decide whether a *private* object *S* was the same object as object S′ presented earlier to the mind. (This is the 'skeptical' part of the argument.)[29]
- Therefore, the ability to reidentify object *S* is infallible – if it exists at all.
- But an infallible ability can never be an instance of rule following, and reference is a rule-governed activity.
- Hence, finally, we cannot refer to private objects.

Wittgenstein's *Remarks on the Foundations of Mathematics* (*RFM*, 1978), surprisingly enough, contains a number of skeptical arguments, all

---

28 Strawson later will take up this theme of reidentification in *Individuals* (1959). The centrality of identity in the philosophy of language was of course emphasized by Frege.

29 I have been asked, particularly by students over the years, why Wittgenstein's argument does not apply to *public* objects. How can we be sure, they want to know, that a public object is the same at a later time? The short answer is: we can't. What is certain is that there is *evidence relevant* to the issue. And it is also sure that we can make mistakes, as in any example of rule following, for Wittgenstein.

tending to show that Platonism – understood as the view that there are peculiarly mathematical facts – is a superstition. His 'intuitionist' arguments, that is his remarks on the infinite expansion of π, are, in particular, to be understood in this way. He exploits Brouwer's arguments to undermine Platonism while rejecting Brouwer's intuitionism.

The skeptical form of the intuitionist argument has, as its conclusion, that if Platonism is true then the law of the excluded middle has no basis. The argument, in my reconstruction at least, goes as follows:

- Platonism says that there is an objective fact underlying the infinite decimal expansion of π.
- This objective fact must underwrite counterfactuals concerning the correct expansion of π by human calculators.
- We cannot call rule following correct or incorrect, unless there is an underlying empirical regularity or agreement by human subjects who are trained the same way.
- In speaking of infinite expansions, however, it is absurd to speak of such empirical regularity.
- There is, therefore, no fact of the matter concerning what a calculator would – *or even should* – arrive at in a calculation unlimited by space and time.
- There is, therefore, no fact of the matter concerning whether, in the infinite expansion of π, there appears, or does not appear, the sequence 7777777777.
- *On the Platonist account*, therefore, the law of the excluded middle has no basis.

Wittgenstein himself, however, has no inclination to drop the law of the excluded middle: this would be meddling in the internal debates of mathematicians. He has explicitly stated in *PI* that no philosophical discovery can influence philosophy, and philosophy cannot revise mathematics. Rather, he suggests, the law of the excluded middle is a 'rule or postulate' (*RFM*, 166).

On this view, however, the law of the excluded middle differs profoundly from other mathematical propositions, which are, to be sure, also rules. Other rules in mathematics are non-conventional: they are empirical regularities that we 'harden' into rules.[30] The law of the excluded middle is different – when applied to infinite expansions it

[30] Cf. Steiner (1996) for a discussion of rules and mathematical theorems.

seems to be a convention. Thus, in the specific choice between classical and intuitionist logic, but not in general, Wittgenstein takes a position akin to Poincaré's position on geometry – as the Texas school teacher replied[31] in an interview with the school board to the question whether the earth is round or flat, 'Ah can teach it either way.'[32]

References

Berkeley, George (1988) *Principles of Human Knowledge/Three Dialogues*, ed. Roger Woolhouse. London: Penguin Books.

Carnap, Rudolf (1956) Empiricism, Semantics, and Ontology. In *Meaning and Necessity*. Chicago: Chicago University Press.

Gjertsen, Derek (1988) Newton's success. In John Fauvel, Raymond Food, Michael Shortland, and Robin Wilson (eds). Oxford: Oxford University Press, 23–41.

Hume, David (1978) *A Treatise of Human Nature*, ed. by L. A. Selby-Bigge, 2nd edn. Oxford: Clarendon Press.

Price, H. H. (1940) *Hume's Theory of the External World*. Oxford: Clarendon Press.

Steiner, Mark (1996) Wittgenstein: Mathematics, Regularities, Rules. In Adam Morton and Stephen P. Stich (eds). *Benacerraf and his Critics*. Oxford: Blackwell, 190–212.

Strawson, P.F. (1959) *Individuals*. London: Methuen.

Wittgenstein, Ludwig (1968) *Philosophical Investigations*, tr. by G. E. M. Anscombe, 3rd edn. Oxford: Basil Blackwell.

Wittgenstein, Ludwig (1978) *Remarks on the Foundations of Mathematics*, ed. by G. H. von Wright, R. Rhees and G. E. M. Anscombe, rev. edn. Cambridge, MA: MIT Press.

---

31 Attributed to Lyndon Johnson.

32 I am grateful to Saul Kripke and Thomas Nagel for comments on this paper, when it was read at the conference in Haifa devoted to Kripke's work. Some of this chapter expands remarks I made in Steiner (1996). This article was written while I was a Visiting Scholar at the Dibner Institute, MIT. I would like to thank the Institute for inviting me.

Part V
Logic

11
The Road to Gödel

Saul A. Kripke

What does this title mean?[1] Gödel's incompleteness theorem, as he originally presented it, seems to be an extraordinary and tricky magical construction. We can now, with modern recursion theory or computability theory,[2] reduce the problem to the unsolvability of the halting problem, or the theorem that there is a recursively enumerable set that is not recursive (computably enumerable set that is not computable) – though that is not the way Gödel presented it himself. A friend of mine of the highest distinction in this very field of recursion (computability) theory once said to me in informal conversation that all of us know how the original Gödel statement was constructed, but no one really understands what it says. It is just an artificial product and has no intuitive content.

Now, I want to do two things: first, to present the Gödel theorem as almost the inevitable result of a historic line of thought. I don't mean that it *did* happen that way; I mean that it *could* have, and perhaps *should* have, but did not happen in that way. Second, I want to show that the Gödel statement, the one Gödel proves to be undecidable in the first incompleteness theorem, makes a fairly intelligible assertion that can actually be stated. Along the way I will do some things that are a little bit more

[1] The present chapter is loosely based on a transcript of a talk delivered at the Hebrew University in Jerusalem, Israel, on June 18, 2006. I have not entirely tried to abandon the conversational tone of the original. A version of this lecture was first given at the conference 'Naming, Necessity, and More', held at the University of Haifa, Israel, on June 21–24, 1999, and was subsequently given to other audiences.

[2] Many now wish to replace the old term 'recursive' with 'computable'. Though I have done this sometimes, I am too used to the old terminology to make the change consistently.

technical, which are, not only as motivation but even as side theorems, unknown (as far as I know) even to specialists. They have to be separated out, because they involve more technicalities, though I will mention them and, to some extent, use them. I should also state at the outset that some of these issues are unnecessary to the main point about the interpretation of Gödel's statement, and can be avoided if one wishes to do so.

Let's look first at Gödel's own presentation, which has struck many readers as tricky and magical, by way of contrast with the present version. Gödel first says:

> Before going into details, we shall first sketch the main idea of the proof, of course without any claim to complete precision. The formulas of a formal system (we restrict ourselves here to the system *PM*) in outward appearance are finite sequences of primitive signs (variables, logical constants, and parentheses or punctuation dots), and it is easy to state with complete precision *which* sequences of primitive signs are meaningful formulas and which are not.[3]
> ... It does not matter what objects are chosen as primitive signs, and we shall assign natural numbers to this use. Consequently, a formula will be a finite sequence of natural numbers, and a proof array a finite sequence of finite sequences of natural numbers. (1931, p. 147)

Now, Gödel gives his main construction. A formula with just one variable free, of the type of natural numbers, he calls a 'class sign'; we can even restrict the notion so that the free variable is a particular one, x_1. The class signs are thought of as arranged in a series (sequence) and the n-th is denoted as $R(n)$. Both the concept 'class-sign' and the ordering relation R are definable in *Principia Mathematica* (*PM*). Any class sign $[\alpha; n]$ designates the formula obtained by replacing the free variable in the class sign α by the sign for the natural number n. The three-term relation $x = [y; z]$ is also definable in *PM*.

---

[3] As everyone knows, Gödel eventually codes finite sequences of natural numbers into single numbers. It is interesting that the coding system he uses in the preliminary sketch is not the famous Gödel numbering used in the detailed version that follows, but it is closer to the types of coding used by Quine (1940) and Smullyan (1961; 1992). However, to see this, some modification of the way Gödel presents it would be required. Personally, I prefer the type of Gödel numbering introduced by Quine and Smullyan, and have my own variant of it (see Smullyan 1992, p. 46). I would also note that for most systems (those containing a Tarskian weak second-order logic), coding finite sequences of numbers into single ones is not really necessary, though it has become famous. Nor need one code finite sequences of such sequences. Gödel's basic construction could still remain.

Then he defines a class of natural numbers:

$$n \in K \equiv \overline{Bew}\,[R(n); n]$$

This means that when we put in a numeral for the number *n* in place of the free variable in the *n*th class sign, which he calls *R*(*n*), what we get is unprovable.[4] That itself defines a class, and so is denoted by some class sign. Hence, it is expressed by a class sign *R*(*q*) for a certain natural number *q*. Then he shows that if we consider the proposition:

$$\overline{Bew}\,[R(q); q]$$

the result is undecidable, and in a tricky roundabout way can be interpreted as saying of itself that it is unprovable. He writes: 'the analogy of this argument with the Richard antinomy leaps to the eye. It is closely related to the "Liar" too' (1931, 149). Pretty clever (if I don't give the details, I suppose you have heard them before) and pretty tricky construction. The result of his construction is that in an almost magical way it gives a formula uniquely applying to itself, which can be proved to amount to its own provability. But what is the formula all about? What does it say? Gödel says in note 15 that the formula states only in an indirect way of itself that it is unprovable. He suggests that this shows the formula doesn't involve any faulty circularity, because only by accident does it turn out that it says of itself that it is unprovable.[5] It says

---

[4] Notice that Gödel here and elsewhere in the paper uses a horizontal sign above a formula to indicate negation. His official notation, however, see p. 150, is the usual '~', and it is used when the system *P* (his version of *Principia*) is officially set up (e.g. pp. 155–7). On the other hand, on pp. 159 and 161 Gödel evidently uses '~' for the material biconditional, and on p. 161 assumes that negation is expressed by a raised horizontal line. This is a bit confusing in a paper that otherwise is set out with great precision. My failure to notice this led me to use a raised horizontal line in another sense, but I hope I have fixed this. If not, let the context show what I mean.

[5] Actually, I disagree with the suggestion made by Gödel's footnote (that is, that a statement saying directly of itself that it is unprovable would involve a faulty circularity). I think we can carry out his construction using a formula directly saying of itself that it is unprovable. See Kripke (1975b, p. 693, note 6). Some people have advised me that my note deserves elaboration, as perhaps I will do elsewhere. Some such elaboration is in Kripke (1975a).

One version of the construction mentioned, using a non-standard Gödel numbering, is independently due to Smullyan. In that footnote (1975b), I do say that I don't maintain that a proposition (as opposed to a sentence, a linguistic object) can be directly self-referential in this sense, and perhaps this is what Gödel may partly have in mind.

that a formula obtained in a certain way is unprovable, and calculation shows that to be the original formula itself.

Unorthodoxly, instead of starting with any of the semantic paradoxes,[6] I want to start with what were ordinarily called 'the paradoxes of set theory' in the old days – that is, that the so-called unrestricted comprehension schema leads to a contradiction.

The naïve or unrestricted comprehension schema is:

$$(\exists y)(x)(x \in y \equiv A(x))$$

For an arbitrary formula $A(x)$, as long as it does not contain y free, it defines a class of all those things where $A(x)$ holds. For those whose intuitions favored the schema, $A(x)$ could contain other parameters $(z_1, \ldots z_n)$, and so the schema would read: $(z_1, \ldots z_n)(\exists y)(x)(x \in y \equiv A(x, z_1, \ldots z_n))$. However, since parameter-free versions already lead to paradox, we shall deal only with the version where $A(x)$ contains no parameters. Some of the classic paradoxes have versions that would be most obviously formalized using extensionality as well as comprehension. Even these can in fact be used to produce versions of the Gödel theorem, but there is no need for excessive complications.[7]

The contradictory nature of the schema shocked a great deal of the mathematical and logical community. Poincaré, whose attitude both to Cantor's set theory and to mathematical logic was hostile, said that the Cantorians overreached themselves and ran into contradictions. Having earlier held that mathematical logic is sterile, now he exulted that it was no longer sterile; it leads to a contradiction (Poincaré 1912, pp. 536–7). Cantor, however, never felt that the contradictory nature of the schema had anything to do with his set theory. I tend to believe that Hausdorff felt so also.[8] But

---

[6] In note 14 Gödel says that 'every epistemological antinomy can likewise be used for a similar undecidability proof'. I take 'epistemological antinomy' to mean the same as what we would now call 'semantic paradox'.

[7] The Burali-Forti paradox is a special case, since in the original theory there is no special reduction of ordinals to sets (or classes) of a certain kind. Moreover, there is the question of reducing relations to sets. There are various possible theories, including no reductions at all. In the latter case, the Burali-Forti paradox would not simply be a consequence of the unrestricted comprehension axiom schema. For the history of this paradox, see Moore and Garciadiego (1981). (Although I agree with them that Cantor did not regard the Burali-Forti result – even with Burali-Forti's erroneous definition of a well ordered set corrected – as paradoxical, I do think he was aware of the mathematical fact that the ordinals cannot themselves form yet another well ordered set.)

[8] Hausdorff refers to the 'so-called paradoxes' of set theory in Hausdorff (1914; 1957, pp. 6, 29–30).

Frege (1902) was certainly shocked. Russell (1967 [1902]), who popularized the paradoxes more than anyone else, was also shocked. Even those in the mathematical community who were more sympathetic to set theory than Poincaré thought there was a serious problem to be solved and that, naively, set theory was most naturally based on the inconsistent schema.[9]

Russell found the simplest and most famous counter-instance to the schema, where $A(x)$ can be a very simple formula, not even containing quantifiers. He showed that the case $x \notin x$ leads to a contradiction, because there can't be any y such that:

$$(x)(x \in y \equiv x \notin x).$$

Of course, as a special case of this, if we had such a y, we would derive:

$$y \in y \equiv y \notin y$$

This is only one of many consequences that are contradictory. Although Russell is really responsible for the recognition of the paradoxical character of other set theoretical paradoxes, such as the Burali-Forti paradox (see Moore and Garciadiego 1981), Quine (see 1951, pp. 128–30) has found perhaps some of the simplest ones. For example, if $A(x)$ is

$$\sim(\exists z)(x \in z \wedge z \in x)$$

a contradiction can be obtained too:

$$(\exists y)(x)[x \in y \equiv \sim(\exists z)(x \in z \wedge z \in x)]$$

This is the class of all unreciprocated classes. Let a class x be called *reciprocated* if it is a member of a class z which is also a member of x; *unreciprocated*, otherwise. Let K[10] be the class of all unreciprocated classes. Then is K itself reciprocated? Plainly not. For if some z reciprocates K

$$z \in K \wedge K \in z$$

---

[9] Gödel's attitude was that the paradoxes 'are a very serious problem, but not for Cantor's set theory' (1947, p. 518). I agree (though with some reservations about the usual formulation of the theory).

[10] No relation to Gödel's use of K above.

since $z \in K$, z would have to be unreciprocated (by the definition of K). But it also would be reciprocated by K itself, which is a contradiction. So K is unreciprocated. Again by the definition of K, this means $K \in K$. But then

$$K \in K \wedge K \in K$$

i.e. K reciprocates itself, which is a contradiction. So this paradox also shows that the unrestricted comprehension axiom schema cannot be satisfied. Like Russell's paradox, it is far simpler than such classical set-theoretic paradoxes as the Burali-Forti paradox.

To me it has turned out to be of some conceptual interest that someone who was simply told that the unrestricted comprehension axiom schema is inconsistent, without needing any particular example, could already derive a (non-constructive) version of Gödel's theorem, proving under appropriate hypotheses (including consistency) that there is a true but unprovable universal statement, and which, on the assumption of ω-inconsistency, is undecidable. We shall prove this below.

Notice that what one has been told is independent of the interpretation of the epsilon relation. It is a matter of pure first-order logic that the unrestricted comprehension axiom schema is inconsistent. Russell already realized this in his example of the barber who shaves all and only those who do not shave themselves – and then the question is whether the barber shaves himself. Or, analogously to Quine's case, one could have the class of all barbers who are never shaved by any barber who shaves him also – or something like that. The same contradiction would go through, because the interpretation of the epsilon relation is irrelevant.[11]

Let us look at this matter in considerable generality. Consider a first order structure having a domain D and some relations R_1, R_2, ... that can have a certain number of places. Let's say that among these relations there is at least one two-place relation R_1. It could have, or it could

[11] For a long time I had never heard of insurance companies that insured other insurance companies against catastrophic claims. (They do exist.) Russell's paradox shows that there couldn't be an insurance company ('Russell's Insurance Company') that insures all and only those insurance companies that do not insure themselves.

not have, designated function letters and constants (whether these are allowed or eliminated[12] is not important):

$$<D, R_1, R_2, \ldots, f, \ldots>$$

We have also a corresponding first-order language L with symbols – the variables range over the domain D, the relations are all primitive symbols of the language, and so on. Assume for the moment that D contains the formulas of its own language L in the domain (I will weaken that assumption in a moment), or at least it contains the so-called Gödelian class signs involving one particular free variable:

$$\ulcorner \mathrm{A}(x_1) \urcorner$$

(As I said one can normalize this by choosing a particular free variable.) Suppose we have a two-place predicate S between elements of the domain D and formulae:

$$aS \ulcorner \mathrm{A}(x_1) \urcorner$$

(Here I am using 'a' as an informal variable over elements of D. $\ulcorner \mathrm{A}(x_1) \urcorner$ also ranges over elements of D, although only over particular elements, namely the 'class-signs'.) Try to interpret this as:

$$a \text{ sat } \ulcorner \mathrm{A}(x_1) \urcorner$$

It is an immediate consequence of the inconsistency of the unrestricted comprehension axiom that satisfaction by a class sign of the language – satisfaction of an element in a class sign of the language L – cannot be what coincides in extension with the two-place relation R_1. Nor can it even coincide with satisfaction when restricted to the subset D^* of class signs in D (though allowed to have an arbitrary extension in D otherwise). Satisfaction in this sense cannot be the interpretation of R_1 (which we are assuming to be a two-place relation), because if it were – and

[12] Russell, of course, showed by his theory of descriptions that function letters and constants could be eliminated. See Russell (1905) and Whitehead and Russell (1910/1925, vol. 1, pp. 30–2, 66–71, 173–5).

even without knowing any particular paradox – it would follow that the unrestricted comprehension axiom schema

$$(\exists y)(x)(x \in y \equiv A(x))$$

holds in the domain in question. Simply take y to be the very formula $A(x_1)$ itself.[13] This would mean that the unrestricted comprehension axiom is satisfied – but it cannot be. You don't even have to know any particular paradox to obtain this conclusion.

The unsatisfiability of the unrestricted comprehension axiom schema is enough to draw Tarski's conclusion that a conventional first-order language cannot fully contain its own semantics – cannot be semantically closed.[14] It cannot contain its own satisfaction predicate, even when confined to formulae with one free variable.

Now, people didn't think of first-order structures for languages L that contained L itself as a part. We could weaken this a little bit by not necessarily assuming it literally contains the formulae of its own language L as elements – though because this is only a matter of structure, it is hard to say whether this is very important. But suppose one has a coding function, which I will suppose to be a one-to-one (though one-to-oneness isn't really necessary for everything I say) mapping of at least class signs into elements of the domain

$$f: A(x_1) \rightarrow D^* \subseteq D$$

(so the range is some subset D^* – it maps the class signs and maybe more (perhaps the whole language L of the structure) onto D^* – which is contained in D). As long as the domain is infinite, there will be such a function. This is purely a matter of cardinality.[15] However, if this is a countable language L, as long as D contains a countable subset, there will

---

13 I have not bothered putting the subscript on the variable in the unrestricted comprehension axiom schema. It is clear that it would hold, regardless of subscript.

14 The matter is often stated in the form that semantically closed languages are inconsistent. But it is really axiomatic formal theories, not interpreted first-order languages, that are not consistent. My own way of putting the matter would be that semantically closed languages, formulated in the usual first-order logic, do not exist. (I make this point in Kripke (1975a).)

15 Put this way the result depends on the axiom of choice. Otherwise, we assume that D is Dedekind infinite, or, equivalently, has a countable subset. A weak use of choice is needed to establish the equivalence of this property with the infinity of D.

be plenty of such functions. Any one of them could be called a coding function. (See how we are getting towards Gödel a little bit?) Then R_1 cannot be satisfied under the coding function, but the two-place relation

a satisfies $f(A(x_1))$

can't be any two-place relation definable in the language L at all – not a primitive one but not a defined one either – because then we would be able to obtain the truth of the unrestricted comprehension axiom schema. Remember, we don't need to know any particular paradox for this, just that the unrestricted comprehension axiom schema cannot be true.

So far we have assumed nothing much about D other than infinite cardinality, and it follows that either the coding function or satisfaction must be undefinable in the language L.

Tarski – I am going backwards, because Tarski was plainly inspired by (dependent on) Gödel rather than the other way around, but we are doing things in reverse order here – not only proved the conclusion that a first-order language cannot be semantically closed, because it cannot contain its own satisfaction predicate (where it contains either its own syntax, so f could be the identity map, or a coding of its syntax (its formulae), so that f could be some other map – there always are such maps, due to cardinality considerations), but also drew the stronger conclusion that truth in the language was undefinable.[16] What premises do we need for that? Why should truth be undefinable? Well, satisfaction reduces to truth, given certain premises. What does it mean for a to satisfy the formula $A(x_1)$? Or putting it backwards, for $A(x_1)$ to be true of a? It simply means that if we put in a name of a in place of x_1, the resulting formula with no free variables

$A \ulcorner a \urcorner$

is true in L. Now, to reduce satisfaction to truth, or at least to make the reduction possible for an appropriate subset D^* of D, one including the (codes of) formulae of L (or at least the codes of the class signs), we

[16] Actually, I am probably being too conventional in attributing this result to Tarski. According to Wang (1987, p. 90), who himself refers to a letter from Gödel to Zermelo (reproduced with comments by Grattan-Guinness), Gödel actually showed that a usual language cannot define its own truth in 1930, before going on to the incompleteness theorem.

must be able to define a naming relation in L that relates each code of a formula to a code of its name in L. As I put it this way, which is close to the way Gödel put it, we have to be able to define substitution too. Alternatively, as probably was first observed by Tarski and perhaps independently by Quine, we could define everything this way:

$$(\exists x_1)(x_1 = \ulcorner a \urcorner \wedge A(x_1))$$

(Here the function of a expressed by '$\ulcorner$' '$\urcorner$' is thought to be definable in L. In the famous Gödelian case, the natural numbers are the (codes of) formulae, and the Gödel numbers of their numerals are the codes of their names. An appropriate defining relation is available in the language.) This is an alternative way of reducing satisfaction to truth, but it still requires a naming relation definable in the language.[17] So to reduce satisfaction to truth, we need a function g mapping every class name or code of a class name into a name of the code:

$$g: A(x_1) \to \ulcorner \mathrm{A}(x_1) \urcorner$$

We are well along the way now, because if truth is not definable, but provability is, under the coding (and this will certainly be true in a rich enough system, like set theory; in fact it is true in first order arithmetic, which is a little harder), then truth cannot be equal to provability, so they must be two different things. Hence, either there is something false but provable, which is very bad, or true but unprovable, which is also bad, but not as bad.[18] And, of course, Gödel opts for the latter case, assuming that if you have an axiomatic system in the language, all the axioms are true. The dilemma involved can be regarded as the weakest and most general form of the Gödel–Tarski result, that is, either a formal system fails to define its own basic syntactic properties, or truth fails to coincide with provability. In the standard cases the second proves to be the case, and provability is even arithmetically definable.

Given this latter fact, we can say more, even at this point. In a famous monograph, Tarski, Mostowski, and Robinson proposed a theory R

---

[17] We don't need names in the literal sense; in Russell's theory of descriptions predicates simply uniquely satisfied by the object, for example, could take the place of names. (What we would need is a binary relation $R(x, y)$, interpreted as saying that x uniquely satisfies the predicate y. So we need a variable y ranging over one-place predicates in the language.)

[18] But see also the remark on this dilemma below.

that was supposed to be a very weak theory such that any recursively axiomatizable theory containing *R* allowed both Gödel's and Rosser's constructions to be carried out. Apparently, the real power of the theory came from the two final axiom-sets. Only one of these seemed necessary to show that the Gödel theorem held in any consistent extension; and this impression was correct for the usual form of the theorem. The last axiom-set clearly gives the impression that the authors thought it necessary to show the same thing for the Rosser form of the theorem, though plainly it is not needed for Gödel's original form of the theorem. But it turns out that the extra axiom-set was superfluous for the Rosser theorem too, since the whole theory *R* was interpretable in the theory with the last axiom-set deleted.[19]

Here I would like to introduce another system I simply call 'School'. It is simply theory *R* without the last two axiom sets.[20] So, it consists simply of the following tables. Assume we have 0 and a successor symbol as primitive. $0^{(m)}$ will stand for 0 followed by *m* successor symbols. There are two primitive functions, plus and times. We have as basic axioms:

$$0^{(m)} + 0^{(n)} = 0^{(m+n)}$$
$$0^{(m)} \cdot 0^{(n)} = 0^{(m \cdot n)}$$

And finally:

$$0^{(m)} \neq 0^{(n)}, \text{ if } m \neq n$$

---

[19] The theory *R* in the classical monograph of Tarski et al. (1953) consisted of the axioms of School as presented in my text together with two axiom-sets:

$$\Omega_4 \quad x \leq 0^{(n)} \supset x = 0 \vee x = 0' \vee \ldots x = 0^{n}$$
$$\Omega_5 \quad x \leq 0^{(n)} \vee 0^{n} \leq x$$

Here the variable x is thought of as universally quantified and for any terms t_1 and t_2, $t_1 \leq t_2$ abbreviates $(\exists w)\ (w + t_1 = t_2)$, where w is a variable not occurring in t_1 and t_2.

The first four axioms including Ω_4 are needed to show that Gödel's original form of his theorem is provable for any system in which *R* is interpretable. Plainly, the authors thought that Ω_5 was needed to obtain the Rosser form, and hence that *R* is essentially undecidable. However, Alan Cobham (1960) showed that *R* was interpretable in *R*- (the system with Ω_5 omitted), and hence we have nothing here that differentiates between the Gödel and the Rosser forms. The system School in the text does differentiate between the two, for one version of the Gödel theorem.

[20] Though I only later on noticed the relation with *R*.

The point of the axioms of School is that they guarantee that any truth-function of the atomic sentences (i.e. any quantifier-free sentence of the language) is decidable in School, and in fact correctly.

Gödel showed that the provability predicates of the usual axiomatic systems were definable in terms of just plus and times. One should not regard this aspect of his work as essential to the main morals, both mathematically and philosophically, of his work, though it is certainly technically interesting. If other functions, such as exponentiation, or even other things needed to define the provability predicate of the formal system, were introduced as primitive, little would be essentially changed. And remember that his basic concern was the provability predicate for *PM*, whose definability within that system is much easier.[21]

Nevertheless, there is a point I am trying to make here. Consider any first-order system S whose axiom-set is definable in terms of plus and times, and which contains School (or really, in which School can be interpreted). It follows from any usual formulation of first order logic that provability is also arithmetically definable. Assume S is consistent. Then by our basic result, truth in S (in the language of School plus conventional first-order logic over numbers) cannot coincide with provability in S. Hence, S either proves some false statement A, or fails to prove some true statement. But given that S is consistent, if it proves a false statement A, it fails to prove the true statement $\neg A$.[22] So there is a statement that is true but unprovable in S.

Now, consider a true but unprovable statement A written in prenex form,[23] where the number of quantifiers n is a minimum for this property. n cannot be zero, since School correctly decides every quantifier-free statement. We can also show that A cannot have the form '$\exists x(Ax)$' where the initial quantifier is existential. By hypothesis the number of quantifiers in prenex form is as small as possible, for a true but unprovable statement of S. Yet, if $\exists x(Ax)$ were true, $A(0^n)$ would be true for some n. By the minimality property of the statement A as having the smallest number of quantifiers in prenex form for a true but unprovable statement, $A(0^n)$, being true, must be provable. But then $\exists x(Ax)$ follows

[21] Suppose Gödel's first incompleteness theorem had been proved only for first-order arithmetic. This might have been ascribed to a weakness in the system. Stronger systems, such as *PM*, still might decide all relevant statements.

[22] This observation is due to D. A. Martin, and replaced a more complicated argument used before.

[23] That is, a bunch of quantifiers followed by something with no quantifiers: $(Q_1x_1)\ldots(Q_nx_n)(\ldots)$.

by existential generalization, so it is provable after all, contrary to our hypothesis.

Hence, the minimal true but unprovable statement A must be of the form '$\forall x(Ax)$'. Since A is true, each instance $A(0^n)$ must be true. So, by the minimality property, each instance $A(0^n)$ must be provable. Hence, in Tarski's terminology, S is ω-incomplete. It therefore is undecidable if S is ω-consistent.

These are the properties of Gödel's undecidable statement, obtained by a non-constructive[24] proof. Smullyan has remarked that most mathematicians have heard that Gödel found an undecidable statement, but not that he showed that there is a formula $A(x)$ each of whose instances is provable but not the general statement $\forall x(Ax)$ (Smullyan 1992, p. 73). Presumably, he meant that the mathematicians in question would find the latter result much more surprising. At least, my own personal experience with one mathematician agreed with precisely that.

Note that in this case the result cannot possibly be improved to give a Rosser form (unlike the situation with theory R, even with the superfluous axiom set deleted). This is true because there are complete and consistent arithmetically definable axiom systems in the language of arithmetic, but it is also true even if recursive axiomatizability is required. Notice that the axioms of School hold in the real and in the complex numbers, whose theories are complete and decidable. This was not, of course, the 'intended' interpretation, but the complete and consistent non-recursive systems don't hold in the 'intended' interpretation either. In the usual terminology, School, unlike R, is not essentially undecidable, even though it is sufficient for all its extensions to satisfy the Gödel theorem.

Up to now, we have restricted ourselves to mere knowledge that the unrestricted comprehension axiom is inconsistent, without knowing any particular paradox. But of course we do know particular paradoxes, of which Russell's paradox is the best known and simplest.

We have already remarked on the relation between satisfaction and truth, and what is needed to get a proof of the undefinability of truth from that of satisfaction. Here, however, let us consider the matter more specifically. The Grelling (heterological) paradox was of course a version of Russell's

---

[24] That this form of the result needs to be non-constructive (i.e. that the independent statement cannot be found by recursive function, given, say, an arithmetical index for the axioms of S) was shown, when it came up in a version of this lecture, by D. A. Martin. His proof uses the recursion theorem. The present writer found another proof, perhaps more conceptual, but I recall somewhat longer.

paradox.[25] Membership was replaced by satisfaction, just as it was replaced in the barber version. In this case, however, we appear to have a related semantic paradox. The following is Quine's exposition of the matter:

> To explain this paradox requires first a definition of the autological, or self-descriptive, adjective. The adjective 'short' is short; the adjective 'English' is English; the adjective 'adjectival' is adjectival; the adjective 'polysyllabic' is polysyllabic. Each of these adjectives is, in Grelling's terminology, autological: each is true of itself. Other adjectives are heterological; thus 'long', which is not a long adjective; 'German', which is not a German adjective; 'monosyllabic', which is not a monosyllabic one.
>
> Grelling's paradox arises from the query: Is the adjective 'heterological' an autological or a heterological one? We are as badly off here as we were with the barber. (1966, p. 4)

The Grelling paradox doesn't really need to apply only to single adjectives, but could apply to whole phrases, nor does it require the invention of any special word such as 'heterological'. As Quine points out, the paradox could be formulated in terms of 'not true of self'. This phrase appears to be true of itself if and only if it is not. 'Not true of itself' is just 'heterological' spelled out. Quine says that he considers this an antimony, that is, a real shock to our intuitions; we can't explain what is wrong with it.[26]

Now Quine turns his attention to the venerable Liar paradox. He considers various forms of it, starting with the 'paradox of Epimenides the Cretan, who said that all Cretans were liars' (1966, p. 6). He finds possible loopholes in this formulation and tries variants such as 'I am lying' and 'this sentence is false'. Finding possible objections to all these reformulations,[27] he finally comes up with a famous formulation of his own:

> If, however, in our perversity we are still bent on constructing a sentence that does attribute falsity unequivocally to itself, we can do so

---

[25] I believe that Grelling's paradox originated in his thesis. The paradox is normally stated for natural language (see below), but could just as well be stated for a formal language. The same type of transformation could be applied to other instances of the unrestricted comprehension axiom schema.

[26] Similarly to the relation of the Russell paradox to the Grelling 'heterological' paradox, we could define a semantic analogue of the 'unreciprocated paradox'. An adjective, or adjectival phrase, could be called 'reciprocated' if it is true of an adjective (or phrases) that is true of it; otherwise, 'unreciprocated'. Then, is 'unreciprocated' unreciprocated? The question leads to a contradiction.

[27] I am not certain that Quine really finds all these ways out completely cogent.

> thus: '"Yields a falsehood when appended to its own quotation" yields a falsehood when appended to its own quotation.' This sentence specifies a string of nine words and says of this string that if you put it down twice, with quotation marks around the first of the two occurrences, the result is false. But that result is the very sentence that is doing the telling. The sentence is true if and only if it is false, and we have our antinomy. (1966, p. 7)

That is a famous and very snappy form of the Liar paradox. Quine goes on to say:

> This is a genuine antinomy, on a par with the one about 'heterological', or 'false of self', or 'not true of self', being true of itself. But whereas that earlier one turned on 'true of', through the construct 'not true of self', this new one turns merely on 'true', through the construct 'falsehood', or 'statement not true'. (1966, p. 7)

Quine's point is that it is a paradox on a par with the 'heterological' one – presumably a *different* one.

But is it really different? If we have a name for an object, say 'Mars', then 'red' is true of Mars if and only if 'Mars is red' is true, or equivalently, 'is red' yields a truth after 'Mars'. As we have emphasized before, if we have a systematic naming function, satisfaction (or 'true of') can be reduced to truth *simpliciter*. In the present case, where linguistic phrases are involved, quotation forms just such a systematic naming function. Something will be true of the phrase 'is long' precisely when the corresponding sentence becomes true with 'is long' filling in the blank position.

When does a phrase yield a falsehood when appended to its own quotation? Precisely when it is not true of itself. The paradoxical example really is:

> 'yields a falsehood when appended to its own quotation' is not true of itself.

Here the subject phrase 'yields a falsehood when appended to its own quotation' is just another way of saying 'is not true of itself'. This isn't a paradox *on a par* with the 'heterological' paradox; it *is* the 'heterological' paradox, given that 'true of' can be reduced to 'true'. Any paradox regarding membership can be changed into one of satisfaction, and then changed into one regarding truth; and the simplest one is the Russell paradox. So this is not, as it is usually thought to be, Tarski's clever and complicated form of the Epimenides paradox – it simply *is* the 'heterological' paradox, using the fact that statements are nameable, here by quotation marks, and perhaps by some other form of code naming in a formal system. So, one shouldn't say it is a genuine antinomy *on a par* with the 'heterological' paradox; it is the same one.[28]

Notice that Quine doesn't realize that he really has the 'heterological' paradox all over again. And we don't have to think of this as a form of the Liar paradox; we don't have to notice that this is a statement that says 'I am false'. If someone did not notice this, there would still be a paradox, namely, the 'heterological' paradox, which is what it really is, souped up. So of course it is true if and only if it is false, because all paradoxes are like that; but if someone did not notice that this was a form of the Liar paradox, we could still get the result.

Now, where, finally, does Gödel's first incompleteness theorem in the form that he stated it fit into all this? Let us forget about basing everything on such a weak system as School. The usual presentation of Gödel's arithmetization does not rely on this. Given a suitable coding (Gödel numbering) of formulae and of proofs, we must be able to decide within the system we are studying whether a given sequence of formulae is a proof or not. The Tarski–Mostowski–Robinson system *R* is sufficient,[29] but as I have already emphasized, we should not forget that Gödel's original purpose was not to prove the incompleteness of very weak systems, even, for example, first-order arithmetic, but of stronger systems such as *PM* (see the title of his paper). Then it is much easier to see that the system can decide whether a given sequence is a proof or not. And indeed, to see the representability within the system of primitive recursive function and predicates.

Suppose now we try to imitate the 'heterological' paradox, only replacing satisfaction (or 'true of') by 'provability of'. Replacing adjectives, or adjectival phrases, by formulae with one free variable (Gödel's

---

[28] In some sense, Tarski seems to have realized the connection. In Tarski (1935, p. 248, note 2), pretty clearly an addition to the original paper since it refers to a specific construction in a paper written later (Tarski 1944), Tarski seems to see that, in natural language, something analogous to the usual proof of the impossibility of a language containing its own truth definition really uses the Grelling paradox. He does not appear to apply his observation to formal languages, however. (I owe this remark to Joseph Almog.)

[29] The main point of the system is of course that it gives an axiom showing that bounded quantifiers are in fact eliminable in favor of finite disjunctions, and hence statements all of whose quantifiers are bounded are decidable.

'class signs' – remember that we could even fix the free variable as x_1), a class sign $A(x_1)$ is naturally called 'provable of' a number n if $A(0^n)$ is provable, or alternatively, as we have seen, if $(\exists x_1)(x_1 = 0^{(n)} \wedge A(x_1))$ is provable. Suppose that we identify formulae with their Gödel numbers. Then a particular formula $Pr(x, y)$ with two free variables says that x is provable of y. $\neg Pr(x_1, x_1)$ is a class sign (in Gödel's sense) that says that a formula is unprovable of itself. It itself has a particular Gödel number n, and $\neg Pr(0^n, 0^n)$ is simply a way of saying:

'Unprovable of itself' is unprovable of itself.

This is precisely the statement G constructed by Gödel.

Thus the basic statement G can be called Gödel's form of the 'heterological' paradox, and to the present writer its content is clearer than if it is regarded in terms of the Liar paradox.[30] If our base system, say, *PM*, is consistent, G cannot possibly be provable. For the proof would be a proof that 'unprovable of itself' is unprovable of itself, and this very proof would show that 'unprovable of itself' *is* provable of itself. Similarly, the reader can complete the argument to show that G cannot be disprovable either, assuming that *PM* is ω-consistent. The argument can be carried through without noticing explicitly that G says something about itself (i.e. that it itself is not provable).[31]

From this point of view Gödel's statement G is not just constructed, but makes a clear and well motivated statement. Sometimes I have used the term 'Gödel heterological' for 'unprovable of itself', so that the statement G is 'Gödel heterological is Gödel heterological'.[32] It is a direct analogue of the 'heterological' paradox, which in turn is an analogue of Russell's paradox.

Similarly, one could give an analogue of Quine's variant of Russell's paradox in terms of the class of all unreciprocated classes; one formula reciprocates a formula when it is provable of it. We have the predicate '$Pr(x,y)$' which says that x is provable of y in the sense defined above. We can call a one-place predicate (formula with one free variable or Gödelian class-sign) unreciprocated in terms of provability if there is

[30] As is usual, given what Gödel says. The same goes for the Richard paradox.
[31] What is really used is that the statement is Π^0_1, or more loosely for present purposes, that it is a universal statement each instance of which can be checked within the system. In particular, the argument uses the fact that a proof of G can be recognized within the system.
[32] Nathan Salmon has suggested 'hetero-Gödel'.

no formula that it is provable of and of which it is provable, i.e. $\neg(\exists y)(Pr(x,y) \wedge Pr(y,x))$. Abbreviate this by $Unr(x)$, a Gödelian class-sign. Let m be the Gödel number of this class-sign and let $Unr(0^m)$ be the formula G^*. Once again, G^* makes a universal statement, each instance of which is checkable. Now can G^* be provable? Not if the underlying system is consistent. For if G^* were provable then $Unr(x)$ would by definition be provable of itself and hence reciprocated by itself, contrary to what it itself asserts, and hence contrary to a concrete and checkable instance of G^*. So if the underlying system is consistent, G^* is unprovable. However, what it says must be true. For it says that, for this particular formula, there is no formula that reciprocates it. If there were one, then there would be some formula H with Gödel number n, and two proofs with Gödel numbers p_1 and p_2 that show that two formulae reciprocate each other. This would be a contradiction, since also these instances are checkable within the system. And what it implies is that H is unreciprocated, when in fact it also shows that G^* reciprocates it. Since G^* is a true purely universal statement, each numerical instance of which is verifiable in the system, it follows that if the system is ω-consistent G^* cannot be disprovable either.

In the case of G, Rosser showed that if 'provable of' is replaced by the more complicated predicate 'provable of with no shorter disproof of', where 'shorter' is given in terms of the Gödel numbering, the statement can be shown to be undecidable without assuming ω-consistency.[33]

---

[33] In 2005 I gave a version of this lecture in Buenos Aires. Alberto Moretti wondered whether it would be necessary to produce a particular undecidable statement as Gödel did given the non-constructive proof of Gödel's theorem, assuming that one was not at all worried about constructive proofs. However, not only is it nice to have a particular example, but it is needed for Gödel's second incompleteness theorem. For one proves within *PM* (say) $Con(PM) \rightarrow G$. Hence, if *PM* is consistent, G is unprovable, and hence so is $Con(PM)$. For this one needs a particular statement G for *PM*, or whatever system is in question. (Nor is the non-constructive proof obviously formalizable in the system as stated, since it uses the notion of arithmetical truth or definability, which in a weak enough language is not itself definable. It is nice of course that Gödel obtained a Π^0_1 statement and this is essential to the second incompleteness theorem as stated.)

I would like to thank Jonathan Berg for transcribing the original lecture. My thanks to Gary Ostertag and especially to Romina Padró for their help in producing the present version. This chapter has been completed with support from the Saul A. Kripke Center at The City University of New York, Graduate Center.

References

Cobham, A. (1960) Effectively Decidable Theories. In *Summaries of Talks Presented at the Summer Institute of Symbolic Logic*, Cornell University, 1957, 2nd edn, Princeton, Institute for Defense Analyses, 391–5.

Feferman, S., Dawson, J.W., Jr., Kleene, S.C., Moore, G., Solovay, R., Jean van Heijenoort, J. (eds) (1986) *Gödel: Collected Works, Vol. I*. Oxford: The Clarendon Press.

Frege, G. (1902) Letter to Frege. In van Heijenoort (1967), 127–8.

Gödel, K. (1931) Über formal unentscheidbare Sätze der *Principia Mathematica* und verwandter Systeme, I. *Monatshefte für Mathematik und Physik*, 38: 173–98; translated as 'On Formally Undecidable Propositions' in Feferman et al. (1986).

Gödel, K. (1947) What is Cantor's Continuum Problem? *The American Mathematical Monthly*, 54: 515–25; reprinted in Feferman et al. (1986).

Hausdorff, F. (1914) *Grundzüge der Mengenlehre*. Leipzig: Von Veit.

Hausdorff, F. (1957) *Mengenlehre*, 3rd edn; translated as *Set Theory*. New York: Chelsea Pub. Co..

Kripke, S. (1975a) Three Lectures on Truth., unpublished manuscript.

Kripke, S. (1975b) Outline of a Theory of Truth. *Journal of Philosophy* 72: 690–713; reprinted in Kripke (2011).

Kripke, S. (2011) *Philosophical Troubles: Collected Papers, Volume 1*. New York: Oxford University Press.

Moore, G. and Garciadiego, D. (1981) The Burali–Forti Paradox: A Reappraisal of its Origins. *Historia Mathematica*, 8: 319–50.

Poincaré, Henri (1912) The Latest Efforts of the Logisticians. *The Monist*, 22: 524–39.

Quine, W.V.O. (1940) *Mathematical Logic*. Cambridge, MA: Harvard University Press.

Quine, W.V.O. (1962) The Ways of Paradox. *Scientific American*, 206: 84–96; reprinted in Quine (1966).

Quine, W.V.O. (1966) *The Ways of Paradox and Other Essays*. Cambridge, MA: Harvard University Press.

Russell, B. (1905) 'On Denoting' *Mind*, 14: 479–93.

Russell, B. (1967 [1902]) Letter to Frege. In van Heijenoort (1967), 124–5.

Smullyan, R. (1961) *Theory of Formal Systems*. Princeton, NJ: Annals of Mathematics Studies, Princeton University Press.

Smullyan, R. (1992) *Gödel's Incompleteness Theorems*. New York: Oxford University Press.

Tarski, A. (1935) Der Wahrheitsbegriff in den formalisierten Sprachen. *Studia Philosophica*, 1: 261–405; translated as 'The Concept of Truth in Formalized Languages' by J.H. Woodger in Tarski (1983), 152–278.

Tarski, A. (1944) The Semantic Conception of Truth and the Foundations of Semantics. *Philosophy and Phenomenological Research*, 4: 341–76.

Tarski, A., Mostowski, A., and Robinson, R. M. (1953) *Undecidable Theories*, Amsterdam: North-Holland Publishing Company.

Tarski, A. (1983) *Logic, Semantics, Metamathematics*, 2nd edn, ed. by J. Corcoran. Indianapolis: Hackett.

van Heijenoort, J. (1967) *From Frege to Gödel: A Source Book in Mathematical Logic, 1879–1931*. Cambridge, MA: Harvard University Press.

Wang, H. (1987) *Reflections on Kurt Gödel*. Cambridge, MA: MIT Press.

Whitehead, A. N. and Russell, B. (1910, 1912, 1913). *Principia Mathematica*, 3 vols. Cambridge: Cambridge University Press; 2nd edn, 1925 (vol. 1), 1927 (vols. 2, 3).

Index

Made in the USA
Las Vegas, NV
28 October 2024

10604213R00144